Yoga in America

To Deborah —

Thanks so much
for all your support
+ for making this
possible for me.

Diane

YOGA IN AMERICA

Passion, Diversity, and Enlightenment

In the Words of Some of Yoga's Most Ardent Teachers

Lulu.com Publishing

To order, ID: 5838139 at www.lulu.com.

ISBN 978-0-557-04633-1 (paperback)

A portion of proceeds from sales of the book supports families of fallen firefighters.

Cover photos: davebernstein.com

With Appreciation

Many thanks to my fiancé, Scott for the idea to compile this book and for his patience with me and support while I worked on it.

With gratitude to my cyber friend and colleague, Bob Weisenberg who supported this project from the moment he learned of it. Bob donated countless hours to edit essays and collaborate with me. This is a much better piece of work because of Bob's wisdom and enthusiasm.

And thank you to the yoga community for contributing your brilliant, funny, heart wrenching and clever works of art that made this book come to life.

Namaste.

TABLE OF CONTENTS

Table of Contents, continued

INTRODUCTION

The call for authors went out to the yoga community on December 26, 2008. One email was sent to a group of yoga teachers, inviting them to answer in 1,000-3,000 words, the question, "What is Yoga?"

Word spread, and by the deadline to submit chapters, January 15, 2009, I had received over 300 submissions. Every submission was unique and special. From January 15-31, 2009, I read and re-read all of the submissions and decided which to include in the book. The only downside to this project was not having the space to include all of the submissions.

An unexpected and exciting thing happened in late January. I stumbled upon Bob Weisenberg's blog and writings. We began corresponding via email and Bob generously offered his time and editing expertise to this project. To date we have not spoken or met, but have worked countless hours "together".

Between February 1, 2009 and February 14, 2009, the 46 submissions that I selected to publish in the book were edited by Bob and me; sent to the writers for approval of the edits and for signing legal contracts. The authors worked within tight deadlines and enabled the entire book to come together in 7 weeks.

The feedback from the yoga community for this project has been overwhelmingly positive and encouraging. Some authors shared that this project gave them a whole new depth to their understanding about the role yoga plays in their lives.

Others indicated they were compelled to contribute because of the charitable nature of the book; a portion of the proceeds supports retreats on St. John for families of firefighters who have died in the line of duty.

And still others were enticed by the opportunity to be published and have their work edited without having to do any of the administrative part of publishing a book.

What drew the authors' interest to the project was fun to learn about as was getting to know some of them through the process.

Each time I read the chapters, both individually and collectively I learn something new or gain a new perspective on an area I thought I knew a lot about.

I am humbled and grateful that the authors of this book have entrusted their art to me. I hope you enjoy reading Yoga in America as much as I enjoyed bringing it into your hands and hearts.

Deborah Bernstein

WHAT IS THIS BLISS, THIS ONENESS?

TRACEY ULSHAFER

BRECKENRIDGE, COLORADO

A fresh blanket of snow covers the mountain. The snow continues to fall in huge billowy nuggets. Atop the apex I am the only person in sight. I gaze about the slope. There is a calmness that I cannot quite explain. It is as though the entire earth is snuggled in a down comforter taking a nap. Even the wind is still.

I push off and begin my slow side-to-side glide down the ski slope. Every now and again I stop, but I know not why. I take a deep breath and sigh. In wondrous amazement I ponder that this must be what heaven would feel like. And then I cry. Tears of a joy that I have never known before begin to stream down my face. Here seemingly alone on the ski slope I feel closer to God than I ever had. Even more so, I feel a oneness, knowing that I am a part of the divine.

What is this bliss, this oneness?

This is yoga.

EVERGLADES, FLORIDA

My airboat sails through the tall grasses of the swamp. The cool wind in my face balances the thick, humid air around me. All that I can see for miles is water and the tall grasses growing out of the mud and murk. I begin to slow the engine, finally coming to a complete stop.

Why did I choose this spot? It appears to be the same as any other, yet it felt right to break now.

I take a seat in the boat and look about. The water laps gently against the side of the boat and then ripples across the swamp, finally fading somewhere out of sight. And at that moment, I see him. About thirty yards away our eyes meet. He floats silently among the grass, waiting, watching. Although we are strangers, I am moved to sit with him, and he with me. I peruse the tip of his scales as they peek out of the swamp and wonder how deep he rests, how long his tail extends. We are both completely still and silent, yet knowing with surety what the other is thinking. It feels as if we are breathing together.

What is this connectedness, this understanding?

This is yoga.

MAUI, HAWAII

The pounding surf thunders endlessly. As I sit and listen, the ocean spray seems to cleanse my body. My eyes are closed as I experience the ocean Goddess wash away my struggles and my worries. For the first time in days, years, I am not thinking. Instead, I am being and feeling. I smile and then giggle like a child playing in the ocean water for the first time.

The radiant sun rains its warmth down upon me and I feel safe. The water mists its freshness around me and I feel pure. My mind is finally clear, and I wonder how I ever let myself get that far into the absurdity of my fears. I realize, for the first time, that I am the maker of my own destiny.

What is this cleansing, this feeling of renewal?

This is yoga.

CHARLESTON, WEST VIRGINIA

The rocking chair sways soothingly back and forth. Softly I push my foot into the boards in a rhythmic pattern that maintains this movement. The porch wraps around the old farmhouse and out of sight. Somewhere from inside the house the sweet smell of home-made apple pie wafts through the air and into my nose. Outside the spring air is just warm enough and just cool enough. I gently lift the cup of lemon tea to my mouth and take a slow sip. The warm tea melts down my throat and into my belly.

In the distance, I watch my dog chase a butterfly. His tail wags and his ears bounce up and down as he trots along. Eventually the butterfly flies away and my trusted friend makes his way back to my side at the porch. He drops his head in my lap and looks up at me lovingly. I massage his ears and he closes his eyes blissfully.

What is this happiness, this contentment?

This is yoga.

NEW YORK, NEW YORK

The energy is unmistakable, undeniable. It is known as the city that never sleeps. It is called the greatest city in the world. Whether it's Broadway, Wall Street, Fifth Avenue or Central Park, the crowd reacts as a living and breathing entity. And every day millions of people call this hustling, bustling energizing island their home. Cultures collide in this roughly 305 square miles of land. From Chinatown to the Harlem, from the East Village to the Upper West Side, never a more eclectic group of people were ever brought together in such a small area. Nearly 170 languages are spoken here. The Nation's most wealthy and the most poor live together just next door.

As I look down from atop a large skyscraper, I can feel her heartbeat. And I know that for a brief time I am a part of that vital life force. Home of the United Nations and the Statue of Liberty, I feel at home and accepted on her shore.

What is this energy, this life force?

This is yoga.

HOME - ANYWHERE IN AMERICA

I spread my fingers and push forward into my yoga mat. Slowly lifting my knees off the floor, I tilt my tailbone up towards the sky and sink down into my heels. My thighs are energized, my mouth is relaxed. My drishtis, my gaze, is towards my naval. My mind is fixed on my slow, steady breathing. Firmly I hug my shoulder blades into my back. Calmly I stay. I am Adho Mukha Svanasana or Downward Facing Dog.

Next I place my knees back on the floor and extend my buttocks back to my heels. My forehead rests softly on my yoga mat. I sigh deeply, allowing the surrender breath to trail off. I relax into the mat. Calmly I stay. I am Balasana or Child's pose.

After my rest I squat down, placing my hands into the yoga mat. I draw my knees into my upper arms and lean forward into the balls of my feet. As I draw my belly in, I gracefully lift my feet off the mat, gazing ahead, breath deep and full. Floating above my yoga mat, I am Bakasana or the Crow. Calmly I stay.

Lying on my back I raise my legs to the sky. I walk my hands up my back bringing my legs in line with my torso. I firm my shoulder blades to my back and gaze at my toes. I breathe as my world turns upside down, yet I am still and peaceful. Calmly I stay. I am Sarvangasana or Shoulder Stand.

Finally I sit in stillness, with my feet crossed up onto the opposite thigh. My hands rest on my knees, my spine elongates. I soften my eyes to the tip of my nose and follow my natural breath. There is a sense of oneness, connectedness, cleansing, contentment and energy throughout my being. Calmly, peacefully I stay. I am Padmasana, the Lotus.

And this is yoga.

Tracey Ulshafer

www.oneyogacenter.net

Tracy teaches Gentle Yoga, Hatha Yoga (all levels), Vinyasa Yoga, Power Vinyasa, Kid's Yoga and Meditation. She is E-RYT, RYS, CMT, and Reiki Practitioner.

In 2003 she opened One Yoga & Wellness Center, which is now a registered yoga school with the Yoga Alliance.

Tracey spent twelve years in the corporate world working her body into knots, chronic sinus infections and severe back pain initially caused by a prior car accident. An introduction to yoga saved her from surgery and opened her eyes to the value of holistic practices. After several years of studies and training, Tracey took a leap of faith and left the corporate world behind to follow a path in the ancient healing arts.

Tracey has taken additional Yoga teacher training with Baron Baptiste as well as many workshops with other Master Yoga teachers including Sri Dharma Mitra, Shiva Rea & Sean Corn.

THE DOWNSIDE TO DOWN DOG

KELLY GREY

"Neti Neti" is a practice in Jnana Yoga--a way of discerning the real from the unreal. In my yoga practice of 25 plus years, I have mostly discovered what is not yoga. And, I have tried just about everything, from living in the more austere ashrams (where you need special letters from your guru and years of service to their ashram to be allowed in, and they still may tell you to go away) to devoting my life to the "spiritual mother".

I have stood on the banks of the Ganges, the Colorado and complete insanity. I have chanted the 1008 names of the mother and sat on rooftops in South India chanting the Maha Mrytunjaya mantra 108 times every morning and every evening for months on end.

I have reached my goal of completing 2nd series in Astanga yoga, only to wonder why, and I spent 8 years doing Bikram yoga every day, hating almost every minute of it (for at least the first 4 years), just trying to find my feet.

I have stood on my head, high on hashish and lain in the dirt channeling Neem Karoli Baba while I was stoned on mushrooms. For days after, I walked barefoot all over the dirt fields surrounding my house singing "ma, ma, ma, ma...." and laughing, and laughing and laughing.

I have been yelled at by swamis, cast out of spiritual groups, shunned by "yogis" and have lain on the stone floor of the Kali Temple in

Trivandrum, India, sobbing and shaking for days, realizing that everything I was chasing was the unreal.

About eight years back, I had it all--everything I had been pursuing, desiring. I had a thriving yoga studio, I had students who respected me, and I had my rituals, my guru, my community, my faith. The man I had been waiting for all my life walked into it finally, asked me to marry him, asked me to have a life together, to teach with him and to travel to India.

We lived in my little one room solar house, hidden down a long dirt road, taught yoga classes together, made love, dreamed. I followed him to the UK to live, excited about the possibility of starting a whole new chapter in my life and I reconnected and reaffirmed my commitment to my spiritual teacher at that time, very intent on serving her and her work in the world.

And as all good stories go, it all fell apart, started to unravel... dissolve. I had the man I wanted and loved and I wasn't happy. I had the faith and the roots of yoga deeply set in me from this life and many lifetimes of practice, and I lost my faith.

I stood in a sweaty little room in Mysore, India, day after day, practicing one of my favorite practices of Hatha yoga –Astanga vinyasa, and while in Chakrasana, Sheshadri, my teacher, crawled under me, picked me up by my feet and swung me up and down over and over, before landing me on my feet (dizzy and shocked) for the 50th time that month, and I just kept asking myself "why?". What was the point? I had gotten really solid in both 1st and 2nd series (as many of you know, no easy feat) and I could care less.

I sat with my Scottish friend later that day in the courtyard, drinking masala chai and with his lovely accent and brilliant smile, he laughed a big rolling laugh and talked of the irony, how we as westerners come to one of the most screwed up countries in the world looking for enlightenment.

The next day, that too familiar, uncontrollable sobbing and shaking set in. For several years I had been experiencing long bouts of endless crying and shaking and heat and pain in my body so intense at times I would actually pass out from it. I wandered up to an Osho center, walked in, wild eyed, still racked with pain and told the man behind the desk that I needed something, anything, now!

Osho was known for his wilder side and more active meditations and this man suggested that we do the "No Mind" meditation. He took me into the back room, put on a tape and we spent the next 40 minutes pacing and gesturing and talking in complete gibberish. After this, a gong sounded and we were to sit silent for 15 minutes and then lie in savasana for another 15.

In all my years of yoga and meditation practice, I had never experienced my mind so completely empty, where I could actually watch the words trying to form, unable to, and the energy behind the words slowly trying to rise and build.

After we finished, the man told me how foolish he thought westerners were, traveling half way around the world, in often hard circumstances, wasting so much money searching for meaning in life. Before I left the center, he told me to go home, plant a garden, have a family, do simple work, be content.

Instead I wandered through India some more, through temples and holy towns and the dirt and the heat until I found myself way down at the southern tip of Kerala, lying on the stone floor of the Kali Temple sobbing, while a very intense priest chanted the names of the mother and bathed and adorned her in her many forms.

The heat in my body was unbearable at that time and lying on that floor day after day, crying was the only relief I could find. I loved the temple and the priest who sang and yet some words of Osho kept creeping back into my mind and heart. He said to be wary of the priests, the politicians and the gurus.

Ultimately, he believed that the gurus and priests were the ones that would keep you from entering the temple (your own true self) because they would tell you that you needed them to arrive. You needed their rituals, their darshana, their blessings. He believed that these gurus would delude you into thinking you were soooo close, only steps from entering the temple and yet as long as you kept your eyes focused on them, you would always miss it.

I was struggling with this idea because I had a guru back home that I knew to be genuine, the real deal, and I was very devoted to her and her life work. When I arrived back in the states, I threw myself into her "work" even more. Finding myself a bit discouraged with intense austerities and Hatha yoga, I moved toward gentler forms and devoted my time to Ayurveda and karma yoga--service.

I soon found myself 'hand-picked' by the guru among a few others to serve her on a deeper level. I was to help spread "the work" around the country and most likely beyond. We were told the time, the people, were ripe to receive this profound work and that we were so karmicly blessed to be in her presence in such an intimate environment.

Two years later and thousands and thousands of dollars later, after leaving a relationship and choosing not to have children (because it might interfere with my service to her and the world) and completely revamping all of my teachings to be solely in alignment with her program (in other words not being able to read a Hafiz poem during a class I was teaching for her because it might be conflictual) I was told by one of her devotees (because guru was too busy) that the whole program was to be dropped, that it was all our fault and that we were to cancel all future scheduled programs immediately.

At that time I had eight programs scheduled throughout the country, one that was to start in less than two weeks. One week before I got that phone call, I had received a phone call from the same devotee telling me that I was doing exceptional work, that I was to go forward with all of my programs and was given "blessings" from the guru.

Having the "rug pulled out from under" is an understatement. How about completely shattered, disillusioned and grief stricken? How about having my faith so completely demolished that I couldn't watch a clip of the Dalai Llama without being suspicious of his "real" motives? How about the kind of heartbreak that you don't really ever recover from, but you just simply move forward with a few pieces missing?

The most disturbing part that I could not resolve was that this was the woman who gave lecture after lecture about accountability only to completely dismiss us and her own actions with the wave of her robes and titles.

I was once told by a friend and fellow yogini, when I was first opening my yoga studio, that it would be the ugliest business I would ever get involved with. While other businesses are more upfront with their motives (money and power), the yoga community ended up hiding behind the words "namaste" and "we are all one", while still having the very human emotions of greed and fear rolling around inside, dictating actions.

Since opening that studio I have been threatened, yelled at and lied to more times than I care to remember. I had a famous teacher's nephew contact me under the pretense of "networking" while he was really trying to get information from me so they could threaten to sue me (for teaching a practice I was certified to teach in).

I had another teacher, whose idea of meditation (as she put it) was sitting in an easy chair with a bong in one hand and a martini in the other, come into my studio and start getting both teachers and students high. During that time I was contracted to teach yoga to kids in a recovery center just outside of town and somehow this same woman manipulated the situation and took over, getting me fired because I wasn't "yogic" in my thinking, because I refused to work with her, because she was smoking hash on her way to teach kids in recovery.

I was told that we as yogis should always be peaceful and get along. When I eventually sold my studio, I did it as honestly as I could, asking for the price I truly wanted and knew to be fair. I was met by a couple who served me tea, talked Vedanta and peace and then offered me a ridiculously low offer (the used car salesman technique) and then eventually came up a little because they really believed I deserved so much more.

It was still way under my asking price but I was moving on, committed to my guru and I needed the money to invest into her trainings, so I took it. Two years later, I found out they were selling the studio for at least eight times the original offer I got.

I was asked to teach at a Vedanta center and then was told I couldn't because I had also studied under another teacher (along with them) and they felt it was conflictual. Both my teachers were Vedanta teachers (you know--NONDUALISM) but both deeply believed the other to be controversial.

My friend was right--an ugly business. And the words Neti neti repeat again and again as I wander through this experience called "yoga". Not this, Not this.

And then the question is "what IS yoga?". Mostly I write what is not.

I don't believe it to be the woman in robes preaching ahimsa and accountability and then not being accountable--someone who is more invested in her status than in truth.

I don't believe it to be in the devotees who are so invested in their status (being close to the guru) that they ignore or close eyes to the hypocrisies and conflictual events that almost always arise, excusing it because we simply cannot understand the real motives of a guru or enlightened one. In my journey, my walk, on this earth we are all human and we are all accountable.

I don't believe it to be in the yoga teacher who postures himself as the authority of your body (not much different than today's western doctors) and tells 55 year old women what menopause is like.

I don't believe it to be in the yoga superstars, the tantric sex gurus or even the austere ashrams (where I was very inappropriately hit on by two swamis and a bramachari and a Reiki master).

I don't believe it's in the ads, the new yoga tights, the namaste bumper stickers or the new approved herbal remedies that are 90 percent grape juice and less than 2 percent herbs.

I do believe it to be in the honest moments, the hard and the gritty and the beautiful. The moments where a man who loves you cares for you while you are sick and heartbroken because you followed a spiritual teacher that simply had a bad moment and can't own it.

I believe it to be in the Mexican mother-in-law who knows absolutely nothing about yoga and is a bit overweight and struggles with her health, but has handmade tamales waiting for you every morning for breakfast simply because she found out you love tamales.

I believe it to be in this little back alley road, in an old gutted house with no electricity and wood floors that slope off and splinter, where people come every Wednesday night to offer a bit of a donation and chant and move and laugh together.

I believe it is the beauty and love and patience I see in my dog's eyes every time I get so busy and wrapped up in teaching and work that we don't have time for a walk.

I would much rather perfect my heart, to unravel and travel its depths, its unknowns and terrifying void and speak from that place, laugh from that place, love from that place, than spend the next 20 years perfecting my triangle or arguing about whether it should be five complete breaths in down dog before jumping back to forward bend or is it the exhale on the fifth breath where we jump.

Carlos Castaneda's teacher Don Juan told him once that there is no path really, only heart. So basically, we can follow any old path we want and it will lead us nowhere. And if you follow a heartless path, that is all it will be. But if we follow the path with heart, then, when the day comes and we realize there is no path, we will have at least followed the heart.

Many years back, a beautiful Italian friend of mine died from AIDS. This woman knew five languages and had traveled the world studying with gurus, living in ashrams, practicing yoga and meditation. She was a body worker and healer and had gone through many forms of training in counseling.

In her last days, too sick to walk or run or stand on her head, she found so much joy in sitting on her porch and feeding the squirrels. She had also been an amazing cook, but could no longer cook for herself and so loved to at least feed someone still.

The day she died she wanted two things. She wanted to see her old boyfriend, a love of her life, one last time, and she wanted him to make her Tiramisu. She wasn't looking for the key on how to do a perfect triangle.

The question is "What is yoga?" I believe the more appropriate question is what is your heart? Your voice? Your essence? What is your love, your deepest most personal truth?

We are all here together, to help one another, to grow, or as Ram Dass says, to provide grist for the mill. But when it comes down to it, in the end, I believe yoga (which means union) to be so deeply personal, that anyone or anything or any idea that stands between you and the temple should simply be removed.

Kelly Grey

Kelly Grey grew up on the east coast and wandered out west early on to find her home in the desert. She has been teaching, practicing and studying yoga since she was 15 years old, starting with TM and chanting with the Hare Krishnas on the Washington lawn, after getting kicked out of the Smithsonian for having no shoes.

She has advanced certification in Sivananda Yoga and as an Ayurvedic Practitioner and teacher. She studied Bikram Yoga and Astanga yoga intensively and is a Phoenix Rising Yoga Therapist. She is also a licensed massage therapist and Reiki master and received certification in India in Pancha Karma therapies and Abhyanga.

Kelly opened up and ran Yoga Shala in Arizona for eight years and started many programs still existing today in the local community colleges, private colleges and health clubs.

Her love is the river. Her guru is her dog, Penny Lane.

Kelly may be contacted at kgreyus@yahoo.com.

BOILER ROOM YOGA

RICHARD WALL

In Nashville, Tennessee, which is the city where I teach, there is a "perfect" yoga studio. I have seen it. It is an oasis, with soft music, perfectly adjustable to the size of the class. The floors are spotlessly clean, yet not slippery. The lights are soft, a combination of direct and indirect lighting, adjustable for any time of day. All the equipment is there, mats, straps, blocks, bolsters, pillows, and wall ropes. It must be heaven to teach in that space. It must be heaven to take classes there.

I teach in a boiler room. Well, not literally a boiler room, but you perhaps get the metaphor. Each week I get e-mail about yoga in Caribbean Islands, pristine havens of quiet and solitude, far from daily life. Often they even are removed from aircraft routes, so there could be no interruption to the silence and solitude, no sound but the ringing of the prayer bowls as the students stretch in the warm sea breezes. I can imagine myself teaching in that place, watching the sunrise and sunset in the quiet.

I teach Boiler Room Yoga. Over the past 10 years I have taught classes in community college classrooms, YMCA "group fitness" rooms, health clubs, conference rooms, and unfinished floors of new office towers. Boiler Room Yoga is far from ideal. The spaces are seldom really clean, and students may have to stack tables before class and reset them at the finish.

One such teaching space was set up for employees of an investment company. The floors were sealed concrete. Fluffy gray stuff covered steel beam ceilings with open ductwork trim, and there were no walls except the outside stud walls of the finished suites. Windows were not covered. It was on the same level and directly next to the air handlers, huge machines that wheezed and squealed to life, usually at the most inappropriate moments of final meditation. At least the air was usually warm.

In most fitness clubs, if you are blessed to actually have a room separated from the weight machines and rock music, the rooms are set to aerobics temperatures, making the beginning and ending of each session a sort of chase against hypothermia. The students quickly learn to like sun salutations, which help them warm more quickly in the frigid air.

In one corporate fitness center, there is no door to the room in order to meet fire codes and regulations; there is a breeze to accompany the regular clanking of lifting weights and fans in the next space, and a constant droning of treadmills, which punctuates our sessions. The temperature varies by the season, in reverse. We freeze in summer and fry in winter.

Wherever I teach there is noise, from the aforementioned clanking, rock music playing, people talking outside the room, traffic or aircraft. One class recently was held in a lovely old chapel, formally a Catholic school, with lovely windows and a perfect wooden floor which could have been cleaner. It turned out that the chapel was in the flight path of the helicopters from the local trauma center a few blocks away, so the windows would rattle nicely during the low approaches and departures. There were helicopters constantly flying above as now and then strangers would wander into the old chapel.

In one teacher training class, we were encouraged to "use the walls" to help teach students. Most places there are no walls available, with various chairs or equipment stacked or thrown into unlikely heaps. At one YMCA, they built a sort of low carpet covered bench around the perimeter of the room, which frustrates any attempt to use the walls. Equipment is not available, missing or nil. New students may have to stand or lie on old carpet of questionable cleanliness. Mats are a sanitary necessity for regular students.

Some of my classes are held in regular classrooms, with the beginning class moving the chairs and tables out of the way, ending by putting them back. The floors are questionable at best, with tossed staples stuck into the carpets like tiny foot-ripping land mines. Some floors are plainly uneven, so that in one class the teacher is on a concrete "hump" covered in carpet, which can throw your balance off in standing poses.

Yes, I often wonder about that perfect studio. Yet, I notice something about Boiler Room Yoga. My students must truly learn to acknowledge but not react to distractions. They perform postures under far from perfect conditions, learning to practice whenever and wherever in "diverse" surroundings, not waiting for the perfect moment at the perfect time. After a while, most learn to relax and meditate, even though there is sound and fury just around the corner.

They learn that the practice is not about "blocking out" the world that surrounds them, but about being aware, yet non-reactive and non-judgmental. As I tell them, "You cannot stop the ocean, but you can learn to surf." This is a metaphor that they quickly learn to appreciate as well as to live. There may be a smell in our yoga classes, but it is not the "stink of enlightenment", of a practice too precious and airy to live in the real world.

Most of my students are not upper class; they will likely not have the money for a week in Curacao at the feet of a master. They learn when and where they can. The lessons learned in the boiler room still work, the postures still have power and energy when performed under less than ideal conditions. Some of my students move on, to practice and even to teach in more perfect places.

Boiler Room Yoga is not easy. It is not easy to teach or to take. For some of us, it is the only yoga we have to give, and so we do. The perfect studio is out there, and some of my students may yet take yoga there and even teach there someday.

Richard W. Wall

I teach an eclectic style of yoga based on Sivananda. I never intended to teach yoga, it was the inspiration of Bill Kuckler which brought me to the head of the class.

In 1994, I taught my first YMCA "stretch relax" class in Nashville, so called because the management there could not call it "Yoga".

The teaching continued, and in the past few years, I began to be influenced further by Erich Schiffmann, John Delmonaco, and Cora Wen, among others. For the past 7 years I have taught in various local corporate, college, university, and private settings.

My Certification is AAAI. I am a former board member of the Yoga Society of Nashville.

HOT YOGA IN AMERICA
ROOTS AND OFFSHOOTS

PETER SKLIVAS

"Where medical science stops, yoga science starts!" -Bishnu Gosh

Hot Yoga in America traces its roots back to a sweaty gymnasium in Calcutta by way of a claustrophobic studio located in the high-rent Shinjuku district of downtown Tokyo. The innovator who piped heat into his yoga classes was a young fitness phenom Bikram Choudhury. He added the heat for a simple reason. Studio members were getting injured doing postures that he had been practicing for years. And he could not understand why. So the yogi asked himself. "What is the difference between Calcutta and Tokyo?"

One of India's foremost physical culturalists Bishnu Gosh had sent his favorite disciple abroad to perform a mission. At the Calcutta airfield before Bikram boarded the eastbound plane Bishnu Gosh issued clear instructions. "I want you to complete my incomplete job." The young man did not need to be told what his guru's job was. As the brother of Paramahansa Yogananda, founder of the Self Realization Fellowship, Bishnu Gosh came from a family of bold spiritual aspirants.

Countless times in his years of training to become an elite yogi and weightlifter Bikram had been driven by his teacher's admonition to assist him in performing his job. Put simply, Bishnu Gosh felt it was his job to save humanity. In all sincerity Bikram answered his guru with the promise to do it. So this young man had to discover why the bodies of his Japanese students were breaking down.

The answer came to him in one word. Heat. As a born and bred Calcutta native Bikram had pushed his body to its limits every day as part of his guru's yoga regiment at annual average air temperature spiking mercury levels twenty-five degrees higher than what he was experiencing in Tokyo. In both cities dew point levels regularly exceeded 80. So the Tokyo air had plenty of moisture. But to Bikram the climate of his new home felt chilling to the bone. Once Bikram added the heat, the injuries stopped happening. Miraculous healings became a regular occurrence. And a new style of yoga was born.

Let's take a step back. To grasp how hot yoga has unfolded after more than four decades of practice, it helps to examine the roots behind its innovator. Starting from the age of three Bikram was immersed in a lineage of yogis vigorously practicing to develop seemingly superhuman powers. Stopping the heart rate so a yogi could voluntarily bury himself underground for a week or longer. A 7-ton elephant stepping on a yogi's chest. Driving a fully loaded truck over the abdomen of a yogi lying atop a bed of nails. As a child Bikram witnessed these amazing feats being performed by his guru and others.

At age thirteen Bikram's intense practice paid off when he won the first of three consecutive National India Yoga Championships. In these teen years he traveled as a member of Bishnu Gosh's troupe of yogis demonstrating the power of the mind to control the body. What this period gave Bikram was an unshakable faith in himself and his guru. This faith emboldened the young Bengali to embark on a journey of challenging people all over the world, from presidents to pop stars, to heal themselves of maladies that medical doctors could not remedy.

The backbone behind these yoga demonstrations which Bishnu Gosh trained his disciples to perform in a traveling show was a sequence of breathing techniques practiced for hours each day. Besides these impressive physics-defying feats, the breathing techniques keyed yogis into the capacity to heal their bodies from injuries.

At age 17 while training to break world records in weightlifting, Bikram sustained a catastrophic injury when a three hundred and sixty-five pound weight fell on his right knee. European doctors informed the young man that they wanted to amputate the leg. Demanding to be carried back to Gosh's College of Physical Education, Bikram knew that if anyone could heal his knee, it was his teacher. Bishnu Gosh had been the first individual to scientifically document yoga's ability to cure chronic physical ailments and heal the body.

As an avid motorcyclist Bishnu Gosh had sustained more than twenty injuries on racetracks. Many times he put his body back together using his yoga practice. In his final racing accident Bishnu Gosh shattered his leg so badly that doctors inserted a metal plate in his knee. Bikram's guru never walked again without help. It was for this reason that Bikram and Bishnu Gosh were determined to save Bikram's leg. Bishnu Gosh would do for Bikram what he had been unable to do for himself.

Six months later Bikram's knee totally recovered. Healing an injury of this severity was the linchpin that sealed the bedrock faith of this young man. From this point forward Bikram never questioned the universal healing nature of yoga. What will work for one will work for all. This became Bikram's motto. At his guru's request Bikram opened yoga schools in India and eventually in Japan.

One of Bishnu Gosh's breathing techniques became the opening signature posture in Bikram's 26-pose Hot Yoga series practiced now at more than 500 yoga studios worldwide. Pranayama deep-breathing (as Bikram called it) has been proven to expand the elasticity of the lungs and increase circulation of the spine's synovial fluid.

Another signature element of Bikram's Hot Yoga is the repetition two sets of each posture in the exact same sequence every 90-minute class without any variations. The first half consists of standing postures. The second half consists of floor postures. Other unique elements include full-length mirrors to correct misalignments and carpeted floors (not wood) to prevent slipping on puddles of sweat.

Teachers do not practice when they teach. Standing at the front of the room teachers issue instructions using a specific monologue first drafted by a California entrepreneur and mystic healer Annemarie Angstrom. Acting as his American guru mentor Annemarie Angstrom taught Bikram the value of creating a reproducible yoga system. She pushed Bikram to open his own yoga studio in Beverly Hills so movie stars could flock to his classes. And she encouraged him to train other teachers so this Hot Yoga could reach a population beyond Beverly Hills and Los Angeles. Over the years Bikram has supervised slight revisions to this monologue.

Another unique element to Bikram's Hot Yoga centers around lawyers, lawsuits and money. Starting in 1985 with Hollywood starlet Raquel Welch, Bikram is the first yogi to sue former students for allegedly stealing the trademark on his Hot Yoga Series. Raquel Welch had written *Raquel Welch Total Beauty and Fitness* along with an accompanying Hot Yoga video closely mirroring Bikram's 26-posture series. Garnering rave reviews, the bestselling book and video converted thousands of suburbanites to home yoga practice, many of whom later sought out Hot Yoga studios to deepen their practice.

Is it accurate to call Raquel Welch a renegade? Or a clever entrepreneur? Once a devoted student and friend of Bikram, she put out her fitness program without gaining Bikram's permission. The net effect of the lawsuit was to pull these products from the marketplace.

While Bikram has never laid claim to the ownership of any single yoga posture, he does claim copyright and trademark rights over the sequence of 26 postures that he developed. His infamous threats of lawsuits are widely recognized as an attempt to control how Hot Yoga is taught in America and abroad.

After 2000 Bikram's yoga teacher trainings started attracting greater numbers of individuals forcing him to expand into a facility where he could host class sizes topping out at 500 trainees. In the last ten years the popularity of Bikram's Hot Yoga has mushroomed across the globe with an army of constantly recycled new instructors acquiring existing studios and opening new ones. Class sizes across the planet also mushroomed to 30 – 50 studio members. In 2009, scheduling 4 to 6 classes daily in approximately 500 yoga studios from Johannesburg to Kuala Lumpur … from Winnipeg to Tasmania … from Santiago to Helsinki, Bikram Yoga is on the cutting edge of redefining how humanity keeps fit.

Stepping away from Bikram's system, some renegades have branched out to innovate their own styles of Hot Yoga. The most widely known of these yogis is Baron Baptiste who incorporated Bikram's heat along with the name that Beryl Bender Birch coined as the title of her bestselling book *Power Yoga*. Baron embodies what it means to be a true innovator. His brand of Power Yoga has adapted elements of Ashtanga Yoga along with traditional dance and fitness workouts which always include a killer ab burn.

Akin to the Bikram approach, Baron's instructors do not practice when teaching. With locations in Cambridge and Brookline, MA, and 39 affiliate studios, Baptiste Power Yoga is a fluid vinyasa style influencing a wide swath of Hot Yoga practitioners and teachers around the world. Baptiste Bootcamps have developed a reputation for rapidly transforming lives. Baron Baptiste's book *Journey into Power* set a new benchmark in the publishing world for sales of a yoga book.

In Fort Lauderdale Jimmy Barkan is training teachers in a morph of Hot Yoga with his moniker The Barkan Method. Another renegade who channeled his energies into innovation, Jimmy has developed a broader curriculum of Hot Yoga, offering teacher trainings that have spawned 29 affiliate studios. Up in Toronto Ted Grand and Jessica Robertson offer Hot Yoga teacher trainings with their own brand called Moksha Yoga. On the Thai island of Koh Samui, Absolute Yoga boasts a Hot Yoga teacher training guaranteed to change your life.

From the Rocky Mountains of Colorado entrepreneur Trevor Tice has launched Corepower Yoga with 30 locations and a sophisticated website offers online yoga classes. Corepower claims to demystify the practice of yoga, making it widely accessible to the masses so that everyone can reap the long-term physical and mental benefits of the ancient practice. Across more than a dozen Texas locations Sunstone Yoga has spread its class offerings out across five different Hot Yoga varieties matching the elements of fire, water, metal, earth and wood.

Whether these entrepreneurial offshoots represent authentic expressions of yoga opens an inquiry best answered directly on the mat. In the decades since Bikram Choudhury first heated up a yoga class back in Tokyo, a steady proliferation of Hot Yoga is setting the stage for a meeting of the influences from India and western fitness and medicine that will bode well for further improvements. Although yoga is touted as an ancient practice, Hot Yoga remains a new phenomenon. In the years ahead it is reasonable to assume innovations will continue to make the practice challenging and safe.

In my studio called Yoga Passion located in Beverly Farms, MA, I teach two styles of Hot Yoga. The first style I call HotCore Yoga. Its standing series mirrors Bikram Hot Yoga. On the floor though, I have inserted a wider range of postures that vary from class to class. Frequently I include more hip openers such as Pigeon or groin openers with Frog and Happy Baby. Or I insert more abdominal work or different transitions into a sequence of three or four postures. In a class, if the studio members are particularly fit, I might put in all of the above. During class I play music which is a no-no in the Bikram universe.

What I endeavor to do with HotCore is retain the very best elements of Bikram Hot Yoga: 1) Heat & mirrors, 2) Challenging posture sequences that almost anyone can do, and 3) Plenty of Savasana punctuated throughout the second half of the class.

Bikram's genius is that he created a posture sequence that my colleague Ted Lehrman could do after a motorcycle accident sent him flying 40 feet through the air leaving him with three herniated discs in the lower spine and two herniated discs in his neck. Doctors had ordered Ted to get rid of his four dogs because walking them posed a serious health threat. Two of his dogs were powerful large animals, a Great Pyrenee and a German Shepherd. One doctor predicted Ted would become paralyzed if he walked the dogs. Ted never considered selling his dogs. In his mind there had to be another option. On the internet after considerable research he found it. Bikram's Hot Yoga.

So picture Ted. Five herniated discs and the rest of his body is a wreck from the accident. What saved his life was turning over mid-air, enabling him to skid on his leather jacket and beeper both of which melted in the process. So this guy is going to attend a physically challenging Hot Yoga class? Come on! How? He could barely move. Well, here's how.

Every day for more than a year Ted did doubles. Meaning he attended a Bikram class in the morning and a Bikram class at night. In the beginning his physical limitations dramatically reduced his range of motion. But slowly Ted worked his butt off to regain core spine strength in the places that were his weak links. I met Ted in the spring of 2000 when he and I completed the certification for Bikram's Teacher Training. For two months we practiced doubles side-by-side in classes with one hundred other yogis.

Ted had already been in his Bikram rehab for about a year. Still working through physical limitations, Ted insisted on rolling out his mat on a spot between the front mirror and one of the narrow mirrored columns so he could see the position of his hips, heels and shoulders when he reached back with his hands in Camel. Burning pain in his spine was still a constant reminder that he was healing his body. But he was walking his dogs every day. Up north of Santa Barbara he and I hiked from Zaca Lake up into the surrounding mountain trails of the Los Padres National Forest.

Shortly after getting his yoga teacher certification Ted opened a Bikram studio in Studio City ten miles north of Bikram's headquarters in Beverly Hills. Today Ted still teaches in this location. So Ted Lehrman is living proof that Bikram Yoga is an effective way to put humpty dumpties back together again. Could Ted have achieved the same result with another style of yoga or some other physical healing modality? Maybe yes. Maybe no. The fact is that there are lots of Teds in the Bikram scene. Lots of people with broken bodies ... as Bikram calls them "junk spine" ... these injured people put in time and sweat to regain their life. And it works. In other styles of vigorous yoga I just can't see how Ted would ever have gotten started.

The second style I teach, *Power Yoga,* is largely influenced by the many classes I have taken with Baron Baptiste. Frequently newcomers ask me to compare HotCore Yoga and Power Yoga. I tell them Power Yoga is like going for a seven mile run while HotCore Yoga is like interval training. Sprint 100 meters. Walk 10 meters. Sprint and walk. Both styles are designed to be an intense psycho-spiritual physical workout. From my experience HotCore Yoga offers a higher rehab value for injuries because the posture sequence shares Bikram's approach. Also with modifications such as using straps and blocks as props and leaning against the back wall to assist with balance issues, almost anyone can do HotCore Yoga.

When yoga teachers and studio members ask me why I broke away from Bikram's Method, I point out limitations in its long-term practice that made it impossible for me to continue. First, I'm only aware of two kinds of fitness instructors who tell their students to lock their knees. The first is ballet instructors. Why do they do it? Because it looks pretty. The second is Bikram Yoga instructors. Why do they do it? Because it looks pretty.

From earliest childhood Bikram was trained to perform yoga postures in a highly competitive environment where physical measurements where taken to decide whose posture was best. It is much easier to kick a leg higher in Standing Bow when the standing knee hyper-extends. Plus, the heat allows studio members to get away with poor body mechanics in the early stages of practice and still derive benefit. When individuals hyper-extend their knees repeatedly, what I have observed is that eventually after three or four years, most people will over-stretch the backs of their knees.

In my own practice I discovered that when I bent my knee slightly, my overall body mechanics improved. Creating core strength has become a popular jingleism in the fitness world which I never understood until I learned how to draw energies up from the base of my spine. In vigorous yoga styles the action of creating core strength is described by drawing up two bandhas (mulabandha and udyanabandha). In the Bikram Method my approach was considered heresy. And it still is.

As a yogi, though, I love the heat. It feels like the great equalizer for those of us not endowed with naturally supple joints. As an athlete and gymrat in my teens and twenties, I competed in sports that ratcheted whatever stiff range of motion I started with down to the point where getting out of bed in the morning required rolling onto my side and slowly undulating my hips forward and back for ten minutes before daring to get vertical. In 1989 my first introduction to yoga came at Kripalu Center where I practiced their soft style of yoga in a 70-degree room.

Okay, let me clarify. Hard styles of yoga are vigorous practices where yogis regularly work their heart rate up and sweat profusely. Ashtanga, Bikram and their growing offshoots such as Power, Jivamukti, Vinyasa and HotCore are examples of what I am

Peter Sklivas

designating as *hard styles*. To an athletic yogi seeking a workout, everything else is a *soft style*: Iyengar, Integral, Shivanada, Kundalini, Kriya, Kripalu, Anusara, Yin, Vini and their offshoots. Hard styles are not intrinsically superior to soft styles. What they offer that soft styles don't is an aerobic workout. Of course yoga offers so much more.

It was three years into my service at Kripula when Yogi Amrit Desai invited Bikram to teach a staff-only weeklong Bikram Yoga intensive. For any master yoga innovator/guru like Amrit Desai to bring another master yoga innovator to teach his method in the ashram is a radical event both for the guru and the disciples, because what the guru does is chart a course that the disciples follow. As an insatiably curious man, Yogi Amrit Desai was always hosting transformation innovators in the ashram. Everyone from the mother of wheatgrass Anne Wigmore and raw food guru Gabriel Cousins to business management consultants and transformational renegade leaders, from The Forum to leading psychologists as well as Indian swamis and gurus from various lineages, but never anyone with the reputation of being as outrageously brash and the seeming anti-yogi that is Bikram Choudhury.

The incredible ashram hype surrounding Bikram seemed antithetical to the purpose of yoga. At the last minute I decided to squeeze my mat onto the carpeted auditorium floor packed with hundreds of mats laid out two inches apart. In the hot auditorium Yogi Amrit Desai was warming up right there with the rest of us. Within minutes of the first posture I got it. The heat made me feel like a superaction hero on a yoga mat. Prowling amidst the forest of sweaty bodies Bikram issued instructions with a rockbed faith and supreme knowledge that made me feel as though I could look up my butt in the half moon backbend. I felt so incredibly supple and strong that I experienced a yoga epiphany that has stayed with me after all these years.

For Bikram teaching a staff of 350 yogis was also a big deal. The majority of Kripalu's sisters and brothers had been practicing yoga for more than two decades. Many of them were veteran workshop leaders. Not the easiest group of yogis to convert to a completely different method of yoga. Bikram's teacher trainings had not taken off yet. And Bikram was famous for telling his students, "If you see guru, run the other way. They are all fakers. Bullshit artists!"

Yet at Kripalu Amrit Desai and Bikram embraced each other as the odd couple of yogi brothers. A tall handsome man Amrit Desai approached his spirituality with a sensitive intellectual boyish appetite to learn more so he could teach more. Short and defiant Bikram didn't have to learn anything. He already knew all anyone could ever need to know. Just ask him, and he'd tell you. Very likely it would be spiced with loads of profanity. At our ashram I had never heard an f-bomb until Bikram's arrival.

On the marble altar where Amrit Desai sat cross-legged in a terracotta robe with his eyes closed chanting mantras, Bikram danced clad in a splashy-colored tiger-pattern silk robe. Despite their enormous differences these two unlikely men became instant friends. Both of them gushed whenever they spoke about the other. Amrit Desai demonstrated the essence of humility with his willingness to show up as a student like the rest of us in Bikram's Hot Yoga classes. At our evening satsangas Bikram glowed with wonder at the phenomenal eloquence that Amrit Desai brought to our community of aspiring yogis.

Within months Kripalu converted a long wide rectangular room into a space devoted exclusively to Hot Yoga with carpet, mirrors and other Bikram specifications. Bikram left Kripalu with the confidence that, if he could convert so many seasoned yogis over to practicing and teaching his method, then perhaps he could expand his horizons to train his own army of teachers. This weeklong training had lasting influences on two important diametrically different styles of yoga in America.

How Hot is too hot when it comes to yoga? Type *'Bishnu Gosh'* into Google and you might be surprised at what comes up. Ten pages of references to an international yoga posture competition called the Bishnu Gosh Cup. The enthusiasts of Bikram's hot yoga are organizing a drive to introduce yoga as a competitive event at the next Olympics. Does bringing yoga onto a global scale of competition count as an innovation? Or a corruption? Bikram's position is that it's better for the youth of the world to compete to perform beautiful yoga postures than it is to let young women and me get lost in drugs, alcohol and trivial inert-body pursuits such as videogames, TV and glomming onto the internet, as a substitute for normal human socialization. But why can't yoga inspire the masses without dreams of wearing a gold metal? Can't working toward creating a golden body be enough?

Stay tuned! If Bikram and his growing worldwide legion of teachers and studio members have anything to say about it, Hot Yoga is going to keep pushing the envelope of how human beings define yoga practice. Personally, while I don't encourage competition with anyone when I am on my mat or prowling my yoga studio as a teacher, I am ever-grateful to Bikram for launching this Hot Yoga revolution. After twenty years of yoga practice I remain thrilled by the opportunities to keep re-invigorating my body practicing my own brand of Hot Yoga. Regardless of whether I get labeled an innovator, renegade or entrepreneur, I love what Hot Yoga has done for me and the people stepping through my door to hurl sweat on the mat.

Peter Sklivas

www.yogapassion.com

At age 15 Peter began daily practice of Transcendental Meditation. During his college years he studied Dzogchen Buddhist meditations & yoga with Tibetan Lama Norbu Nomkai.

For 6 years Peter worked as a staff member at Kripalu Center studying numerous facets of yoga with Yogi Amrit Desai & other senior Kripalu Staff.

In 1999 Peter founded Yoga Passion & has taught 5000+ yoga classes in the following styles: Kripalu, Bikram & Power.

In 2007 Peter created his own style of Hot Yoga called HotCore Yoga which is now the mainstay of his practice & service. In 2008 Peter created a TV series called Yoga Passion dedicated to exploring the many nuances of yoga which he is shopping to network or cable channels.

I WALK ON IN PROFOUND JOY

HALLI BOURNE

I sought out yoga for one reason only: I wanted to walk.

On a rainy morning 17 years ago, my car hydroplaned, violently twisting into a crescent around a hapless tree.

At 21 years old, I sped through life as though I were being chased, an insistent, inner clench anticipating calamity around every corner. Narrowly surviving the car accident, I spent two arduous months in a wheelchair, left with no other option than to *slow down*. Routine tasks became major feats. The next four months brought me onto crutches, to a cane, and then, miraculously, to my first yoga class.

All prior concepts were obliterated the moment my car crashed. Surviving death was, in many ways, the easy part of my healing journey. Choosing to continue to live from that point forward has been the undeniable challenge. Through breaking my ribs, my pelvis, and shattering both of my legs, my perception has been altered forever. The doctors told me I might not walk again. They told me the best I could hope for was to walk with a limp, uncertain whether the shards that remained of my legs would heal with any uniformity.

At the time of my car accident, I would have claimed that I had been *forced* to slow down. Today I would say instead that I had been *invited*. I see people's lives become more and more compressed in this breathless culture of "you are what you produce." Recipient now to an unlikely wisdom, I invite my yoga students to also slow down, to become aware of their wondrous breath, that they can see the truth of their lives.

Slowing down provides an opportunity to discover our True Nature as divine human beings, seeing instead that we *are* who we *are*, regardless of any labels we attach to ourselves. We miss this understanding when we are flying breathlessly through our lives. In the "Yoga Sutras", the seminal, classical text on yoga practice, Patanjali asserts that all human suffering is caused by the ignorance of the True Self. Echoed in numerous ancient teachings, it is only through the act of becoming still that one can access the deeper callings of the heart, therefore shedding the bottomless, unquenchable dissatisfaction of the noisy mind.

When I walked into my first yoga class, I had been walking unsteadily without a cane for only a month. As many do in the beginning, I sought out yoga for physical healing, seeking relief from a pervasive, dogged pain, ignorant then of yoga's more penetrating potential.

Beyond the challenge of performing yoga asanas, over time I noticed a fledging sense of calm. While practicing the poses certainly increased my strength and stability, it was this perceivable calm that became the true motivation to continue practicing yoga.

Most of the scars left by the car accident are not outwardly visible. I walk without any obvious sign that I have endured anything at all. Yet I hold both the visible and invisible scars as trophies for wisdom I realize I asked for; yet, I could not have known the suffering that would be involved. Injury and limitation have been my noble and wise teachers. Chronic pain has taught me compassion and empathy. Learning how to walk again has become a metaphor for an odyssey of self knowledge. Yoga is my practice for acceptance of the experience, and the inherent wisdom that lies therein.

In my journey, I have learned that while an aspect of yoga *is* physical exercise, yoga, in truth, is an exercise in awareness. Yoga is a means for transformation. When we move with consciousness, we discover that we are more than our bodies, and the first signs of peace arise, like a tender, sapling tree. I now see that peace for the world begins with peace within me. Through the limitation that severe injury has brought to me, I have come to understand the *necessity* of the human form in the soul's evolution. To transcend and discard the body without this understanding is to miss the point. To be physical *is* the point, for the spirit cannot know limitation. The ego/self constructs the *illusion* of limitation in order to create relativity. Restraint brings knowing and wisdom, which the soul desires above all. The soul, or the "Observer" (Patanjali's term), understands without interruption, that It swims in the ocean of Brahman---the beginning, the end, and the middle of all that is and all that ever will be.

I am a practitioner and teacher of the Kripalu yoga tradition. Kripalu is a practice of "meditation in motion," a compassionate, empathetic approach to practical, accessible yoga practice. Each movement is linked to the breath and to the sensation of the movement, therefore *informing* the movement. Detail to alignment and to the engagement of musculature invites liberation, spiritually as well as physically. The breath flows and so energy flows unimpeded. Self-knowledge is the unfolding result.

I envision a world in which breathing deeply becomes a widespread practice. Through my yoga and meditation practice of 17 years, I have come to see that the breath is the reason that we are having any experience at all. The breath is what links us to life and to the potential for fulfillment, contentment, and a sense of unity, which is yoga's true purpose. Through an effectively deepened breath, we find dissolution of repetitive, often misinformed thoughts and perceptions of ourselves. Coupling a deepened breath with a conscious yoga practice brings ease to the body and a gentle stillness becomes possible.

The Sanskrit term, "samskara", refers to the grooves made by repeated patterns. The nature of the mind is to relentlessly cycle invariable thoughts we have about ourselves and others, maintaining a worldview that imprisons us into a well-worn, constricted groove, or rut. The mind is captivity. Yoga is liberation. Patanjali states concisely and conclusively, "Yoga (unity) is experienced in that mind which has ceased to identify itself with its vacillating waves of perception" (Chapter 1, Verse I,2, <u>Yoga Sutras of Patanjali</u>, Stephen Mitchell). The mind's nature is to analyze and categorize. The heart's nature is to open, to beat the pulse of life. When the mind is dominating the voice of the heart, imbalance and misperception naturally result. Yet through the balance of the two, and the balance of all the aspects of our True Nature, we learn how to see ourselves and others more clearly. Fostering this balance, as a yoga practice will do, can yield a reflective, integrated life.

Skilled paramedics and physicians on the night of my accident gave me the ability to survive my injuries. The practice of yoga has given me the ability to thrive, and to ultimately transcend the limitation of a mind-dominated paradigm. Through yoga, my healing journey continues and I walk on in profound joy.

Halli Bourne

www.deeprootsyoga.com

Halli, the owner of Deep Roots Yoga & Healing Arts, has been teaching yoga for ten years, while she has been practicing yoga and meditation for 17.

Halli is a certified Kripalu Yoga Teacher, a licensed Massage Therapist, a certified Craniosacral Therapist, a certified Yoga Trance Dance Teacher, and creator of Elemental Yoga Dance.

Deep Roots Yoga & Healing Arts includes public and private yoga classes, yoga retreats, yoga trance dance events, meditation classes, and healing arts including craniosacral therapy.

Halli has a B.A. in Theatre Arts. She is also a writer, a poet, a singer/songwriter and a visual artist. She performs kirtan regularly with Dharmashakti and Christian Pincock.

FOR MEN ONLY – IS YOGA FOR YOU?

JEFF MARTENS

Attention all Men! Do your joints sound like a Fourth of July celebration gone horribly wrong? Does the only time you breathe deeply occur when police lights flash in your rear-view mirror? Does the extent of your stretching routine take place during commercials when you reach between the sofa cushions into a sleeper mattress that nothing but a hairball, a half bag of Cheese Whips and the lost TV remote has used in over a decade?

"Maybe," you say after looking around to see if anyone is watching you read this. Okay men, now consider this: Would you like to be strong enough to carry your mate through the doorway, focused enough to watch a golf match AND the playoffs (using picture in picture technology) and STILL have the flexibility to bend over and clip your own toenails without sounding like you were just tackled by the entire "Steel Curtain"? If you answered "yes" to any of these questions, then yoga is the path for you. If you answered "yes" to any of these questions out loud, then yoga is definitely the path for you!

Wait a minute, you say, what is yoga anyway? And aren't most yoga classes all filled with women? Well, in a word, yes. And, you boldly continue, isn't yoga all squishy with chanting and music and meditation and womanly stuff? To which we respond: are you sure that you want to be using that word, "squishy"?

First of all, men, you need to know that there are dozens of different styles of yoga including Yin, Bikram, Raja, Iyengar, Jnana, Ashtanga, Neopolitan and Tutti Fruiti. Men also need to know that Yoga offers far more benefits than just silencing your knee joints when you stand up from your lunch break, thereby saving you from the embarrassment of having to explain to all your coworkers who ducked under the table that they weren't actually the victims of a drive-by shooting. A regular yoga practice will help you to experience more strength, focus and flexibility in your life. And isn't that a good thing in these trying times when they have not yet invented a TV remote with cell-phone capabilities that you can call to find out where the darn thing is hiding?

Okay, you say, so there are lots of women in a yoga class. Maybe I'll give it a try. At this point most men will divide themselves into one of three different camps. The "I want to go to yoga because there are so many women there" camp, the "I don't want to go to yoga because there are so many women there" camp, and finally, the "I never heard of yoga except that some female celebrities are doing it and they look fairly hot and maybe I should give it a try because my toenails are getting pretty long" camp. In technical Sanskrit terms, learning which camp you belong to is called "Knowing your 'Yo!sha'." Let's explore together which camp you belong to and then see which type of yoga might work best for your camp. Then we'll see if there are any bears prowling around the campfire.

Camp One: The "I want to go to yoga because there are so many women there" camp. If you belong to this camp you will show up for yoga class freshly showered and doused in cologne, most likely purchased from the same convenience store where you get your groceries. Your eyes will be wandering like a kid in a candy store and you will choose to set up your mat next to the most fit woman in class. Just as you try to make eye contact, the class will begin and you will find that not only is the woman next to you able to 1) stretch further, 2) hold poses longer, and 3) breathe deeper than you have since you were in the womb, so too can just about every other woman in class, including the 72 year old grandmother in the back who is suddenly looking to you like an Olympic athlete in disguise. After five minutes of intense embarrassment (perpetuated solely by you since no one else is even glancing in your direction), you may collapse under the pressure of constant mental comparison while choking on the vapors of your own cologne. Best type of yoga for Camp One: Heated or Bikram yoga where the ratio of men to women is a little more equal and you will be forced to focus on your own practice in a full-length mirror while feeling the sting of aftershave mixed with sweat rolling into your eyes as soon as you walk into the room.

Camp Two: The "I don't want to go to yoga because there are so many women there" camp. Men, if you find yourself in this coalition, take heart! Women are your friends! Women are your support group! And it will most likely be a woman who calls 911 if you find yourself trapped in a difficult pose. If you belong to Camp Two, you are usually shy and unobtrusive in class, trying to squeeze into the furthest corner of the room. In a misguided attempt to blend in with the female crowd, you might purchase the best yoga supplies and wear bona-fide, color coordinated outfits. After 10 minutes of class you may notice that you are initially more flexible than you thought but still wonder why you can't hold your own arm over your own head for more than five seconds without crying your very own tears. In the meantime, the women in front of you actually look like they are having fun. As you wipe the tears away, pretending they are sweat, you also notice that the only other guy in class smells like he rolled in cologne samples from a popular men's magazine. Best type of yoga for Camp Two: Level One or Slow Flow classes where you can explore your tightness carefully and come to realize just how astronomically high the pain threshold is for women, all the while offering thanks that, for your gender, giving birth is not an option.

Camp Three: The "I never heard of yoga except that some female celebrities are doing it and they look fairly hot and maybe I should give it a try because my toenails are getting pretty long" camp. If you belong to this camp you will not make it to the yoga studio because something came up. Best type of yoga for camp three: Clipping your own toenails.

So there you have it: a thorough and complete male guide for knowing your Yo!sha. We hope you realize by now, men, that women are pretty harmless in a yoga class if you follow some fairly basic guidelines: 1) Do not ask someone out for tea after class unless you are able to speak without gasping for air. 2) If you feel squishy, consult a doctor or health care practitioner. 3) Leave the toenail clippers at home. This concludes our campfire exploration of finding out your Yo!sha and it's a good thing too, as all that manly cologne is raising the interest of several nearby bears!

Jeff Martens

www.innervisionyoga.com

Jeff Martens has been teaching yoga and holistic principles since 1989. His understanding flows from diverse sources including a Psychology and MFA degree, a deep love of sacred stories, and a three year study of the world's sacred texts.

Jeff's classes combine timeless wisdom, internal adjustment, practical philosophy and inspiring affirmation in a dynamic flow unifying the teachings of Classical and Tantra Yoga.

Jeff is a writer, teacher trainer, co-founder of the Yoga-Vision Yoga Conference, founder of the Student Yoga Program at Arizona State University and co-owner of Inner Vision Yoga in Chandler, and Tempe, Arizona.

Check out his DVDs YogaFlow and YogaPower at his website.

THE WONDER OF BEING ALIVE
YOGA PHILOSOPHY DEMYSTIFIED

BOB WEISENBERG

I'm writing this because I'm excited about Yoga. It's not the type of Yoga most people think of as Yoga--the exercise program and pretzel poses, although that's part of it. Rather it's about Yoga philosophy.

Yoga has filled my life with wonder and joy. Not by itself, of course. The sum total of all my other experiences has prepared me to be receptive to Yoga's power. It has become a life philosophy that both complements and builds off all my other accumulated life philosophies and spiritualities.

Yoga is a 5,000 year old tradition of trying to achieve ultimate inner peace and happiness. What I like most about it is that, even though it has a rich and complex history, with hundreds of variations, branches and sects, its basic tenets are elegantly simple and livable.

Let me be quick to say that I am not an expert on Yoga. But I have read widely and learned about Yoga from many knowledgeable people. My insights come from my personal encounter with Yoga at a conceptual and daily practice level, particularly inspired by the writings of Stephen Cope of the Kripalu Center and Rod Stryker of ParaYoga. (See "Recommended Yoga Resources".)

Initially I took up Hatha Yoga to enhance my tennis training. I felt I could use some greater flexibility. Like most Americans' first encounter with Yoga, it was mostly a stretching and workout routine. My wife and I would go to class two or three times a week.

But then I found that Yoga meditation and philosophy started to interest me as well. I read Stephen Cope's wonderful book, <u>Yoga and the Quest for the True Self</u>, and I was on my way.

WHAT YOGA MEANS TO ME

Here is what Yoga has come to mean to me, sublimely simple, yet utterly profound and transforming:

1) Each of us is already infinitely wondrous--miraculous, awe-inspiring, unfathomable. (This is well hidden beneath the distractions and emotions of everyday life.)
2) Our wondrous nature is the same as the infinite wonder of the universe.
3) The way to experience our wondrous self is to fully experience the present moment, since each moment of consciousness is infinitely wondrous in itself.
4) The mind, body, and spirit are inseparable.
5) Experiencing our wondrous self leads to an abundance of joy and goodness.
6) The techniques of Yoga, leading to "pure awareness", are one method for discovering our true wondrous nature.

It took me a while to fully appreciate the truth and depth of these six simple gems, but now I've pretty much internalized them and they have made my life immeasurably richer.

Let's look at my six key points one at a time:

THE INFINITELY WONDROUS SELF

1) Each of us is already infinitely wondrous--miraculous, awe-inspiring, unfathomable. (This is well hidden beneath the distractions of everyday life and emotion.)

Ask yourself this question: "Which is more wondrous, the entire universe or an individual human being?"

Think deeply about this. Most people can't honestly choose between the two. The question is, of course, unanswerable. The entire universe is so wondrous (miraculous, awe-inspiring, unfathomable— whatever words you choose to use.) Yet, when seen objectively, so is a thinking, breathing, feeling human being.

The fact that it's not easy to choose is fascinating in itself. And it's a dramatic argument for the most basic Yoga idea that just being alive can be infinitely joyful and wondrous in itself, if we let it.

For me this is a blockbuster, mind-blowing insight, and undeniably true. I had always thought of the individual human being as small and insignificant, like a grain of sand on the beach. And we are, in a way.

But each of us is also infinitely wondrous--so wondrous, in fact, that it's hard to decisively declare even the entire universe to be more wondrous.

The universe is complex and unfathomable, indeed. But a human being, in body alone, is equally complex and unfathomable, and, in addition, we are conscious. We are able to perceive the miracle of our own being.

Yoga often uses the word "divine" for this. The most basic finding of Yoga is that each of us is already divine. I prefer the word "wondrous" instead of "divine", because "divine" has too many other religious meanings which Yoga doesn't intend to convey.

According to Yoga, this wondrous, blindingly amazing self is the "true self" referred to in the title of Cope's book, <u>Yoga and the Quest for the True Self</u>, and the process of self-realization, or "enlightenment", is not the process of "becoming" something, but rather simply "discovering" the joy of who we already are, buried beneath the pressing distractions and emotions of everyday life.

For me the conclusive, objective realization that each of us is as wondrous ("divine" if you prefer) as the entire universe is like a light switch that changes everything about the way I think about myself and my life.

THE INFINITELY WONDROUS UNIVERSE

2) Our wondrous nature is the same as the infinite wonder of the universe.

What fills you with wonder and awe? Is it the staggering beauty of the Grand Canyon? A Mozart opera? Walking through a garden blooming with flowers? A jumbo jet passing overhead? The birth of a child? A Brett Favre touchdown pass?

The big things are obvious. We all know what that kind of wonder feels like.

The wonder of a galaxy is obvious. Think about its hundreds of millions of stars rotating around a central axis, and the whole galaxy itself barreling at an incredible speed through space. And then think about the fact that there are millions and millions of galaxies!

What about a paper clip? In many ways a paper clip is as wondrous as a galaxy.

To begin with, like the galaxy, a paper clip consists of millions and millions of things (molecules, atoms, and the even smaller quarks) interacting with each other in complex ways. Then consider what happens to all these tiny elements and how they have to interact with each other. They're not spinning around an axis like the stars in a galaxy, but, then again, a galaxy can't bend and spring back into shape like a paper clip can. If you were small enough to stand on the nucleus of an atom within a paper clip, it would be a lot like standing on earth surrounded by stars.

Now, consider what it took to design and make that paper clip--the metallurgy and engineering that led to the precise formulation of just the right flex, the mines that had to be dug to extract the raw materials, the processing plants that transformed the raw materials into the right metal, the machines that had to be designed and built to manufacture thousands of paper clips a minute.

Somewhere in the world, there is a person who is an expert in paper clips, for whom the whole world revolves around the design and manufacture of paper clips. He or she can tell you the entire history of the development of the paper clip, and what people did before there were paper clips, and who invented it, and what are the advantages and disadvantages of all the different possible designs and materials for paper clips, and the future of the paper clip, and where we go from here, etc. etc.

Convinced yet? In reality, everything within our perception is utterly fantastical and pretty much unfathomable. If a paper clip is wondrous, is not everything wondrous? What's surprising is that we are not in a continual state of gaga just perceiving whatever is in front of us at any given moment.

Really, living is like walking though an incredible kaleidoscope. Consciousness would be like a perpetual hallucination if we didn't have automatic mechanisms for just getting used to the pure wonder of what we see, hear, and feel. But instead, most of time we are simply oblivious to it.

Yoga seeks to put us back in touch with the infinite wonder of just being alive, starting with the wonder of ourselves, then the wonder of the universe. And then Yoga wants us to understand that these wonders are one and the same, because our wondrous selves are an integral part of that infinitely wondrous universe.

But if we and the universe are so wondrous, why don't we experience life like that most of the time? How do we turn this blockbuster insight into an everyday experience?

THE PRESENT MOMENT

3) The way to experience our wondrous self is to fully experience the present moment, since each moment of consciousness is infinitely wondrous in itself.

One of my favorite Yoga stories is the one about the young American who makes an arduous journey to the farthest reaches of the Himalayas, seeking to learn the secret of life and happiness from one of the greatest Yoga gurus.

Once in the Himalayas, he travels five days up into the mountains, through many trials and difficulties. Finally he reaches the high mountain pass where the great old man in a white robe and long flowing grey hair sits in lotus position, staring peacefully off into space.

The young man sits down next to the guru and assumes a similar pose, waiting for his words of wisdom. An hour goes by. Then several hours. Then a day, then several days. Finally the young man says to the old man, "What happens next?"

The guru answers, "Nothing happens next. This is it."

Every moment of life is precious and magical. We experience this not by striving to be happy, but by focusing, in a relaxed way, on the present moment. Most unhappiness comes from regrets about the past or worries about the future, both of which are greatly diminished by gently focusing on the present moment.

Yoga makes no attempt to change the regrets, worries, or other suffering we face, but merely to provide a different perspective on them by making us aware of the wonder of life beyond our current preoccupations, no matter how important or serious they are.

Focusing on the present moment, we cannot help but become tuned into the wonder that is just being alive and conscious. No effort is required, just a relaxed shift in consciousness--a simple receptivity to the indescribable wonder of being alive and conscious at this very moment.

We don't need to try to force ourselves to feel good, as in "positive thinking". When regrets and worries occur, we don't need to fight them. Instead, feel them just as they are, without judgment, then gently refocus on what's going on right now in the current moment. The current moment is rarely unhappy in and of itself.

You might say, this is all well and good if one is already content and happy, and one's problems are relatively small. But what about the truly serious pain and anguish that happens in everyone's life, to one extent or another?

It would appear that the more stressed and troubled one is, the more helpful Yoga might be. Yoga and Yoga-like techniques are being used today for the treatment of even the most overwhelming grief and health problems, including tragedies like terminal illness and the loss of a loved one. Like acupuncture before it, "mindfulness" meditation is starting to be studied and proven scientifically in the West.

You might think if one is "present-focused", one would just sit around like a wet noodle all day and do nothing.

Surprisingly, I find the opposite is true. Since my regrets and anxieties are reduced to relative insignificance (still all there, but put into perspective by the awareness of continual wonder) I find myself with more pure energy to do everything.

I'm able to give myself more completely to other people in conversation. I find myself enjoying or easily tolerating things that would have made me very unhappy before. I am more objective and creative about solving problems.

And, without being false, forced or even effortful in anyway, I do have a much more constant and abiding appreciation of the everyday incredible magic that is being alive.

MIND, BODY, AND SPIRIT

4) The mind, body, and spirit are inseparable.

Yoga in America is best known as a popular exercise program and health club fitness class. Hatha Yoga--the physical poses, is practically synonymous with Yoga in the U.S.

However, just because Yoga poses and movements are popular doesn't mean they're not important to Yoga philosophy. In fact, they are an integral part of Yoga traditions.

Yoga has always taught that whatever we think affects our body, and whatever our body feels affects our mind. The poses of Hatha Yoga are nothing more than a unified meditation involving both the mind and the body. And much of Yoga literature describes the body as though it were one big brain, with its "chakras" (energy centers) and energy flows.

Today the "mind-body connection" is pretty well accepted as part of our thinking about psychology. But it was still a fairly radical idea 15-20 years ago, much less 5000 years ago when first proposed by Yoga gurus. (Actually, maybe it wasn't a radical idea back then. Maybe it just became a radical idea more recently with all our emphasis on the intellect.)

Before this starts sounding too abstract, let me give you a very down-to-earth example. Sometimes, when I'm feeling a little stiff, stressed, or worn out, I get up, spread out my Yoga mat and just run through some basic Yoga poses for ten or fifteen minutes, focusing on the present moment.

This leaves me feeling completely invigorated in mind and spirit. My Yoga routine is like a cup of coffee for me. It works almost every time, no matter how lifeless I feel before I begin.

Let me give you another simple example, this time how the mind affects the body.

I am a serious tennis player. You might recall that all this Yoga stuff started for me when I took Hatha Yoga classes to improve my flexibility for tennis. Yoga was great for this. I did become much more flexible and it did improve my tennis.

What happened next was unexpected. I found that the philosophical practices of Yoga, especially focusing on the present moment, and detaching my ego from the results, had a far more beneficial impact on my tennis than the flexibility. The Yoga of the mind had a bigger effect on my tennis performance than the Yoga of the body.

Many religions (and even some Yoga traditions), treat the body as though it is something to escape from, into the purer world of the spirit. The body is treated almost like the enemy to be overcome in one's spiritual quest, particularly in the ultra-orthodox Catholic tradition I grew up in and struggled with as a kid.

Yoga is the opposite (at least the branches of Yoga that appeal to me). The mind, body, and spirit are inseparable and the same. We are unified beings, and our physical presence and actions are an integral part of our quest for happiness, not separate and distracting.

ABUNDANCE OF JOY

5) *Experiencing our wondrous self leads to an abundance of joy and goodness.*

"What did the Yoga Guru say to the hot dog vendor?"

Answer: "Make me one with everything."

Good joke. But this is, in fact, kind of the way we feel when we're most happy—one with everything.

The great gurus of Yoga and other Eastern traditions achieve inner peace and experience the ultimate joy in life by cultivating the boundless wonder of a child. For them every moment is the occasion for innocent amazement, even in the middle of the most trying circumstances. They still experience all the ordinary pain and difficulty of being human. They just process it differently.

There are certain types of experiences that can suddenly thrust anyone into truly appreciating the utter joy of being alive. The most dramatic example is a serious illness or a near-death experience, in which we are suddenly on the verge of NOT being alive. Another example is temporary blindness. Imagine being blind for a while and suddenly being able to see.

But we can also be moved to this kind of ultimate appreciation of being alive by great music, or overpowering natural beauty, or reading about an amazing scientific discovery, or by the experience of great art.

I'm relatively new to Yoga, but in a way not so new if the subject is "transcendent consciousness" rather than Yoga itself. One of the reasons I'm so attracted to Yoga is that I've had semi-ecstatic "one-with-the-universe" experiences all my life. They are like the experiences Cope describes in his book as the initial basis for his interest in Yoga, but far more plentiful. I seem to be prone to them, in fact, with or without Yoga. I consider this a great blessing.

I've had them in music, in nature, in literature, in relationships, in tennis, occasionally in religion, in business, in my family, in windsurfing (especially in windsurfing, where one must focus intently on the wind and the angle of the sail for hours at a time), etc.

I know Yoga is a new and different kind of pursuit, but I believe it is closely related to, and encompassing of, these other experiences I've had with transcendent consciousness.

The practice of Yoga seeks to make this type of ecstatic, wonder-filled, one-with-the-universe consciousness commonplace and readily available in our everyday lives. In a nutshell, it seeks to give us unlimited joy. (Sound ambitious enough?)

Yoga knows it doesn't have a monopoly on this kind of joy, of course. Yoga assumes itself to have discovered universal truths. If you look at almost any moment of pure joy it usually has this character of total absorption in the present moment, where all other concerns and preoccupations fade into insignificance.

So it's not surprising that one can come up with countless examples of Yoga-type present-focused joy in every aspect of human life. Yoga is just a powerful way of discovering and exploring this aspect of our existence. Yoga didn't invent it.

That's the joy part. What about "goodness". Why would all this self-absorbed consciousness-raising necessarily lead to goodness?

Yoga scriptures have strong and clear teachings about the moral requirements on the path to happiness. These are similar to any religion's. But Yoga also assumes that when we see ourselves and the universe in their true natural wonder, we will be moved to act in a highly moral way. We are much more likely to do the right thing in any circumstance if we see ourselves, our fellow human beings, and the entire universe as wondrous, divine and inseparable.

PURE AWARENESS—YOGA TECHNIQUES

6) The techniques of Yoga, leading to "pure awareness", are one method for discovering our true wondrous nature.

You might have noticed that I haven't even mentioned Yoga techniques so far, except in passing. This is because the techniques are just a means to the philosophical end.

The poses, meditation, and breathing techniques of Yoga all have a central aim—to achieve "pure awareness." Pure awareness is non-judgmental, egoless witness of ourselves and our emotions. It is what allows us to experience the full spectrum of consciousness--the universe and the "universe within". Pure awareness is how we experience more fully all the wonder and awe I have been talking about.

If you are unfamiliar with Yoga, try this deceptively simple Yoga approach to see what I mean:

> Focus on the current moment--what's going on right now at this moment.
>
> Breathe deeply, relax all the muscles in you body.
>
> As a thought or feeling enters your mind, let yourself feel it as deeply as it goes (whether it is a regret about the past, a worry about the future, or just a neutral thought).
>
> Accept and completely allow yourself to have that feeling.
>
> Mentally step out of yourself and watch that feeling as though from the outside.
>
> Gently focus back on the present moment.

You can see this is the opposite of "positive thinking", which involves pushing yourself to think certain positive thoughts, and to push out all negative thoughts.

In contrast, Yoga philosophy involves not trying to think anything in particular, and not controlling your thoughts at all, except to gently focus on the present moment, or to focus your mind on one particular thing. This is actually not that easy to do at first, hence the many branches of Yoga that teach a variety of techniques. With time and habit, however, it becomes truly effortless.

At this point, the magic often just happens on its own. You might find, as I have, that this simple habit eventually starts to bring out the amazing nature of everyday existence, without the often counter-productive effort associated with trying too hard to "figure things out" or searching for something outside ourselves to "turn us on".

Most other Yoga techniques are just expansions and variations of this present-focused philosophy. Poses help us become more aware of our bodies in the present moment. Meditation helps us get into the present moment more and more deeply. Breathing exercises get us in touch with our most primal source of energy—our breath.

Some Yoga techniques have you focus for an extended period of time on just one thing, anything. It could be your breath, or your heartbeat, or a mantra, or a single leaf on a tree (or even a paper clip, I guess). By focusing so completely on one thing, you not only become super aware of your object of concentration, but also kind of clear out your brain to be more receptive to every other sensory perception.

Other Yoga techniques are the opposite—they expand your awareness to take in everything at once instead of a single thing. I call it "ultra-awareness". You become very still and allow yourself to be ultra-sensitive to all the immediate sights, sounds, and feelings around you.

Yoga techniques can have a strong impact on everyday emotions. My own experience, paradoxically, is that I tend to feel emotion more directly and strongly than I did pre-Yoga, but I don't struggle with it as much.

This is because, while I'm struggling with it, I shift into pure non-judgmental awareness pretty much at will, and this helps me see the struggle in perspective, and thus deal with it better without diluting it or avoiding it.

In this way, yoga enhances and informs all our human feelings and actions—it does not replace them or mask them.

If you decide to get into Yoga, you need to pick and choose what is most meaningful and useful for you. The whole picture can be overwhelming and intimidating. The insights you get are more important than the specific practices you adopt. And, even though it has a sprawling 5,000 year old history, ultimately Yoga needs to be about simplicity, not complexity.

IN A NUTSHELL—CONTINUAL WONDER AND AWE

For a simple renewing meditation, I often just recite these same six key points in my head as I relax all my muscles and breathe comfortably:

1) Each of us is already infinitely wondrous--miraculous, awe-inspiring, unfathomable. (This is well hidden beneath the distractions and emotions of everyday life.)
2) Our wondrous nature is the same as the infinite wonder of the universe.
3) The way to experience our wondrous self is to fully experience the present moment, since each moment of consciousness is infinitely wondrous in itself.
4) The mind, body, and spirit are inseparable.
5) Experiencing our wondrous self leads to an abundance of joy and goodness.
6) The techniques of Yoga, leading to "pure awareness", are one method for discovering our true wondrous nature.

As persuasive as I hope these cosmic truths are after reading this essay, it really takes considerable (but relaxed) practice to work them into one's habitual everyday life and consciousness.

I once wrote to a friend, "Just relax, breathe deeply, and experience each moment, non-judgmentally, as it's happening, no matter what is happening." That's a summary of Yoga wisdom in a single sentence.

The central message of Yoga is that just being alive contains infinite and unlimited wonder (and meaning) all by itself, regardless of what else is happening in your life. Yoga reduces the complexity of our lives to the elegant simplicity of continual wonder and awe, without losing any of the other things we treasure about being human.

A FEW RECOMMENDED YOGA RESOURCES

These two books and website are an excellent guide to the philosophy and practice of Yoga:

Yoga and the Quest for the True Self by Stephen Cope. An inspiring exploration of Yoga philosophy, and its relationship to Western religion and psychology—for me the single most influential Yoga book.

Kripalu Yoga--A Guide to Practice On and Off the Mat by Richard Faulds and Senior Teachers of Kripalu Center for Yoga and Health. The title is self-explanatory. Warm, thorough, and very well-written.

www.parayoga.com   Rod Stryker's website—excellent synthesis of Tantric Yoga for modern devotees.

Bob Weisenberg

www.myyogabook.wordpress.com

Bob Weisenberg is a Yoga philosopher, writer and blogger. This chapter is an excerpt from his online book/blog, "The Wonder of Being Alive—Yoga Philosophy Demystified."

Bob leads the Philosophy Group for the Yoga Journal Online Community, where, as Bob puts it, "we discuss Yoga's lighter topics, like The Meaning of Life, The Wonder of the Universe, Pure Awareness, and How Can I Achieve Happiness?" See:

http://community.yogajournal.com/reweis

Bob's other great passion is flamenco guitar, which to him is another form of Yogic spiritual expression. (It's even said that the Spanish Gypsies originally came from India!) Hear his music at:

www.myspace.com/padreehijo

"Instead of finding the time to practice Yoga, practice Yoga all the time."

FIRM BUTTOCKS OR SELF-REALIZATION?

LAURA SACHS

I have been practicing yoga for nearly 30 years and even though there have been times I have had to put my practice on the back burner, what has remained constant is my LOVE of Hatha Yoga. My practice has taught me about myself and has assisted me on my journey as a human being.

I introduced hatha yoga classes to a health club in 1990. Up until that point, yoga was taught in "studios" which offered only yoga classes. I was managing a group exercise program and knew the benefits of yoga to all ages. Management was skeptical because of liability issues. I promised to not teach head or shoulder stands initially. They agreed. The rest is history.

It is commonplace to have "Mind/Body" sections of health clubs now where mind/body disciplines such as yoga and Pilates are taught. Hatha Yoga classes seeped into many health clubs. According to the January 2003 issue of Newsweek Magazine, 15 million Americans are practicing yoga. Americans, I think, had stepped into a yoga class perhaps for superficial reasons, such as a "firm buttocks" to start. They soon discovered the deeper dimensions of this ancient practice, and this it the reason for its continued popularity.

The word yoga means "yoke" or "union", but union with what? Hatha Yoga is one of eight limbs of this body of knowledge. Traditionally Hatha, the physical body branch of yoga, was a means to master the body so that one could master the mind. If our body is uncomfortable in lotus position how will we be able to open our attention to the practice of meditation?

The asanas as we know them today were not the main focus of yoga until the mid-1800's. The objective of yoga is Self-Realization, not firm buttocks. The real pearl inside of the oyster, the true benefit of a Hatha Yoga practice is its inherent design as a vehicle to Self-Realization. I am referring to union with "Self" as in capital "S" or "Higher Self", as distinct from ego or little "s".

We, as modern day people, can practice this art and glean the inherent treasures of this body of knowledge. We can use it as a foreground to discovering the gifts of our life, our own unique purpose, the intelligence within our bodies and the attributes of our Higher "Self". One of the adjunct benefits and possibly the lowest common denominator of these yoga postures may be firm buttocks. I say, "Yes!" to that! Having firm buttocks is perhaps a self-esteem enhancer. We feel good about how we look! This system, Hatha Yoga, goes way beyond being a self-esteem enhancer. I have identified three dimensions, stepping-stones, if you will, to increased self-awareness: focus, attention and mindfulness. These may be baby steps to "Self Realization", but they are doable!

Focus is fostered by a yoga practice. In order to execute a demanding posture such as the Standing Bow Pulling Pose, or Dan Day Amana Dhan U Ra Sana, we must focus our attention on one spot. Our eye gaze, fixed, then becomes the forefront of all other thoughts and sensations that arise. This one-legged balance is a serious back bend. It is a beautiful form; it is balance in action. What are you thinking about while performing this posture? Where is your attention drawn? Certainly it's not to your grocery list or to your next professional meeting or even a night out with friends.

On *what* are you focusing? As new students we are imitating the postures. As we progress we begin to seek guidance asking, "Am I doing this properly?" As we progress we begin to notice and appreciate how well another student is executing the posture. We begin to compare ourselves to other students. We are focused on the proper mechanics of any posture, and this never entirely goes away with demanding postures.

However, as we continue to practice, new layers of awareness arise one breath at a time! This is the mental training that is fostered by our practice. Through focus and attention we become acquainted with the art of mindfulness in this pose. During the execution of the standing bow pulling posture, we become acquainted with the process of doing and the process of being. This is the pearl we are seeking.

For the last 10 years I have taken class in San Francisco from Mary Jarvis. Mary is a very inspiring teacher. She is technically very knowledgeable, but the one liners she shares during class enrich my life and point to this art of mindfulness. At some point she will remark about how we have "done it again". She will say, "Thank you for giving me some of *That*, again!"…*That* feeling of union, peace, "at-one-ment" that yoga class provides. In the true sense our practice is recreation: *re-creation*. We reset ourselves each time we practice.

Do you then leave class and forget about this mental training, the clarity that you feel during class, in posture? Have you had the experience of leaving class feeling aglow only to find yourself glaring at a driver that cuts you off? Our practice is about bringing yoga/union into our daily lives. Our practice is about bringing non-judgment and peace into our lives and our world, one moment at a time.

When I teach yoga I ask my participants to differentiate. This word means, "to perceive a difference", for instance between a sunken rib cage and a lifted rib cage, to distinguish between a lifted and a reaching rib cage. Triangle posture or Trikonsana is a way we develop or enhance our discernment. Any wide base posture grounds us. We take a stand and we spread our wings in this posture.

We are taking a stand and holding our ground as we connect with our heart and lungs – or our feelings and breath. We are imitating the structure of the Tri/Angle – a beautifully balanced, basic form! We are opening our heart and lungs and nurturing this relationship in this posture. We are reaching for what is above as well as to what is below.

The same process is possible in our daily lives through mindfulness. We are able to differentiate the subtle nuances of our attitudes toward others and ourselves. Opening our hearts allows us to take a path that has heart. We feel it! We know it.

Are you familiar with the vow of "Ahisma"? This vow originated, as did yoga, 5000 years ago. Later it was adopted by a religious sect called Jain, which began in India in the 8th Century BC – at the time of Moses. Simply put, the vow of "Ahimsa" is "Harm to none". The distinction is made that this includes all sentient (feeling, emotive) beings – even "ourselves".

As teachers many of you may have had the experience of students who are blatantly competitive during class. Our concern is one of safety - one can hurt herself if she pushes too hard. "Harm to none" means accepting ourselves as we are in the posture in any given moment--having enough compassion for ourselves to celebrate the fact that we are in class!

"Harm to none" is a tall order, one that requires attention, and focus, a "mindful-ness". Asking the following question really helps: "How can I honor the light, the life force in this person, within this situation?" Ram Das, the ex-Harvard Professor who has written and lectured on spiritual exploration for the past four decades in such books as "Be Here Now", "Grist For The Mill" and "How Can I Help?" illustrated this quite well in one of his early talks.

He related the story of a woman who was involved in the process of Spiritual Awakening, this Mindfulness to which I am referring. She was on a New York freeway when a truck changed lanes and came dangerously close to hitting her car. She opened her window and yelled, "You, You weird expression of God, You!" Bless her for expressing her feelings in the highest manner possible in that moment. Even in a moment when she was reacting to what felt like a life-threatening incident, she adhered to her commitment of spiritual awakening, to her vow to honor the light in each person.

We learn about ourselves by simply showing up and executing the postures. I lecture on wellness to corporations. I invite my participants to define the word, "Fitness". I have come to define Fitness as the ability to respond to a situation, or the circumstances that make up our life, in a proactive not a reactive manner. Our practice assists us in being responsive rather than reactive. This respons-ability is required for spiritual awakening.

In my mind, mindfulness is the most important gift of a regular yoga practice. Hatha Yoga is meant to assist us in our daily lives, make us more responsive, stronger and more committed to our values. We learn so much about ourselves by just showing up and executing the postures. Through our practice we develop the ability to stay in posture. This endurance can translate into our lives. We are able to hang in just a little longer in difficult situations, or when life doesn't seem to be going our way. We learn how to dig down and find the focus and attention, the strength, really, that is required. Namaste.

Laura Sachs

http://bodymindfitness.net

Laura D. Sachs has been actively involved in the fitness and health fields for over twenty years.

She is certified by the American Council on Exercise, Aerobics and Fitness Association of America, and is a Registered Yoga Instructor with Yoga Alliance.

Laura has contributed and written for IDEA Fitness Journal, FitYoga, American Fitness, Shape magazines and Natural Health.

She is the creator of E-MOTION® Mind/Body Fitness Video Program, E-MOTION® Relaxation CD and Yoga Walk CD.

Laura also practices Jin Shin Jyustu and Cranio-Sacral Therapies.

YOGA'S REMARKABLE IMPACT ON OUR LIVES AND ITS SCIENTIFIC BASIS

TOMMIJEAN AND BENJAMIN THOMAS

In 1978, we began our life-changing relationship with Yogacharya B.K.S. Iyengar. "Yogacharya" is defined as a teacher and master of the yogic traditions, and as a guru who practices the yogic exercises and teachings. We began our training with him and his family in 1979 and have continued to the present (2009).

We managed to stay focused on the path of yoga while raising our large family with six children and pursuing additional careers. We have taught thousands of students over the years from all walks of life and they have learned from us while we have also learned from them.

In November of 2008, we published *Iyengar Yoga: The Integrated and Holistic Path to Health*. Iyengar gave title to our book and wrote the foreword. Our book covers, in a condensed form, the main concepts of yoga and how to perform the postures, meditation, breathing, philosophy, chanting, and anatomy. It contains over twenty original illustrated series to help both teachers and students learn to sequence and link the postures to make for a fulfilling yoga practice session.

Yoga has been a truly remarkable life-changing experience for each of us. We would like to tell you about it individually:

WHAT YOGA MEANS TO ME (TOMMIJEAN)

Yoga is my salvation. I came to yoga training with a hidden handicap in my legs that greatly prevented me from physically functioning like others and that gravely limited my physical activities. I had severe varicosities and edema that resulted from four back-to-back pregnancies. I was in pain almost all of the time.

Standing and walking, which is taken for granted by many, was a challenge and very painful for me and I was unable to be ambulatory for any prolonged period of time. Modern medicine was unable to alleviate my pain.

Within a month of intense daily yoga training I experienced such a true miracle of medical gains in my legs, that to this day, I rarely miss a daily personal practice of yoga. Yoga has also provided other gains for me, such as a way to manage minor aches and pains, my weight, stress, and my emotions.

With the practice of yoga, I find I am calmer, have more mental clarity, focus, better concentration, and improved interpersonal relations. Yoga also inspires creativity and productivity. Spiritually, I developed an intimacy, a trust, and faith in the Supreme Being that I had never before achieved.

WHAT YOGA MEANS TO ME (BEN)

It is with great joy that I have watched the transition of yoga here in my country, the USA, between 1976 and 2009. When my wife, Tommijean, and I first began yoga practice, we were certainly considered as and viewed as outsiders to the mainstream of America.

In the beginning years of our yoga history, we lived in the South for seven years. Not only were we a black and white mixed couple, but we were practicing a "strange California cultish practice." We did our best not to be bothered by our public reception.

I suffered with a severe speech disorder of stuttering beginning from a very young age. In addition, I had reoccurring and excruciating migraine attacks. Both of these medical problems found no relief with modern Western medicine. These conditions seriously affected my career and my relationships.

Today, both of these conditions are practically non-existent. However, as our Guru taught us, "stop and you will lose." My yoga miracles were so blatant, that only a fool would have discontinued the yoga. Now, at this later time in our lives, we both intend to increase our time in our private practice of yoga.

Although I followed Tommijean into the training of yoga about a month after she had started, I quickly developed enthusiasm for it. Tommijean had experienced such miracles with her leg problems and seemed to be going through such a vivid and positive transformation, that I had to see what she was doing. With my lifelong speech difficulties, I never expected to be leading and teaching chants and virtually singing solo as I now do in my classes and seminars. Yoga is my exploration and development of the self.

OUR SCIENTIFIC RESEARCH

Over the last decade, Iyengar encouraged us to use our education and skills to research the benefits of yoga and to then publish the results for the public. This we did in our recent book, *Iyengar Yoga: The Integrated and Holistic Path to Health*. Our research on yoga consists of three separate studies involving 614 assessed subjects and additionally includes a Comparative Analysis that examines the similarities and differences in yoga benefits by those who are newcomers to yoga, long-term practitioners, and a group of professional teachers.

This research project revealed that there are significant and positive physical, psychological, and spiritual benefits from the practice of Iyengar Yoga. It also validates the Thomas method of approaching Iyengar Yoga. The motivation behind our research was based on the fact that oftentimes yoga teachers have to rely on appeals to authority or unconfirmed reports of success when justifying their interventions. We felt that ignoring the methodology of contemporary science would diminish the creditability of Iyengar Yoga as it increasingly gained worldwide fame and acceptance.

Our research revealed that physical gains were the primary motivator to begin the practice of yoga. Spiritual interests, though, increase over time. Many American practitioners now use yoga as a complimentary alternative to medicine (CAM). It is becoming known as an effective adjunct to Western medical treatment. Integrative medicine, a combination of complementary alternative medicine and mainstream medicine is now becoming popular.

When we studied our research subjects, we were amazed to see how very many diverse medical problems and illnesses were helped by the practice of yoga. Although our Guru told us that yoga is not a panacea, it appears that yoga has a profound healing effect on a great number of physical ailments. Yoga physical practice provides all the gains that other exercises do, such a stretching and building strength, and it can include an aerobic workout. A restorative practice is also available. This is a more suitable way of performing the poses when one is very tired or has an ailment that needs to be attended to. It is surprisingly powerful.

Yoga practitioners often demonstrate an uplifted feeling following a session. The student of yoga typically feels more energetic, less stressed, greater equanimity, and increased self-control after yoga practice. One's mood improves and various types of emotional disturbances are reduced.

Our recent research, published in our book, gave empirical evidence that yoga provides many psychological benefits. Research subjects were assessed and evaluated using standardized tests. Results were very significant showing that yoga contributed to increased psychological health.

A good yoga session typically evokes peaceful, happy, and loving feelings. Overtime the practitioner goes through changes and develops more patience and understanding. The state of mind is different after practicing yoga, for negative thoughts vanish, and it's as if one becomes a different person. Our research revealed that there were higher levels of mental acuity and clarity in yoga practitioners.

A FEW CONCERNS IN A SEA OF SUCCESS

It is truly exciting to see the various styles and methods of yoga develop worldwide. Yoga is becoming more and more diverse and specialized. For instance, there are classes for children, classes for those with specific illnesses, classes for various age groups, and classes for the elderly. There are classes for the businessman, the housewife, and the student. As we showed in our research, yoga is for ALL. Those from different races, ethnicities, religions, both genders, and so forth can participate in yoga and gain from it. America's melting pot of differences is now being seen on the floor of the Yoga studio.

The reception to and acceptance of yoga has greatly increased over the last decade. Yoga studios are sprouting up all over. One might even say yoga has become like a fad. And this is okay as long as the traditional essence and meaning of the yoga does not get lost or abolished in all the current-day activity. And we hope that the interest in yoga does not fade over time as it does with some fads.

Our desire is that some of the Sanskrit terms will be maintained, for if various people pick out different names for the same posture then the authenticity of yoga may be lost and the ability for people to communicate well about a posture could possibly break down.

Another concern is that teachers are now being certified in various styles of yoga with minimal training. One can get hurt with improper practice just like in any other type of physical practice and the teacher clearly needs to be qualified to present the yoga properly and to prevent the students from getting hurt. We are also concerned that too much emphasis in yoga may be now placed in the physical realm when the ultimate goal of yoga is spiritual.

INTO OUR YOGA FUTURE

This year we will be 68 and 71 and are experiencing the aging process. Iyengar tells us that yoga will allow us to age gracefully. By grace we mean accepting the inevitability and realities of aging, adjusting our practice and life-style accordingly, and, through sustained prior yoga practice, having the skills and tools to maintain agility and range of motion.

This would also include acquiring the mental acuity, understanding, consciousness, and awareness of the life-cycle, including death. This grace is the applied knowledge and ability to change what need not be endured, and to endure what cannot be changed.

Having practiced for over 30 years, with the fortune of being well-trained by a great master of yoga, being part of the yoga-lineage, it is rewarding and comforting to truly experience with greater clarity the wonderful, all-encompassing aspects of yoga, the Spectrum of Life. Truly, yoga is the study of the Self, Life, and how to live life well. In America and throughout the world, there is a growing community of people who now have access to this bestowed tool and knowledge.

A BLESSING FOR MODERN MANKIND

Yoga is a blessing for modern mankind. It positively affects all parts of our beings, mind, body, and spirit. The greater the amount of time a practitioner can devote to yoga, the greater the benefits. We have remained devotees of B.K.S. Iyengar and his style and method of yoga for over 30 years now. Our Guru is world renown for his innovative, unique, and superlative presentation and teachings of yoga. His yoga is distinct from all other systems and known for its intricacies, timings, sequencing, therapeutics, alignment, and props.

Guruji tells us that yoga brings "health, happiness, prosperity, and hope." We prostrate to him with devotion and gratitude for his teaching of us, his caring and direction over all these years. We believe our lives have been significantly blessed and enriched due to our yoga endeavors.

Tommijean and Benjamin Thomas

www.thomasyoga.com

Tommijean Thomas, Ph.D. and Ben Thomas, B.S. have been yoga practitioners since 1976. Their teaching of yoga has spanned over 30 years.

The Thomases are Senior Yoga Teachers certified by Yogachara, Dr. B.K.S. Iyengar of the Ramamani Iyengar Memorial Yoga Institute (RIMYI) in Pune, India. Their original certifications were granted by B.K.S. Iyengar in 1983.

The Thomases have traveled to Pune, India to study with B.K.S. Iyengar, his daughter, Dr. Geeta Iyengar, and his son, Praschant Iyengar, on eleven occasions. They took additional trainings with Iyengar and his family at seminars held in the United States.

SKIP THE MIDDLE MAN AND
GO DIRECTLY TO BLISS!

SARITA-LINDA ROCCO

You can't talk about *yoga* without talking about the mind. In all of its dualistic glory, it is the master of ceremony of life as a human being. The mind is our greatest asset and our biggest challenge, sometimes within moments of each other. It's always there--choosing, judging, challenging, assessing and protecting our lives, moment to moment.

True to its nature, the mind is pleased when desires are met. It loves stimulation such as reading magazines, playing internet games and puzzles, and more. The mind enjoys observing others' problems and desires by watching TV shows and movies. It loves entertainment. When it is occupied, the mind is happy.

It is our mind that takes us outside ourselves on the search for happiness. "If I can just get this job I'd be so happy!" "Oh, I'll feel great once I have that house, car, lover, designer outfit, and _____". You can fill in the blank. The list goes on and on. It prods us to keep going until the desired object is achieved. Then, for a short time, it stops wanting. In those spaces, where the desire stops, we experience satisfaction. "Ah, I did it!" or "Whoo, I got it!"

Of course, that feeling wanes and, before long, the next desire is born, and it's up and at 'em! Out we go for the chase, which is exhausting. The endless activities wear us out. The body becomes tired and the mind keeps pushing! More thoughts, more desires. Some call it "the rat race".

You can't fault your mind. It is perfectly designed to "want". It's one of our most important survival mechanisms. The problem is we identify our mind as "who we are", and become totally absorbed in chasing desires. This is a common challenge called "being human".

How many times have you reflected on your personal "rat race" and thought, "Isn't there a better way? There has to be more to life than this!" Each time our family vacations at the beach, my sister says, "I feel fantastic here! If I could bottle this feeling and sell it, I'd become a millionaire!" That "feeling". What is it?

Remember when you were a child? True happiness and contentment just "happened'". It was easy and natural. Simple things like staring at the sky, feeling the wind, and smelling flowers and grass could trigger the "feeling". No worries or fears. Remember?

Where is that feeling? I asked a few friends to describe their feeling of joy and contentment. Here is what they said:

"The feeling wells up, starting from my toes and tingles all the way to the top of my head."

"It feels warm in my belly"; "It makes me laugh or cry."

"It feels like my heart grows bigger than my body. I am inside my heart instead of my heart inside me."

All of these descriptions have one thing in common; they arise from inside our own body, not the 'thing' that caused it outside.

Yoga teaches that true contentment is already inside, like a flowing river. Achieving and acquiring isn't necessary to access the real river of contentment. Yoga calls it "Your True Nature" or "The Self" and it is independent of, yet includes, the things. It is ancient, infinite and omnipresent--present before the desire. In other words, you can skip the middle man (things) and cultivate pure contentment or the state of "Yoga" Itself.

My cousin's family is farmers. While growing up, I had the privilege of many weekend farm experiences. One of my most vivid memories was the fresh milk at breakfast. Having come from the cow just moments before, it was pure, creamy, rich and delicious. When I returned home and back to "milk from a carton", it was apparent to me that the milk from the carton was not nearly as good as the milk from the farm. Adding enrichments from the "outside" did not make the natural milk better. Milk is sweetest in its purest state.

Our capacity for contentment is much the same--sweetest in its purest state. It feels good mixed with achievements, but it is sweetest in its purest form, which is Yoga. Like raw milk before the processing and additives, deeper contentment is pure and delicious, richest when experienced for no reason outside itself. No fear, no desire.

Things appear and disappear; the state of yoga does not. It is the river, the purest form of peace untouched, unfiltered. Bliss is alive inside of you. Desires rise and fall like puppets, your mind the puppeteer. Yoga teaches that there is a state deeper than contentment, more subtle and refined than the one brought on by the job, the car, the partner or the clothes. It is Pure Awareness, the real you, beyond and including the mind, Eternal and Divine. It is the pure milk of All Being. The yoga texts call it "Shiva – the embodiment of knowledge and bliss".

To personally and directly experience this "state of Yoga" is the birthright of every human being, the most important journey of life. Yoga practice and study is the map and pathway to that continuing experience of bliss.

My favorite yoga scripture below reflects this teaching:

NIRVANA-SHATKAM-*Chid Ananda Rupah Shivo'Ham Shivo'Ham*

(Aadi Shankara Acharya 788 AD- 820 AD)

I am not mind or intellect. Nor am I the thought or the consuming ego. Neither am I the sense of hearing, tasting or seeing. I am not the sky, nor the earth, nor fire, nor wind; for I am consciousness and bliss. I am Shiva! I am the embodiment of knowledge and bliss.

I am neither the sign of breath (prana) nor the five fold vital airs, nor the seven elements of the body, nor the five sheaths, nor the organs of action like mouth nor hands, not feet genitals and the back; for I am consciousness and bliss. I am Shiva! I am Shiva!

I know no aversion, nor any attachment; I covet not, nor does illusion shroud my eyes; I have no pride, nor any touch of envy; neither duty nor selfish purpose; neither desire nor freedom; for I am consciousness and bliss. I am Shiva! I am Shiva!

I am neither virtue nor vice acquired, neither pleasure nor pain, neither mantra nor sacred place, neither scriptures (Vedas) nor sacrificial fire. I am neither the enjoyer (subject) nor the enjoyable (object), nor the enjoyment (action); for I am consciousness and bliss. I am Shiva! I am Shiva!

Death cannot claim me, nor fear shake my calm; division of caste or creed I know not; I have no father, no mother , no birth, no brother, no friend, no teacher, no pupil; nor have I another life, for I am consciousness and bliss. I am Shiva! I am Shiva!

I am changeless, formless, enveloping all, omnipresent, untouched by sensory organs, unfathomable, beyond the realm of freedom or bondage. For me there is always evenness; for I am consciousness and bliss. I am Shiva! I am Shiva!

SAT CHIT AANAND-Truth Consciousness and Bliss

Sarita-Linda Rocco

www.yogainlet.com

Sarita-Linda Rocco, CSYT, Yoga & Ayurveda Teacher, Therapist and Consultant.

Own/Operate YOGA INLET -Yoga and Ayurveda Center in West Reading, PA.

Certifications: Wise Earth School of Ayurveda® Advanced Teacher, Master Yoga Teacher Institute Svaroopa® Yoga; Master Yoga Teacher Institute Meditation Teacher; Erich Schiffmann Freedom Style Hatha Yoga Vinyasa Flow; Bikram Hatha Yoga

Created & developed "YOGA on the BALL" (VHS, DVD).

YOGA AIN'T WHAT YOU THINK IT IS

CHARLES FARIS

SETTING A FOUNDATION

It's the middle of October, 2009, and I am spending the week with John Friend, founder of Anusara yoga and my yoga guru for all intents and purposes. And like the title says, yoga ain't what you think it is, probably. And yet what is it? There's been a lot of ink spilt over that question, and given just how ineffable this thing called yoga is, how slippery the slope to self-discovery can be (I think I just dropped a clue!), let's see what happens if we look at it sideways, and in an attempt to eff the ineffable and get a grasp on the slippery eel of yoga we'll just turn our gaze for a moment to another much more scary word, guru.

BRING ON THE KOOL-AID

Ah yes, guru. Visions of the Beatles, long haired hippies in loin cloths, gibbering bearded monkey-faced shysters with a taste for American dollars and Rolls Royces and maybe even things of a more sinister nature, of thousand dollar purchases of meditation lessons, and of families wrecked by the departure of earnest youth dropping out of college in order to journey into the light. Yes, guru. Lots of baggage with that word.

And yet in all of that imagery only one word really applies to the pure meaning of the word guru; light. Yep. The word guru just means light bringer. It's an honorific, which can be challenging in contemporary America. And when I say that John Friend is my yoga guru I'm just saying he's my teacher whom I honor for bringing me closer to my true nature, which means happier, more comfortable being me; funnier, sexier, all that stuff you think you need to be happier. And being closer to your true nature is what brings all that stuff.

LET'S START OVER

Yoga ain't what you think it is. It's a system to bring you closer to being the person you truly deeply madly want to be, know you are, and yet fear that you may not be, and are terrified that you will never be. And I'm studying this week with the guy who has helped me the most in that regard, and who promises to help me even more.

WOODS FOR THE TREES

So let's get into something useful. Take a minute and sit up straight. Take a deep breath and open your heart. There. Now we can progress.

We started this thing on a Monday, with a day devoted to what John calls the five universal principles of alignment, which begs the question; aligning with what? Aligning with your true nature, of course. This is yoga after all. So forget all that stuff about jumping around on the floor with your foot behind your head, wearing sexy duds while listening to music with indecipherable words.

SHALL WE START AGAIN?

Come to the front of your seat, fill yourself with breath, feel your heart. Feel how much you want to be that person you truly madly want to be, know you are, fear you are not, quiver that you may never be.

The first principle that will bring you into recognition of that self is called opening to grace. What's that? Open to grace. Let yourself feel your connection with your maker, your source, the life energy that flows through you, that moves you, however stumblingly, through every day of your life.

Yes, we stumble. We stumble because we are not aligned. We are off balance. There are ruder ways of saying this. And you know that. So to end the stumbling, to speed up the recovery, we follow the principles. And we start with principle number one. Open to grace. Soften up, open your heart, feel your connection to something bigger than you. Something as big as big gets, and then magnified by a really big number. Something bigger than that.

SO WHAT HAPPENS WHEN WE DO THAT?

And why should I care? What happens is that we get happy. We feel joy and connection. We delight in our own freedom.

Or to put it another way: we get into the zone. Stuff happens with exquisite grace (that word again). We glide through the yuckiness without so much as soiling our shoes. That thing that was so hard back in (insert time frame) with (insert person, challenge, task, etc.) suddenly eases up, starts to shimmer, and it's like you are Keanu Reeves in The Matrix, minus the machine guns, walking up walls, doing backflips and landing in the right place at the right time to say the right thing to the right person.

SOUNDS GREAT, WHERE DO I SIGN UP?

Of course, we live on planet Earth, not a computer program, so there is the very earthiness of our existence that we have to work with, which brings us to day two and the second principle, muscle energy. Say what? Well, you didn't think it was all just breathe deep, feel your heart, and now everything is bliss, did you?

Or maybe you did and that's why I am here to say, once again with exclamation point; yoga ain't what you think it is!

So let's look at a famous picture to make sense of both of those principles at once.

The first photograph of planet earth, taken on November 10, 1967, just after the summer of love. This big giant heavy hunk of stone, floating in empty space. Floating.

SPACE IS GRACE. EARTH ENERGY IS MUSCLE ENERGY.

So there we go. We float in this grace. We feel this connection. And...well, if we are going to do anything, make any sort of action, we have to have some hold-to-it-ness. Some gravity. Some place to do things from. We have to draw into ourselves our strength, our love, our muscle, in order to provide, as the Earth does, a platform for action.

And now imagine that big beautiful planet once again. Floating through space. Being pulled though space by an object so large that we can't comprehend its size, mass, weight, gravity. Really. An object of such mass that it creates unimaginable heat, and light! Just through the gravitational force of pulling itself into itself. And now get that this unimaginably large and unbelievably gravitational object, our sun, our own bringer of light, our guru, is also floating in space, held aloft by the grace of Universe.

Now remember, these are just two of five principles. And this is just one system of hundreds. We can make this yoga thing as complex as we wish. And we can make it as simple as we wish. And it always comes down to aligning with your true nature. Finding your right relationship with the infinite. Being truly madly deeply happy. Now, sit back and soak all of that in, float in a bit of bliss, and hold it together. Peace.

Charles Faris

www.creative-lifestyles.com

In my hatha yoga classes I incorporate an active physical style of slow movement with long holds and a steady attention to flowing internally and externally with the breathe.

I incorporate as much as I can of the training that I have received from all of my teachers, primarily John Friend and Todd Norian in the tantric Anusara tradition, and including Ganga White and Tracey Rich of the White Lotus Institute, and David Swenson, who teaches Ashtanga Yoga as explicated by Pattabhi Jois. All of these lineages flow from Sri Tirumalai Krishnamacharya.

I also incorporate heart meditations from sources as diverse as contemporary Sufism, the Tantric Buddhist lineage of the Dalai Lama, and the Institute of Heartmath, a contemporary research organization located in Boulder Creek, California, as well as various new thought philosophies, in particular the work of Mike Dooley of Totally Unique Thoughts.

HOW YOGA SAVED MY LIFE

MAUREEN SPENCER

My journey into the world of yoga started when I was 15 years old in Boston in 1968. I remember picking up my mother's *Women's Day Magazine* and there was an article about yoga. As I read the article I saw the words "mind control". My attention was riveted to the description of what yoga meant and the pictures.

The story was about a woman in her 40's who taught yoga, a housewife from Massachusetts where I lived. Excitement soared through my body as I saw how she did these amazing contorted postures. I didn't quite understand it but something stirred inside of me that wanted to pursue it.

I examined each pose carefully with my innocent young eyes and wondered how she got into them without injuring herself. I also wondered why? Her words described how peaceful the practice made her feel and that aroused within me a yearning and hunger for that kind of internal peace.

When this profound epiphany happened, I was a chubby teenager, feeling lost and confused, angry (and not knowing why) at my parents, brothers and sisters. Being the oldest of 13 siblings was taking its toll on me. There were so many diapers, bottles, kids screaming, fights, dishes, and laundry to do, that I was mentally depleted.

While my parents were loving caretakers, and tried their best to care for the brood they created, to an overwhelmed mother's helper it was pure insanity. I was raised in a strict, Irish Catholic upbringing that was filled with such hypocrisy most of the time. How could we outwardly accept and honor God, yet at home there was anything but feelings of goodness and spirituality.

My parent's world was so out of control that the thought of having a mind in control was intoxicating to me. I didn't realize then what I came to understand years later--that all the schedules I created for cleaning the house, doing the dishes, and taking out the trash were the initiation into being a future control freak.

As I developed an outward appearance of being mature for my age, the inside terrain was a sea of turmoil and out-of-control feelings and emotions. As I tried to control the external craziness we lived in, I couldn't control what I felt inside.

Overeating was my comfort – candy and cookies to calm me down temporarily. Now we understand that sugar temporarily raises the hormone serotonin, and makes us have a brief period of happiness. Back then, I had no idea how overwhelmed and depressed I had become and sought comfort in sweets. Thus, the weight gain and continued feelings of being overwhelmed.

Many times I wanted to run away, but like most kids, it was a fantasy because I had nowhere to go. I was attending a Catholic high school in South Boston. My mother decided to send me there. She figured it would be good for me not to attend the local city high school where I might get into trouble.

My rebellious side was brewing and the rough culture in the city would have been the worst thing for me at that time. There was a lot of social unrest during the 1960's in Boston, with large movements of families relocating from the South to the city neighborhoods. We lived in a "tough" neighborhood and experienced inner city living at its worst.

When I hear today of horrendous releases of emotional rage in high schools and colleges I can relate on some level. I just never built it up to the point of external explosion. It was bottled up nicely in a good girl image, being as perfect as I could to get acceptance from everyone.

Then along came YOGA! After I read that article, I started to practice the poses in my bedroom every day after school. I was hooked. I laid out the magazine and followed the instructions for the various postures and meditation techniques. I remember they included the lotus pose, the cat, the downward facing dog, the sun salutation, the shoulderstand, the headstand, back bends and forward bends. The magazine article had just enough to get me started in my practice.

Soon after, I purchased my first yoga book, *Lilias, Yoga and You* by Lilias Folan. At that time she was on PBS television early in the morning with her bright smile and long braided hair, teaching yoga to the world. She still teaches it today, as graceful as ever, in her mid-sixties.

Richard Hittleman's books on yoga were the next door that opened to me. There were no studios or classes in those days for a young teenager in Boston. The yoga books were my only source of comfort and strength. It made you feel like you knew the authors personally, following their lead in and out of contorted movements, but knowing something profound was happening inside. Then along came yoga LP records, which played through a class while you followed along with a small handout. I still have two of those in storage as memories of how far yoga has come in America.

Inspired by this power over my body, and the feeling of wellbeing, I began to eat more sensibly and gradually started to lose weight. In less than three weeks, I lost 25 lbs. I started to get more firm and tight, and improved my grades in school. I was clearly more centered and focused. I looked good and exuded a genuine peacefulness inside.

During my 11ᵗʰ year in high school, when I started my yoga practice, I fondly remember this one particular nun, Sister Jesse, who saw the subtle transformation in me. She would ask me questions about what I was doing and reading. In desperation to understand what I was experiencing in altered states while meditating, I started to read Timothy Leary's books on altered states of consciousness from LSD. I could relate to what he described while he was on heavy hallucinogenic drugs.

Sister Jesse was concerned about my reading and quizzed me about it, but she could see I was following a very different approach from Leary in my quest for personal transformation. His description of increased awareness, expanded consciousness and direct perception was what I was experiencing from all the yoga poses and deep meditative states. I was slowly becoming more enlightened.

That year she moved me up from the back of the room to the first row in the class and would often keep me after class to carry on profound discussions about what I was learning from yoga. I had her intrigued to say the least. I made her question her Catholic paradigm more than once, quoting and explaining yoga philosophy and what I thought was the true essence of what religion should be about.

I found my family life was more manageable and not so overwhelming. It gave me the peace I was trying to find. As I became more centered, the randomness in my family sought out my order, and things changed for the better. I was the surrogate mother to my siblings, so this new inner strength had a positive effect on them.

If I had not stumbled upon yoga in 1968 as a teenager, I don't know what would have happened to me. I wonder if I would ever have gone to college. I really wanted to be a doctor but knowing my parents financial state, I settled for being a nurse. Nursing school came easy for me as I entered the training at seventeen years of age in 1970. I introduced some of the nursing students to yoga and got permission to use one of the classrooms to start a yoga class. My first yoga teacher job!

In 1978, I attended my first yoga teacher certification program at a small place north of Boston called the Ashram. I became pregnant halfway through the course but plowed on to graduate. It was exactly what I needed to learn and use the breathing and meditation practices during the delivery. Through the years I attended other teacher certifications and courses, feeding the inner hunger for more information and awareness from yoga.

I have taught a weekly yoga class since 1970, over 35 years now. In 1995, I finally opened a yoga business and named it *Finding Inner Peace*. I understood my karma, my calling and gift, was to teach yoga and share this profound spiritual practice with others. At each hospital where I have worked as a nurse, I have taught a yoga class. In the early days we were met with much skepticism, but now the practice is widespread, accepted and honored by many people, young and old.

It was in 1996 that I established my own yoga teacher certification course and have been certifying yoga teachers since then. I wrote a curriculum with lesson plans, learning objectives, homework assignments and weekly asana practice for a six month program. I was fortunate to be invited to participate in the first meeting to develop standards for yoga teacher certification programs.

The first meeting was held in October 1997 at the Kripalu Yoga and Wellness Center in Lenox, Massachusetts. The founding members included many well-known leaders in the yoga community. We created standards for five areas of practice and the group's efforts eventually were the basis for the National Yoga Alliance. It was one of the milestones of my yoga career, being invited to participate with masters from various styles of yoga. My professional nursing background helped me in collaborating and establishing standards of knowledge for yoga curriculum development.

It has been an interesting journey for me with yoga. Having been a practitioner my whole life, I sit back in dismay at times at how commercialized it has become. Studying and practicing the basic moral precepts is what it really is all about. I wish more instructors and teachers were more authentic in living the yogic lifestyle. It is not about the style of clothes, the competitive edge you feel in some settings, the elitism presented in some programs or centers. It is about the journey within, to our own personal temple of light, to meet our higher self and God in bliss and self-actualization.

Now I am 55 years young, I enjoy health and freedom from disease. I practice yoga every morning and evening and teach it weekly at a health club. I direct a Registered Yoga School and train over 100 teachers a year, in six locations with 15 faculty teachers.

Yoga will be with me to the day I pass into the subtle matrix from where I emerged as an infant and took that first breath. The science of yoga is my life, my savior and spiritual paradigm. It is wonderful that Yoga in America has grown, transformed, and expanded into all walks of life.

Maureen Spencer

www.findinginnerpeace.com

Maureen Spencer, M.Ed., R.N. is the founder of Finding Inner Peace Yoga School and Integrative Medicine Program. Maureen is recognized as an Advanced Registered Yoga Teacher with the National Yoga Alliance and is the Program Director of Yoga Teacher Certification at Finding Inner Peace.

Maureen has completed yoga studies with the American Yoga College, International Yoga Studies, Integrative Yoga Therapy and Meridian Hatha Yoga Therapy. As a Nurse Healer - she is trained in Therapeutic Touch, Quantum Touch, Ear Candling, Magnified Healing and Reiki Master/Teacher.

Maureen lectures locally and nationally on the Science of Yoga and Energy Medicine and teaches nurses and therapists Reiki Energy Healing at the New England Baptist Hospital in Boston, where she is the full-time Manager of the Infection Control Program.

YOGA IN AMERICA IS...

HILARY LINDSAY

YOGA IN AMERICA IS:

The bar in *Cheers* where everybody knows your name

A support group

The joy of community and the awareness of one's singular peculiarities

The first solitary foray into the wilderness

The awakening of a budding teen

The first trip to a foreign land

The promise of peace

A step toward the truth

The struggle to be creative and the fight to be competitive

The running of the bulls

What your friend did to lose weight

The sweetness of Satchidananda and the sternness of Iyengar

Competitive, corporate, and consumer driven

Clothes, gear, and music

A traveling circus of superstars

The video on the television set of the Kansas farmwife.

The workout of the suburban housewife and the Hollywood star

An option on the fitness menu at The Golden Door Spa

A small class at the community center

Offered in rehab and at the local church

The silence of meditation and the hip hop on the deejay's playlist

Recognized as" Hot"

Forever considered cool

A rapt audience

The innocence of the unsophisticated offering obeisance to the cloth

The condemned tenement on New York's lower East side transformed into a multi-million dollar Mecca

An ingredient tossed into aerobics and strength training classes

An escape from stress

A chance to improve

Where East meets West

Used to be patchouli and now it's nag champa

Disguised by different titles

Confused with enlightenment

A step toward enlightenment

The memory of the first kiss and the practice of the last breath

An open marriage with secret resentments

Where groovy meets greedy

The Age of Aquarius in the time of the Kali Yuga

Mommy and Me and AARP

Invisible things happening as you watch your body change

The Libertarian mat and the Liberal mat side by side and next to the Right Wing Republican mat

The Unitarian partnered with the Evangelist

Birkenstock communing with Cole-Hahn

Not knowing who will put on the Birkenstocks and who will put on the Cole-Hahn's after class

A cup of Starbucks before class and a cigarette afterwards

What you do Friday after work before cocktails

Heralded by revolutionaries and captured by entrepreneurs

In *Reader's Digest, Prevention, Men's Health* and *Cosmo*

A third world understatement into a new world phenomenon

A New Age diamond from ancient carbon

The exploration of a perfectly balanced universe

A haven for the insecure and a stage for vanity

A studio you keep tidier than your own home

A copyright, a series, a chain store

Never stepping in the same stream twice

Literature, history, physical education, science, and philosophy

Popularized by Hippies, carried forth by Yuppies, and embraced by the masses

Introduced at Woodstock

Validated by The Beatles

Originally a philosophical approach, then a physical means to well being

On course to reclaiming its philosophical approach with a physical practice

Flow

Freestyle

Architecture

Innocence

And

Ambition

Why does Yoga in America have such diverse expressions? How is it that people who would not appear to have much in common cross invisible boundaries to enter common ground? What is the nature of the tie that binds us together in this endeavor?

America is a young country. Americans look for God, for the meaning of life, in an earnest way that is unlike the populace of older countries who either take these things for granted or have a common religious philosophy as the general doctrine. America is like a child in her formative years soaking in the world before she has formed a filter. As Americans we are headstrong and innocently reckless. We grasp for shiny objects. We are the center of the universe. We need to be the best. We are exhausted and we don't know when or how to stop. We want to be loved.

At the same time we are competitive. We are insecure and vain. We want to be good. We want to be admired-- observe the popularity of Power Yoga classes in their many styles.

At the same time we want safe and clear borders--observe the popularity of Iyengar classes.

At the same time we want friends and community and we want to be loved--observe the popularity of Anusara classes.

Americans share these human qualities in abundance, so we frequent a variety of yoga classes to meet our different needs at different times.

We also want to know who we are and it's not that obvious as the country changes faster than we can keep pace. As we are like a small child without a filter, we are also like an adolescent with growing pains. We are part of a changing picture. We embark on spiritual journeys with enthusiasm to make sense of things. Yoga has become a means to approach life with a philosophy that is acceptable to many, especially because it doesn't require a dismissal of one's religious background or religious practice.

When I began teaching yoga in Nashville about 15 years ago, the teaching of Yoga was limited to a couple of individually operated Iyengar studios and a small number of teachers offering classes in offbeat places. I had come from L.A. where a fellow named Bryan Kest was making a name for himself teaching what he called "Power Yoga", an exciting new approach based on Ashtanga.

I had come from the dance world and had been teaching a class combining dance and yoga. I carried the inspiration of Bryan's work to Nashville and taught my version of Power Yoga to people who had never experienced much if any Yoga, and all corners of the population embraced it. I also found them eager to be offered a philosophical approach to the physical practice which surprised me because Nashville as the buckle of the Bible Belt is steeped in Christianity and I thought that my approach would be too radical.

I was wrong. Here where there is so much energy directed toward the discussion of God and purpose, the inquiry was larger than discussions in individual congregations. That has led to an open hearted and open minded group of yogis which has grown to include hundreds of teachers, many diverse studios, and the long overdue change of the class title "Stretch and Flex" to "Yoga" with my class at the YMCA.

Why is there such a dramatic rise in all things Yoga in America? The answer may be in the accessibility of the first two limbs of Yoga. The social restraints and ethical observances of yoga, the *yamas* and *niyamas*, serve as guidelines for conduct that can be experienced immediately without any intermediary, in the very actions and reactions expressed in the postures. At a time when Americans are waking up to a shared belief that we need to find equilibrium, to reassess our priorities, to face up to our effect on the rest of the world, to balance the desire for prosperity with the desire to remain healthy, many look to Yoga to put things in order.

When the restraints and observances are the basis for our postures, what we learn through our bodies becomes a metaphor for the effect of individual actions on the whole. We may experience this awareness on a conscious or subconscious level depending on the depth of our individual practice; however, what is often recognized as "mindfulness" serves us well on any level.

When we practice asana we work on various parts of the body for the good of the whole. This correlates to the *yamas*: the nonviolence of *ahimsa*; the truthfulness of *satya*; the respect for the integrity of others which is *asteya*; the respect to oneself that is *brahmacharya*; the resistance to the allure of sense and memory that is *aparigraha*.

The *yamas* inform our whole practice: the way we consider that doing injury to oneself for the sake of the pose is wrong; the way we consider that dishonesty about our abilities is a disservice to our self; the way in which we do not want to create a dependence by being too charitable; the way we do not sacrifice the body for the sake of a "successful" limb or steal the health of one part of the body for the glory of another; the way we consider that overexerting ourselves or pushing where we don't belong is wasteful and obnoxious; that coveting a pose because we had done it or seen it done before is arrogant and insensitive; and the awareness of countless grey areas requiring extreme sensitivity which comes with practice.

According to Patanjali's *Yoga Sutras* , the second limb of Yoga known as *niyama* describes the conduct of people living within their own sound architecture. *Niyama* affords us the opportunity to get into oneself, to enjoy oneself through the contentment of *santosha*, the bright clear spirit of *saucha*, the energetic drive and desire to work that is *tapas*, the emotional space to be introspective that is *svadyaya*, and the surrender of *Ishvara-pranidhana* which allows us the peace to accept life as it is.

The ethical limbs of Yoga allow us to experience ourselves both as a collective and as individuals. The *yamas* allow us to reap the fruits of our intentions both in asana and in life. The *niyamas* give us the opportunity to tune into a universe that reflects us in our best moments—meeting the people we are beyond our personalities, before our experiences shaped us. The integrity inherent in the independent practice as well as the collective conscience resonates with us Americans as it is the basis of our philosophical spawning ground.

We know that violence, dishonesty, stealing or grasping for glory, insensitivity and arrogance, exerting too much control or taking over responsibility for able people as to make them weak has destroyed nations. Implicit within the philosophical DNA of our country is our inheritance from the English philosophers John Locke and Thomas

Hobbes, who popularized the notion that man needs laws to protect his goodness as well as to protect him from himself. Our concept of individual happiness was predicated on social restraint. One does not come without the other.

The founding fathers took measures to ensure Americans a basis of government that would avoid self-destruction, and laid that design out in *The Declaration of Independence*. The life, liberty, and pursuit of happiness that Americans believe is their birthright comes with the same discipline of self-restraint outlined in the first of the eight limbs of Yoga as described by Patanjali thousands of years ago.

Given that underpinning, no wonder that Yoga resonates with modern Americans. We share the basic assumption that when the community is healthy, the individual has the opportunity to pursue happiness.

Americans live in an uncharted territory in uncertain waters. We look different from each other, speak different languages, and come from different backgrounds, different countries. We have many different governments within the U.S. government. We keep expanding, with technology rapidly changing our interactions, our communication, our trust or distrust of each other.

We are pressed to evolve more quickly than our parents or grandparents to balance progress with the safety of the planet. Parents are vigilant watching for predators and drug abuse. We are assaulted with information that tells us we can look better, feel better, measure up, if we just ante up. And we expect ourselves to set the standard for many things, for the rest of the world.

Within that context, the simplicity of paying attention according to the guidelines of thoughtfulness, kindness, and integrity toward self and others, free from the bait of Heaven or the threat of Hell is a welcome beacon to many of us. Add the physical component that exorcises through exercise many of our restless demons as well as the rehabilitative and restorative benefits and you have in Yoga an essential tool for any American household.

Hilary Lindsay

www.activeyoga.com

Hilary Lindsay has created yoga programs for corporations, choreographed videos for celebrity clients, and works one-on-one with high profile clients.

She teaches comprehensive yoga classes for children, empowering classes for teens, and inspired instruction for adults.

Hilary has been covered by popular magazines and television shows and continues to work for a variety of publications as a yoga expert.

She aims to energize people to be empowered by the experience of gaining physical strength and self-awareness in a joyful environment.

HALLMARK COULDN'T SAY IT BETTER

CYNTHIA OVERGAAG

What is yoga?
I needed to know
To have confident wisdom
When my students asked me

So I learned about union
And prana and chi
Chakras and OM
And Patanjali

What is Yoga?
I am trusted to know
Guiding chants, meditation
And vinyasa flow

Speaking of koshas and doshas
And Shiva
Relaxing under blankets, while listening to Bija
What is Yoga?
My students tell me

They trust their own wisdom in bodies set free
They understand Sanskrit, alignment and nadis
And that balance is more than gazing at drishtis

What is Yoga?
It's all that you need

It's the light...it's the water
It's the Earth...it's the seed

Its love, devotion and sweet Namaste
And knowing that peace is but a breath away

Cynthia Overgaag

Cynthia Overgaag is an advanced level teacher certified in the Kripalu tradition. She was a former professional ballet dancer with the Eliot Feld Ballet of New York City.

As Kripalu is the yoga of compassion, Cyndy has studied and continues to practice Iyengar, Ashtanga, Kundalini, as well as the Anusara styles of yoga. It is the belief of the Kripalu tradition to explore the many facets of yoga, so that they may share the blessings of all approaches with their students.

DOORWAY TO MY SPIRIT
THE VOICE OF MY SOUL UNDILUTED

JAMIE DURNER

Yoga is the cornerstone of my spiritual experience through which I explore and deepen the connection of my human embodied self with my larger cosmic Infinite Self. It is through my Infinite Self that I connect to the universal energy and everything and everyone within the cosmos. This Infinite connection allows me to acknowledge and embrace the interwoven web of all humanity and living beings, to walk a path of compassion and reflection in our united journeys.

The philosophical and spiritual roots of yoga provide a roadmap to allow me to personally and intimately connect with my Infinite Self through a non-dogmatic approach. Rather than a religion, yoga merges energy technology with the exploration of consciousness and spirit. I am poked, prodded, and compelled by the teachings to question, to examine, to search, and to explore my conscious relationship with spirit through an ancient wisdom that remains timelessly relevant today.

Yoga is a set of spiritual teachings that cross the borders of culture, of religion, and of race to bring us together, large and small, in union. It is at once both a unique and an individual journey, yet also a shared path of connected growth.

YOGA IS THE DOORWAY TO MY SPIRIT, THE VOICE OF MY SOUL UNDILUTED

Yoga is the gateway to my inner wisdom, the place I can connect deep within to my ever-changing yet consistent truth. I seek solace and refuge from confusion and chaos in the rhythm of my breath, in the vibration of the chants, in the flowing motion of my movement. I shake off the worries of the moment, the trivialities of my monkey mind, the chain of my habitual fears.

I rise from my mat and meditation blanket with new awareness. Answers arise within the space of quiet to questions I hadn't even yet formed. And those questions that I consciously bring with me to explore, upon rising, I leave with new perspective and with inspired guidance about how I want to go forth.

From my inner connection I can approach and engage in the world with greater mindfulness. I step outside of automatic patterning and instead make choices with conscious actions. I am driven and guided by a sense of my inner divine purpose. I walk with greater peace as I am covered in a blanket of cozy trust.

Yoga allows me to gain access to deeper understanding. I open and expand beyond the limitations of my mind and cultural expectations to the greater reality of the MORE of universal consciousness. Yoga deepens my intuition, opening my eyes to see others as part of my connected energy. This shared connection offers a bridge to understanding and compassion and allows me to live in greater harmony both within myself and in community with others.

YOGA IS A WINDOW TO MY THOUGHTS, MY HABITS, AND MY PATTERNS

Through the precise science and technology of Kundalini Yoga and its hundreds of yoga kriyas (sets) and meditations, I dig beneath the habituated surface of my seeming reality. I delve into my unconscious habits, bringing them closer to the light in order to see what needs to be cut loose, what needs to be re-shaped, and what needs to be nurtured and developed.

In meditation I free the clutter of my mind to defog the lens of clarity and to remove my illusions in order to see the path of truth more clearly. I push up against perceived limitations to make room for new possibilities.

Following the yogic timelines to change and expand habits, I have joyfully engaged in holding specific meditations or yoga kriyas for 40, 90, 120 and 1000 days with powerful results. Holding a three minute meditation for 1000 days literally turned my mindset of scarcity to one of abundance. And from this space of abundance I opened my life to a flow of love and light, success, and prosperity.

It is to my yoga that I first look for my tools of change, for specific, time-tested techniques to effectively allow me to shed unneeded and outgrown patterns. And it is as I acknowledge, honor and then shed that old skin, which may have once served me but no longer does, that I can awaken to the life I am ready for in this moment. As I release the old, I am able to welcome in new habits and lifestyle practices that guide me towards greater health, happiness, and wholeness.

YOGA IS THE KEY TO MY SUCCESS

Beyond the yoga postures, the breathing exercises, and the sounds of resonating mantra, exist the basic elements of how to be at one in life. While I revel in the strength and flexibility which the physical aspects of yoga provide, it is my inner core that has received the greatest gifts through my daily yoga practice. Each day that I practice yoga, I strengthen and stretch more than my muscles...opening and expanding my nerves, my mental possibilities, my ability to go out into the world and face the challenges and opportunities of life with grace and ease.

With each success in my yoga space, I expand the parameters of my definition of success itself. Whether it is deepening my ability to move into a posture or being able to hold a 31 minute meditation for 40 days, each time I succeed in yoga, I create a new level of success in all areas of my life. From my expanded view of success, I go into the world with greater trust. This trust is the core foundation that provides me with new skills and confidence with which to approach challenges and with the courage to try something new.

YOGA IS THE ULTIMATE BODY/MIND EXERCISE

Yoga is flow and stillness, tension and ease, the balance between dualities. It is my heaven and sometimes my hell. It is my daily practice into remembering and living my truth.

To me, yoga is one of the most powerful transformational tools we have available for this critical time in our culture. This unique time in our lives, on the cusp of the Aquarian Age, is full of modern complexities and shifting energies. We need tools that take us to a new level of awareness, to create a sense of trust and confidence in ourselves so that we can become the healthiest and happiest people we can be…and then spread that energy on to others…one person at a time…creating a ripple and then a wave of joy and peace in the world.

YOGA IS MY DAILY DOSE OF HEALTH

Better than a vitamin pill, my yoga keeps my body fit from top to bottom, both inside and out. Each day I try to move in some way-- warming, stretching, and strengthening my muscles; lubricating my joints; stimulating the guardians of my health, my glands; breathing in new life force, and flushing out the excess. With the connection of body and mind, I know that I can affect my inner being by also keeping my body relaxed and in alignment. And vice versa, I know that when I practice a meditation, I am infusing my body with openness and energy just through my breath.

Yoga provides the ultimate structure for health, offering thoughts on food and nutrition, lifestyle recommendations on almost every aspect of life and health, and ways to nourish both body and mind. It is a complete guide to optimal health.

Yet, one can choose to follow even a small part of the path and gain benefits. Start where you are and simply begin. Your health will improve, your life will change, and your yoga will deepen. It is both a guide and a reflection, connected in the cyclical nature of cause and effect.

YOGA IS THE ANCHOR TO MY SANITY

I once thought of enlightenment as an end point, a static place I would reach if I was good enough and worked hard enough. Instead I have learned through yoga that enlightenment is the ongoing, ever expanding connection to myself and my ability to stay centered and thoughtful despite the external chaos.

Yoga is the anchor to my balance and the tool that empowers me to not only move above the chaos, but even to change the nature of chaos as it exists within my reality. Beyond simply making better choices and responding to life with thoughtful actions, I know that through my very energy and thoughts I create my own reality. Not only can I reprogram my mind and alter the very nature of my brain, but through my yoga practice I can channel my energy to create the peaceful space of success and ease which I desire.

YOGA IS A TOOL FOR MY CLIENTS
AS A BODY/MIND COACH

Kundalini Yoga is one of the primary tools I offer to my clients as a way of assisting people to live life with conscious habits and patterns which support them on their path to balance, abundance and fulfillment. As Kundalini Yoga was designed for the busy householder, the techniques and meditations don't require large amounts of time in order to be effective. Small starts make a large difference. And reasonable expectations allow people to more easily integrate these powerful tools into their lives and create success which in turn creates more success.

Yoga and meditation are the gateways to helping my clients develop a transformative partnership with their inner wisdom. I believe that each of us has our best answers already; the key is to recognize them. Yoga provides an accessible gateway to be able to understand and listen to the inner wisdom which holds those answers. From this inner connection, individuals discover how they can bring healing & harmony to all areas of their life…from the inside out.

Jamie Durner

www.jamiedurner.com

BodyMind Coach™ & Kundalini Yoga Teacher.

Registered Yoga Teacher in the Kundalini Yoga tradition.

Yoga practitioner of Ashtanga, Iyengar blends, and Kundalini Yoga.

THE ART AND SCIENCE OF
TRUE LASTING HAPPINESS

GYANDEV (RICH) MCCORD

Yoga has become well known in the West for its many physical and psychological benefits, such as improved muscle tone, lower blood pressure, stress relief, increased vitality, and mental clarity. Yet the original purpose of yoga was—and its highest purpose has always been—spiritual: Yoga is the art and science of attaining true, lasting happiness.

Yoga is a science because it offers specific, practical methods for obtaining these benefits. It is an art, because its highest benefits come only through sensitive and intuitive practice; otherwise it yields only superficial results. To understand these points more fully, let's take a look at yoga's lofty goal: true, lasting happiness.

THE HIGHEST ASPIRATION

Yoga maintains that underlying all that exists is a single consciousness that not only created the universe, but *became* the universe. That is, it formed the universe out of itself, there being no other "building materials" with which to work.

People call that consciousness by many names: Spirit, God, Truth, Love, The Divine, Absolute Existence, etc. Yoga teaches that the essence of that consciousness is joy (*ananda* in Sanskrit), and since we are part of that consciousness, our own essence, too, must be joy. According to yoga, our innate desire for happiness is the desire to "come home" to our true nature. Whatever people seek in life—love, wealth, fame, power, etc.—they seek it always for the same reason: the happiness they expect to find through it.

The ancient sages of India asked: If lasting happiness is the goal, then why try to find it through things (love, wealth, etc.) that end when human life ends—and usually much sooner than that?! Why not instead seek happiness *directly*, in the only way that it will last: through uniting our consciousness with the everlasting joy of Spirit? The sages' explorations gave birth to the many tools and precepts of yoga.

There are numerous yoga traditions, handed down from teacher to student over millennia.[1] Each has its own special emphasis, but all have the same goal: to unite limited human consciousness with the unlimited, ever-joyful divine consciousness. Hence the word, "yoga," which in Sanskrit means "to yoke" or "to unite."

THE TOOLS OF YOGA

The emphasis of yoga is not on *belief*, but on direct *experience*. Yoga says: Believe whatever you want, but try these practices and discover the way to happiness through your own personal experience.

Many people equate yoga with its most visible tools: the *asanas* (yoga postures), which offer many of the physical benefits of yoga. Depending on how they are practiced, asanas can also give psychological and spiritual benefits. For example, Ananda Yoga (the asana style that I teach) draws upon the power of the mind and heart to amplify the asanas' natural uplifting effects on consciousness, thereby taking us closer to the joy we seek.

---

[1] I follow the yoga tradition of Paramhansa Yogananda, author of the spiritual classic, *Autobiography of a Yogi* (Crystal Clarity, Publishers).

Yet asanas are only a tiny sliver of yoga. Yoga is a complete way of life, giving us practices and insights to enhance everything we do—mundane as well as spiritual, outward as well as inward. Uniting and reinforcing them all is the supreme technique of yoga: meditation.

By quieting our thoughts and feelings, meditation enables us to perceive directly the joy of our true nature. So long as we are active—even in pleasant ways, even just mentally—that deeper joy eludes us. Other yoga techniques convey many benefits, but their greatest value lies in how they support inner stillness. Throughout the ages, yogis have proved that deep, daily meditation is the ultimate tool for experiencing divine joy.

THE ENERGY-MIND LINK

There is a highly practical, common thread that unifies all these aspects of yoga: energy.

Since the time of Albert Einstein, science has said—and later proved—that all matter is simply energy. For millennia, yoga has gone a step farther, saying that energy (*prana* in Sanskrit) not only constitutes our physical bodies, but also intelligently governs the operation of all bodily systems, and is intimately linked to the workings of the mind. To emphasize the "intelligent" aspect of prana, yogis often call it "life force."

Since the goal of life is a state of mind (i.e., happiness), prana's connection with the mind is especially relevant. A simple experiment will demonstrate this connection, as well as provide an important insight into why yoga is the science of happiness:

Sit upright with a straight spine, close your eyes, and relax your body. Breathe evenly, and relax your mind as well. Now imagine that, all of a sudden, a friend brings you some stunning good news: "You just won the lottery!" If you imagine this vividly enough, you will feel an inner "lift" that straightens up your body—perhaps even turns your eyes to look upward—and you will inhale. That lift is only partially physical; primarily, it is due to energy rushing upward through your body toward the brain.

Then, just as you're excitedly planning what you'll do with your lottery winnings, your friend says, "Sorry, my mistake. You didn't win after all." The reverse happens: your body sags, your eyes turn downward, and with an exhalation, you sigh (or curse). Here again, the sagging sensation is only partially physical; it's mainly due to energy pouring downward through your body.

All this is so familiar that few people bother to take a closer look. Most people simply accept it as an obvious fact of life: Things that we like *lift* our spirits, and things that we dislike *depress* us. Thus they continue their "yoyo" existence, reacting positively and negatively, *up and down*, all day, every day.

The ancient Indian sages, however, *did* take a closer look. Here's what they discovered: If our reactions to life's happy and sad events are always accompanied by upward or downward movements of energy, then by learning to control those inner movements of energy, we can better control our reactions—and thus begin to find the inner joy that doesn't depend on outer circumstances.

This insight is crucial, because our likes and dislikes (which give rise to our reactions) are far too numerous to correct, one by one. But they all have one thing in common: their link to the inner flow of energy. If this flow can be brought under control, then we can more easily improve our state of mind.

Those sages developed a broad spectrum of yoga practices that help us, each in its own special way, to bring the energy-flow under control. When done correctly, those practices give us the strength and clarity that bring us ever closer to true, lasting happiness.

THE HIGHEST ART

That phrase "done correctly" is where the "art" of yoga comes in. For while the mechanics of yoga practice are important, mechanics alone can never govern the subtle realm of human consciousness. Even in the physical realm of asanas, more than mechanics is needed for maximum benefit. The highest success in any aspect of yoga requires that we have the "feel" of the yoga techniques.

In fact, that's how it is in any field: the highest success requires more than intellect, training, willpower, or motivation. All those are valuable, and no doubt many physicists had as much of them as Einstein, and many artists had as much as Michelangelo. Yet how many could equal those two geniuses? Almost none, because Einstein and Michelangelo had something more: an *intuitive* understanding of their fields, which took them beyond the limits of the intellect.

How can we gain such an understanding of the art and science of true, lasting happiness? Yoga teaches that the heart is the key—not the physical heart, but rather the heart *chakra* (energy center) in the middle of the chest. This is where we feel love, and can receive intuitive insight.

But the heart can also be agitated by our likes and dislikes, which keep us in an up-and-down existence. The ancient sage Patanjali put it this way in his *Yoga Sutras*[2]: "Yoga (union) is the neutralization of the whirlpools of likes and dislikes." When the heart is perfectly calm and receptive, our intuitive ("feeling") faculty enables us to experience our true essence; when the heart is *not* calm, our feeling faculty gets caught up in the swirl of emotional reactions, dimming our inner capacity for deep understanding.

---

[2] Patanjali's *Yoga Sutras* is one of the two main scriptures of yoga, the other being the *Bhagavad Gita*. Both date back more than two thousand years.

Thus it is that many yoga techniques—above all, meditation—involve calming the heart energies. The calmer and more receptive the heart is, the clearer our understanding of anything toward which we turn our attention. Yogis turn their attention toward a deeper understanding of their own essence.

INVALUABLE AID

Some rare individuals are able to attain an intuitive understanding of yoga seemingly by themselves, but most need a teacher—someone who has that understanding, and can impart it to the receptive aspirant through means subtler than words or even thoughts. Much progress can be made without a teacher, but to attain that pinnacle of human aspiration—everlasting joy and complete inner freedom—yoga maintains that a teacher is needed.

Thus we come to the much-misunderstood concept of guru. Some spiritual seekers think they do not need a guru. Others fear that a guru will impose upon their free will. To such concerns, Paramhansa Yogananda replied: "People have no idea how to get out of their mental forest. Every path they attempt ends in a confusion of dense undergrowth, or leads them back to where they first started out. In time, the realization dawns on them that they are lost.

"Then, if someone comes and says, 'I know this forest well; let me show you the way through it,' will they consider his offer a menace to their free will? Won't they view it, rather, as an opportunity to accomplish successfully what their own will has been trying for so long, but always in vain, to accomplish?

"The purpose of the guru is not to weaken your will. It is to teach you secrets of developing your inner power, until you can stand unshaken amidst the crash of breaking worlds."[3]

---

[3] *The Essence of Self-Realization*, Paramhansa Yogananda (Crystal Clarity, Publishers).

We can gain that ability through the art and science of yoga, aided by the invaluable support of one who has it already. Then we will surely find the true, lasting happiness that we all seek.

Gyandev (Rich) McCord

www.expandinglight.org

Gyandev (Rich) McCord is the worldwide director of Ananda Yoga, director of Ananda Yoga Teacher Training, and a co-founder of Yoga Alliance. He has been teaching all aspects of yoga since 1983, and has authored numerous books, DVDs and CDs on yoga and yoga therapy. He lives in Northern California in Ananda Village, a yoga community of nearly 300 disciples of Paramhansa Yogananda. Gyandev teaches at Ananda's spiritual retreat center, The Expanding Light, as well as at various sites across North America, Europe and India.

The foundation of his teaching is his practice and study of the teachings of Paramhansa Yogananda, and of Swami Kriyananda, the direct disciple of Yogananda who founded Ananda. His own daily *sadhana* (spiritual practice) consists of three or more hours of Ananda Yoga, meditation, and Yogananda's Energization Exercises.

Gyandev finds much encouragement in these words from *The Essence of Self-Realization* by Paramhansa Yogananda: "Self-realization is the knowing in all parts of body, mind, and soul that you are now in possession of the kingdom of God; that you do not have to pray that it come to you; that God's omnipresence is your omnipresence; and that all that you need to do is improve your knowing."

YOU ARE DIVINE AND PERFECT

KAREN PIERCE

Most of us were raised with the social belief that there is something between us and God (a church or the Pope, for example...) and we need to be on a quest. This philosophy of "There is a higher power" is dualistic and assumes you are a lower power. We've all been affected by this thinking of trying to get somewhere, as if we're not already somewhere. The idea of human imperfection is deeply ingrained in our minds. This type of thinking blinds us to the perfection that is already us, as Life itself.

Traditional Yoga is a non-dualistic practice of your direct participation in the extreme intelligence that beats in the heart and moves the breath. There is a great power moving in you, as you. When you cut yourself, you don't have to ask your body to heal itself, it just does. And thankfully, you don't have to remind yourself to breath.

We would rather go on a 10 day retreat to a mountaintop than participate in our own breath. Just INHALE! It is unfortunate that we think of pranayama as a "practice". Pranayama is nothing more or less than conscious breathing. It isn't something we DO, it's something we ARE.

You are not here to become "enlightened" or "self-actualized". You already are! Seeking enlightenment assumes you don't already have it. You are already an extreme intelligence. Now, if there is a source to this extreme intelligence (call it what you will – God/Goddess,

Divine, Great Spirit, Allah, Yahweh, Jehovah), can that source be absent from this physical expression that is you? There is no separation. If they are one and the same, then there are no steps to be taken. You ARE the divine expression of this extreme intelligence. The looking, the seeking IS the problem.

People all over the world try to meditate so they can find "enlightenment". What happens when you try to make yourself go to sleep? Trying to sleep prevents sleep. Just like you can't make yourself go to sleep, you can't make yourself meditate. It just happens. Don't try to meditate; it sets up struggle in the mind. Meditation may or may not happen. If it does, it happens spontaneously and it is a gift.

We are all extreme intelligence and self-existing perfection. You are formed from this wonder – the body, the breath, the heartbeat, and all of nature. Yoga begins when you let go of ideology and accept the self in its natural state. Yoga is a reminder of what you ALREADY are and have. The divine is not within you, it IS you. You are divine and perfect.

Karen Pierce

www.innerspacesbykaren.com

Karen Pierce is a professional organizer and yoga teacher. She helps people transform their lives, inside and out.

Karen was introduced to meditation and yoga as a teen and holds many certifications including her 200RYT through Yoga Alliance and is a certified Yoga Ed instructor.

A student of yoga for over 25 years, she has been blessed to have learned from many world renowned yogi masters in Ashtanga, Iyengar, Anusara, Power Yoga, Jivamukti, Kundalini, Bikram, and Viniyoga. But her heart belongs to the teachings of Krishnamacharya and her dedication to her mentor Mark Whitwell.

Karen is a gifted teacher dedicated to bringing the practice of authentic yoga to all populations in a safe format that is rooted in exercise science as well as filled with the true spirit of yoga and the essence of how it was taught over 100 years ago.

Karen is also the author of "Yoga Bear: Yoga for Youngsters", a children's book published by Northword Press (2004).

YOGA IS WHATEVER
YOU WANT TO MAKE OF IT

ADRIENNE REED

I have owned my own yoga studio in Tampa for over five years, and have been teaching for a little over seven. It seems like almost every day I learn something new about what Yoga is. Some of my most memorable examples are:

I taught a class with an older gentleman who fell asleep on his mat before class started, and continued to snore loudly throughout the entire session. From this, yoga became a way for me to learn laughter and how to respect another's personal space and personal situation.

I taught a class with a large body builder who moaned rather sensually in every pose. From this, yoga taught me how to smile inwardly and see the pure joy that people can feel from experiencing yoga in their own way.

I taught a class with a woman who rolled up her mat, gave me a dirty look, and left my studio because I was teaching a class with all partner poses. From this, yoga became a lesson on how to not take things personally and how the age old saying "different strokes for different folks" applied to me and my classes – no matter how much work I put into them.

I taught a class on a day when I was rip-roaring mad, and everyone who attended was in a very foul mood. We decided that the "f" word was going to be the theme of our class, and everyone in the room dropped the word as much as we could throughout the hour.

We left laughing hysterically and watched our bad days and bad moods disappear to nothingness. From this, yoga became a way for me (and the others who attended) to choose happiness and learn that even the nastiest of things have a lovely little silver lining.

I taught a class of poses that were each held for several minutes, and during each pose one person would share a personal story that was inspiring or a part of their lives they are most proud of. We learned things about each other that were so profound, so intimate and so beautifully honest that none of us will ever forget that class. From this, I learned that yoga can be freeing, surrendering and so honest that you can laugh and cry all at the same time.

The word "yoga" incites so many interesting responses from people in America. Some believe it's a religion. Some think it's some sort of cult following. Many have the notion that it's a bunch of old ladies sitting around "stretching" and "breathing". Most think it will be boring and/or weird, and it's certainly not for them.

Yoga is whatever *you* want to make of it. There are classes across America that offer a myriad of yoga styles. Some classes are quiet, meditative and introspective. Others are sweat-inducing, challenging and fat burning.

Most classes are somewhere in between, offering a little bit from each end of the spectrum. So, before you take a yoga class, decide what you want *your* experience to be and find a class that suits *your* needs.

When I first started with yoga, I was drawn to it for two reasons. First and foremost, I enjoyed the physicality of power yoga and the lean body I had as a result of consistent practice. For the first few years, however, I remember standing on my mat and very often thinking, "You want me to do WHAT?!?!"

I would inwardly laugh at the crazy instructor who was asking me to put my right elbow on the outside of my left knee. But, when I tried it, hey! My elbow would and could actually go there!

But the thing that made me come back to yoga versus any other form of exercise was the mental benefit I received. When I practiced yoga, I didn't think of anything else but what I was trying to do in each moment of class.

I quickly realized that the complex postures and requirement of me to be *there*, in the moment, also allowed me to check out of the rest of my life and receive a well-deserved mental break. There were no "to do" lists. There were no worries about babysitters, or what I'm cooking for dinner. There was only me, my mat, and a bunch of poses that seemed to be ever-changing, always challenging, and incredibly fun and laughable.

Those challenges allowed me to forget about the rest of my life for a full hour. They allowed me to return home stronger and healthier, both physically and mentally. So, yoga to me, at the beginning of my journey, was my stress reliever, my weight manager, my muscle toner, and my sanity keeper.

As I progressed, I decided that I was going to make the leap into instruction and began teaching yoga to some friends in my home. I quickly learned that teaching was much harder than all those calm instructors made it seem. And learning the ropes of how to teach it drastically changed my view of what yoga is. It was, at that time, more of a technical body of work for me to study, embrace, and ingest.

I studied and worked hard to make my classes creative, fun, exciting and unpredictable. But most importantly, I wanted to make the people who attended feel as though they received a part of me with every experience. So, yoga during my teacher training time became methodical, anatomical, and a creative outlet. The experience felt to me to be more extroverted, rather than the personal experience I'd previously cherished it to be.

I now teach and practice many styles, from easygoing basic yoga to intensely challenging power yoga. Yoga to me, as an instructor, is so beautifully different in each and every class I teach or attend.

It is the breath that we all share as we move through the postures. It is the mood that is felt and created by everyone on their mats. It is the grace and beauty in each and every pose from each and every yogi experiencing them.

It is the journey of body awareness, satisfaction and self exploration that we experience both personally and as a group as we progress through a class. As the people, the mood, the postures, and the bodies in the classes change, "yoga" changes for me as well.

Yoga in America may seem like it is only a form of exercise. I often hear criticism that it has become "Westernized" and we've lost all the spiritual aspects of it. I completely and respectfully disagree!

For me and everyone I meet who approaches their practice with an open mind and a commitment of regular practice, it is so unbelievably intimate, personal, and soul-filling. It is what keeps us young, makes us laugh, makes us scream, and warms our hearts. It is most definitely spiritual. And it is definitely more than just a way to lose weight. It is a way to learn more about ourselves, and to experience a way of letting go that permeates every part of our lives.

Americans may *come* to their mats looking for a good workout, but most *leave* their mats with a sense of self they cannot get from any other style of exercise. I experienced this happening to me personally. Over the years, I've watched it happen to hundreds of people in studios across the country. And, I know it can also happen to you.

Adrienne Reed

www.AdrienneReed.com

Adrienne hosts the nationally syndicated public television series, *"Power Yoga: Mind & Body"*, with a reach of over 53 million households. She has released ten award-winning DVD's.

She is the founder of Namaste Yoga studio near Tampa, Florida.

Adrienne has appeared on Daytime, ABC News, Fox News and other television programs, and appeared in the magazines Self, Fit Yoga, Fitness and others.

She is currently co-authoring a fitness book, which she hopes to release in 2009.

DAWN MUSE

BRIDGET BOLAND

At 5:58 a.m. every Wednesday morning, I find myself facing a moment of truth: I'm awake, mat unrolled, class sequence planned, yoga studio warm and inviting. I'm ready to teach. But is anyone going to show up? This is a drop-in class. No one pays or registers ahead of time. As a former loather of early mornings, I stand in awe of my students who are not only able to get up in what feels like the middle of the night to practice, but do so willingly. (Confession: on the rare days I promise myself I'll get up early to do my own practice, more often than not I succumb to the alluring heat of my husband's body curled around mine and switch off the alarm instead of hoisting my body out of bed and onto the mat. My dedicated students might flash in my mind, a brief pang of guilt might pierce my half-awake state, but give me another moment and I'm happily back in dreamland.)

But today is a great morning: my eyelids opened before the alarm went off. I dressed in the dark, brushed teeth and hair, inserted contacts, and in less than ten minutes I was ready for work. Minimal upkeep is just one of the perks of teaching yoga for a living. I like driving in the quiet to Dragonfire Studio here in Dallas. I enjoy the subtle sounds of the earth slumbering, so I refrain from turning on the cd player and instead roll down my window to let the breeze sing me a song. As I get out of the car, I look overhead. A crescent moon tattoos a tiny arc of light on the skin of the darkness. Under it a single star hangs like some celestial punctuation mark. Texas summers are searing hot but now that autumn's arrived, the air in the morning is soothing as a cool hand on a warm forehead. When I unlock the studio door I leave it open, invite the breeze inside with me.

I love the Dragonfire Studio. It's a cozy, artsy space in a slightly dilapidated white building. In better days, the structure was a sprawling single family home. But in its current rundown condition, the back half has been divided into three apartments. The yoga studio is the former kitchen, dining room and living room. Laura, the studio owner, has decorated it in funky country Zen kitsch. There are pretty Chinese paper lanterns adorning the ceiling around the perimeter of the practice space. Two-feet tall wooden dreamlike animal sculptures stand quiet guard in the corners. I believe they ward off nightmares and bad energy.

Two red distressed leather couches in the entry lounge open their arms like grandmothers beckoning for a hug, inviting students to take their time before and after class. Atop the front desk sits a pretty lacquered box where students deposit their money or punch cards. And a sprig of bamboo in a chipped blue glass vase offers new shoots of good fortune every few weeks. There's a subtle hum in the air in this gem of a place, as if the walls have paid attention during countless classes and learned the art of *ujjayi pranayama*: long luxurious breathing.

I'm the only one who drives to morning practice at Dragonfire. Since the studio is in a residential neighborhood, most of my students live close enough to walk. It's the moment of truth again: 5:58 a.m. I peek my head out the screen door, peer out into what feels more like night than morning. Here come my regulars: Robert ambles up the road with his mat bag slung over one shoulder. He raises a hand in a silent salute. A couple of yards behind him I see Crispin, padding barefoot on the warm pavement. Her long brown hair shines in a halo of moonlight. For a moment it looks as if she is a sleepwalking angel, floating along in her nightgown. But as she draws near, I see she has thrown a pretty floral shift over her yoga tights. Yogi, the studio's unofficial mascot, trots alongside her. Yogi's a smart cat; he knows Crispin will take pity on him and feed him breakfast after practice if he's patient enough to wait until 7:15. Jenny turns the corner from the other direction. She resembles a friendly ghoul with her white hoody atop her head, so I quip "Hi there, Casper," as she floats in sleepy solitude past me into the studio, a ghost of a smile passing over her lips in response.

As the regulars unfurl their mats, an unexpected guest scoots in the door. It's Shanda. She's a faithful attendee of the Tuesday evening class. She has told me before that she's not fond of morning practice, so I'm happily surprised to see she made the effort this morning. I ring the Tibetan chimes lightly, a soft but sure calling of our bodies and our minds back to the moment, back to the breath.

There's something about practicing yoga in the early morning hours that feels more sacred than any other time. Even the getting ready has its own special energy. When I studied in Mysore, my fellow yoginis Sadie, Beth and Dianna, and I rose every morning to the raucous din of Indian life that never seems to cease. The cacophony of auto rickshaw horns bleeping, roosters crowing, dogs barking and men laughing were both our lullaby and our alarm.

The morning routine in Mysore was almost exactly the same as at home in Dallas. In some ways it was a comfort, a balm of familiarity against all the disorienting differences you encounter when you're in a foreign country halfway around the world. In India, we made two changes in the litany of dressing for practice: We brushed teeth with bottled water. No sense tempting Kali into striking us down with some bacteria or parasite. And we threw saffron hued wraps woven with pretty gold trim around our shoulders before stepping outside our hotel room. India in February was plenty warm enough to go out in our tank tops, but Mysore is still very much a traditional city. The wraps covered our bare arms and demonstrated modesty. The saffron color indicated that we were on a spiritual pilgrimage. They warded off another form of parasite, young Indian men intent on meeting "loose" Western women!

The four of us walked about a mile down rutted stone streets to the yoga shala. In our uniform saffron shawls we must have looked like a coven of nuns en route to morning liturgy, which was not far from wrong. More often than not we walked alongside one another the whole way in reverent silence.

Some mornings in India it was easy to get up and go. Others, especially the day after a particularly difficult practice, it felt like I had lead in my legs. But even on the days when if felt as if we were "trudging the road to happy destiny," the trudging never overshadowed the happiness. I glowed in India; I thrived on performing the primary Ashtanga series daily.

One of my students recently read an article in National Geographic which said that there is a very short period each day when the world is completely still. "It's a tiny window of time," Caroline gestured, measuring a miniscule frame with her thumb and index finger to make her point. "Somewhere right around three thirty in the morning, every living thing sleeps. The birds tuck into their nests, the other animals quiet down. And if the wind isn't blowing and you hold your breath and listen hard, you would almost swear the earth had stopped turning." Her eyes shone like a delighted child at the revelation. "Imagine," she continued, savoring her discovery. "Everything still. No television, no radio, no car alarms. Nothing but quiet."

In the summer of 2005, I assisted at the Chicago Forrest Yoga Teacher Training. It's an arduous twenty-four days: teacher trainees arrive at the studio for meditation at 6 a.m., followed by a two-hour intensive asana practice. They get a two-hour break, then return for a full afternoon of instruction. They learn how to teach and how to make adjustments on students. They also journal, answering questions such as where they hope to be and what they hope to accomplish in the next year, three years and five years, and what obstacles stand in the way of their success. They contemplate mortality through a sobering Zen death meditation. It's an emotional time, with just a two-day respite mid-way through the training. More than once during my own training in 2001 I had wondered whether I had the stamina and emotional wherewithal to complete the course.

I got to measure my progress and dedication toward my practice by my attitude about rising early in the morning. As a teacher trainee in 2001, I got up at 5:15 each morning. I remember grousing to anyone who would listen about how much I missed the luxury of staying in bed until 6:30 or 7 a.m., and feeling smugly superior to anyone who confessed to a later wake up time. When I agreed to assist at the 2005 training, I discovered Ana Forrest required her assistants to practice with her *prior to* the students' meditation and practice. Our practice was two hours long. The students arrived for meditation about quarter to six. This meant we met for practice from 3:30 to 5:30 a.m. Yes, a.m.

I groaned when I learned we'd be getting up in the middle of the night every day for twenty-four days. Was I a masochist? Was practicing really worth my precious time in bed? Would I hear an alarm going off at 3 a.m.? I could recall nights when I hadn't gone to bed until that hour, but I was pretty sure I had never gotten up then. And before the training, there was only one word I could think of to describe awakening at that hour – ungodly. I told everyone who would listen about my plight. Most were sympathetic, though some pointed out that I was *choosing* to participate. I stopped talking to them for the duration of the training.

Morning one found me fueled by adrenaline. I'd flown into Chicago the night before and had dinner with my mom, then tried to go to bed at nine, but read for two hours because I just wasn't tired. It felt wrong to turn in while the sun was still shining. I bolted out of bed when the alarm buzzed, excited to see my teacher and to practice.

Day two was agony. By 8 p.m. on day one, I was looking for toothpicks to prop my eyelids open, literally falling asleep in my dinner plate. I crashed hard, and although I got eight hours of sleep, at 3 a.m. I yearned to crawl back in between the sheets instead of onto the mat.

Days three through seven passed in a sleep-deprived blur as my body struggled to adjust to the new schedule. But by day eight, realization dawned: I was beginning to enjoy and even look forward to my middle of the night sojourns. I awoke in the dark and often went to bed in the light, but the quiet of the early morning hours had somehow snuck its way into the rest of my life. I found it easy to make excuses for afternoon naps, and everyone understood why I couldn't stay out late on a "school night."

There's something compelling to me about the mystery of the night, and I found a comfort in the dark hours, the lull of the day. Every morning I drove down Chicago Avenue to the studio. Most mornings there were only a few cars and hardly anyone on the streets. But Fridays and Saturdays, revelers poured from smoky bars onto the sidewalks out front, looking in vain for an errant cab or necking with drunken passion in shadowy alleyways. I drove slowly past. My body might have been achy and sore from lots of inversions, and backbends, but seeing those people left me grateful for the hangover I wouldn't have when the sun came up.

I'd meet Ana, her partner and the other assistants at the studio. The Shaw's Crab House neon sign lit up the night immediately in front of us, but beyond that lay a dark frontier. We'd climb the steps to the second floor studio space of Moksha Yoga, lay out our mats and get down to breathing and stretching. We alternated days between practicing with music and practicing in silence. Each had its own gifts. After we warmed up, we'd step to the top of our mats, and in faithful expectation we'd begin surya namaskar, the sun salutation. What an act of faith, to flow through vinyasa after vinyasa, convinced that regardless of the thick cloak of blackness covering the city outside the studio window, the sun would eventually come up to say hello!

If you stay awake willingly, the hours between dusk and dawn seem like a bonus, like you're cheating time into giving you more than you're entitled to. It's a great time to scrub floors, organize closets, go for a long, long walk. A great time for any activity that leaves your mind free to wander your inner darkness.

Out of dedication to my practice, I've seen and experienced the sun rising from the mysterious dark of night in cities across the United States. Back at Dragonfire, it's 6:35 and still pitch black out. I smile to myself as I realize that I know from firsthand experience that it stays darker here later in the morning than in the Midwest. Ten minutes later, the first faint tinge of light rolls the darkness away. It's that time again. I turn to my students and direct them into the sun salutations. And together we witness this wonderful, ordinary miracle: the dawning of another day.

Bridget Boland Foley

www.bridgetfoley.com

Bridget Boland Foley is a yoga teacher, energetic healer, writer, birth coach and former attorney.

Trained in Forrest Yoga in 2001, Bridget strives to provide a sanctuary for students to go inside and explore the emotional landscape of their life experiences through breath and movement in yoga ceremony, or practice.

Bridget offers group and private instruction, corporate classes, pre/postnatal yoga and yoga/creative writing workshops. She also provides hands-on therapeutic healings based on her studies of energetic healing and Biosynthesis.

For Bridget, well-being arises from creating balance in the physical, emotional and spiritual realms of life.

EVERYTHING I EVER WAS
AND WILL EVER BE

CAROLINE COZZA

Every yoga class I've ever experienced has been the answer to the question: "What is yoga?" Because the more one practices yoga, the more one understands that the question really isn't "what is yoga?", but rather, "what isn't?".

I wake up to the sensation of warmth on my face and on instinct, without coffee or a digested newspaper article, I make my way to my mat to salute the sun that finds me day after day, no matter how far I travel, or how much I'm sure I've changed. That's yoga.

And sometimes, in the evening, when the moon is just so in the sky, when it's shape eclipses my emotions and its luminosity shames the stars, I'll salute it too, even though it's way up there and I'm way down here, because it's yoga.

When it's coming down so hard, such that I can't tell my tears from the rain, when everything that could be wrong, is wrong, despite my efforts or lack thereof... that's yoga.

And when everything fits together as though my life were a song or a plot from a book, when I smile despite myself, that's yoga.

In July, when my grandfather died after 89 years of life, that was yoga. And when Adar's body finally exploded with life, and diapers, and baby monitors, that was yoga too. Indeed every single moment of my life since it took shape has elaborated on what yoga is.

Even the times I was sure were too sad to be true - when I learned how fur coats are made, when I caught myself learning to ignore homeless people while living in Chicago - even they were yoga. And their being yoga, their being the yin to the yang that is compassion, has enabled me to see them without the distortions that ignorance provides.

When I was doing my yoga teacher training, they told me yoga is "union". The inevitable question that hung like a cloud above my head and kept my Trikonasanas and Sirasanas company might seem obvious: what does yoga unite?

In answering this question, or in trying to at least, I became increasingly aware of the relationship between seemingly oppositional realities. I realized that even things diametrically opposed lost their meaning in the absence of their counterparts.

I recalled my college years, when I was studying the thought exercise aimed at elucidating philosophy that underscores the Einstein-Podolsky-Rosen Paradox: if the whole world were red and red were the only color that existed, would the color red exist or would it's meaning be lost in the absence of other colors?

I wondered, is yoga a holistic equation that accounts for the good and bad by illuminating the impossibility of one existing without the other? Or is it simpler than that?

Is it the reason why so many people gather barefoot at retreats and in yoga studios when they could just as easily practice in the comfort and privacy of their own homes? In other words, is there something intrinsic in the practice and philosophy of yoga that compels us to join together with other people?

I spent the first several years of my practice contemplating these questions. Eventually, and with the meditative awareness that yoga inspires, the answers found me.

And in the end, or perhaps the beginning, I realized that the answer to this question of what yoga unites is both simple and infinitely complex; because yoga, I've come to understand, unites EVERYTHING.

The breath and the body, the warrior and the child, the tangible and the ethereal, the male and the female, the baby and the corpse, pleasure and pain, solitude and company – all of these experiences have their place and their purpose in the context of yoga.

So I hung my mat on that – the idea that yoga encompasses all things. But as I continued my practice, I found that there was a depth this conceptualization failed to reach. How could that be? How could everything fall short of anything?

The problem, I realized, was not with yoga, but with what my words had done to it. The semantics I used to articulate my ideas were not simply providing a means of communication, they were determining the end product.

I realized that the words and ways I thought about yoga were passive. Things are nouns, after all, and a stream of nouns in the absence of verbs is like a lake frozen over. Nothing seems to move or change, and even if one tries to they are stopped by the cold hard properties of matter.

But I knew yoga to be a flow. And I knew this, because I felt it. I felt each pose bleed into the next. I enjoyed the unfolding modifications that enabled my asanas to grow and evolve, changing to accommodate the changes in the environment that is my body.

I also found myself growing increasingly displeased by the distinctions that classifications and names illuminate. A tree is a tree because of x and y and z, which is different than a mountain, which we know is defined by a, b, and c. Differences are made paramount in the context of nouns, so where is the union in that?

Enter purusha, prakriti's compliment. To speak of one without the other is as meaningless as a sentence composed only of nouns. The integral relationship between prakriti and purusha is the means through which trees and mountains are one and the reason that one is Atman. It is thus the means and the end.

And it is only by understanding this reasoning that we attain the liberation from which we were never separated, but instead bound, in the same way that suffering is bound to compassion and red bound to blue.

I would like to think that my ability to speak about this reality in spite of the restraints words pose means that I understand it. But I know not all of me does. My mind might have finally grasped the logic that underscores this reasoning, such that it is appeased. But I know my emotions and body don't.

I know this, because I still spend more money on myself than on others. I know this because I still value my brother's life more than a stranger's.

But I also know that beneath the greed and fear and suffering, this knowledge exists. I know because it finds me sometimes. When sitting cross-legged for hours with only the company of The Heart Sutra, it finds me. When my compassion is so strong it's like a magnet seeking the suffering that is its counterpart, it finds me.

And when I close my eyes in Shivasana, and feel the rhythm of my at last balanced breath, when my heart beats in time with the fan's hum and the fly's wings, this truth finds me. All that is yoga lays itself down before me so I can see that it is and has always been everything I ever was and will ever be.

Caroline Cozza

www.bluepointyoga.com/staff/teachers/caroline.html

Having worked as a personal trainer and aerobics instructor for years, yoga seemed like a natural progression for me. I'd been practicing Mahayana Buddhism before being introduced to yoga and thus found it to be a rather organic synthesis of two seemingly competing interests – physical exercise and eastern spirituality.

After receiving my certification from Yoga Alliance, I began teaching yoga at Duke University and Blue Point Yoga Studio in Durham, North Carolina. As an experienced personal trainer I strive to integrate my knowledge of physiology with my understanding of eastern spirituality by offering a holistic yoga experience aimed at increasing strength and flexibility by focusing on isometric movements in the context of flow sequences.

In addition to teaching at Blue Point, I am a doctoral candidate in Duke's clinical psychology program and enjoy working as a therapist in this capacity. My primary research interests focus on mindfulness-based treatments for psychopathology including Mindfulness-Based Stress Reduction (MBCT) and Dialectical Behavior Therapy (DBT).

INVENTING YOURSELF WITH YOGA
(AND A LITTLE HELP FROM JESUS,
BUDDHA, EINSTEIN, AND MARLEY)

SUMYA ANANI

Everyone on this planet has a great mission. Yoga helps one discover what that purpose is. Yoga is the practice of understanding and realizing the Self. But what does that really mean?

Yoga taught me that all of life is thought. All the masters teach us how to train and discipline our mind. Why is that important?

We think of reality as things that we see, things that we touch. But what is reality?

Where does reality start?

It starts in our mind. What is "real" begins in our mind. This nature of consciousness is the Ultimate Reality. The invention process begins in the mind. An idea is a thought. The invisible realm (thoughts) creates the visible realm (matter).

Everything you see in this world began as a thought in a person's mind. A light post, electricity, chewing gum.

Mind precedes matter.

Jesus taught meditation. Jesus said, "In my father's house, there are many mansions...As ye sow, so shall ye reap." One interpretation of that could be the many states of consciousness we all carry in our mind, the many thoughts. As ye sow in the mind (realm of heaven), so shall ye reap in the body (realm of earth).

If you plant thoughts of jealousy, you will be jealous. If you plant thoughts of kindness and love, you will be kind and loving. If you plant tulips, you don't get squash. You reap what you sow. The most fertile soil in the world is the soil of your consciousness.

As above, in the mind, so below, in the body.

Jesus also said, "Finally, Brethren, whatsoever things are true, whatsoever things are honest, whatsoever things are just, whatsoever things are pure, whatsoever things are lovely, whatsoever things are of good report; if there be any virtue, and if there be any praise, think on these things." (Phil. 4:8).

Some versions of the Bible say dwell upon these things, some translations say meditate on these things. Jesus understood these aspects of thought and the importance of training our minds. What we think about ultimately expands.

THE MOST DIFFICULT POSTURE

Patanjali, the author of the Yoga Sutras, told us that the most difficult posture is the posture of your mind. The mental posture is the most important pose in yoga.

So to come to an awareness of what you're thinking is the most awesome power you can ever have because the thought level is the creative level.

Yoga is about asking yourself these vital questions: What do I dwell upon?

What are the thoughts that dominate my mental landscape? Yoga teaches us to pay attention.

"Wake up," said Buddha.

Buddha taught meditation too. Buddha said, "We are what we think. All that we are arises with our thoughts. With our thoughts we create our world."

The mind is the creator. The mind's nature is to think. But Yoga has taught me to make my practice of "just thinking" a very intentional practice.

I listened to an audio tape by Louise Hay. In it, she says that science has found that we have about 60,000 thoughts a day. Most of these thoughts are dwelling on the past. "Woe is me, what happened to me, what they did to me, I'm a victim." If we're not living in the past, we're worrying about the future.

We become scientists on the yoga mat.

Watch your mind.

Observe your mind.

Study your mind.

In the Bhagavad Gita, Krishna tells Arjuna that trying to control the mind is like trying to capture the wind. It's difficult to restrain, difficult to achieve.

But it's not impossible. That is the beauty of it. It can be achieved through the twin practices of abhyasa (practice) and vairagya (detachment.)

CREATE YOUR OWN REALITY

The more I study Yoga, the more amazed I am at this practice and how it teaches me about myself, where my mind is dwelling, and how I'm creating my reality one thought at a time.

Yoga taught me that I have responsibility to envision and create my future, no matter what happened in the past. The past is gone, it's an illusion. All we have is now, this moment.

What patterns are you creating through your daily diet of thinking?

What kind of thoughts are you cultivating in the soil of your mind?

What are the thoughts you regularly entertain?

A good healthy thought is like a good guest in your home. You want guests to have a good time and you want them to come back.

But you want to entertain the right guests. If people come over and trash your house, break dishes, and insult you and your family, you're not going to invite them back.

We should guard our mind like we guard our home. Train yourself not to invite unhealthy thoughts into your mind. Don't let them wreak havoc.

Yoga continues to teach me to consciously choose thoughts of blessing, gratitude, generosity, acceptance towards myself and others, love, tolerance and abundance. These are some of the guests I want to entertain.

The Yoga Sutras begin like this: Atha Yoga Anushasanam. Now, the study and practice of Yoga begins. The message of the Yoga Sutras is "Choose again." Now, this moment, you can choose again.

Each of us is an artist. Artists create. What do you want to create?

Create abundance.

Create health in your body.

Create joy.

Create generosity.

Create everything that you want in your life, for the highest good of all concerned.

Think about what you want.

Focus on that.

What do you want in life?

Meditate on that.

What "reality" in the world do you want to have?

Dwell upon that.

What do you want to have manifest in the world?

Imagine that.

Albert Einstein said, "Imagination is more important than knowledge."

Once we become aware of these thoughts that dominate our life, we have power to undo those thoughts that don't serve us anymore.

In Bob Marley's Redemption Song, he sang, "Emancipate yourselves from mental slavery, none but ourselves can free our mind."

What we think about we become.

Yoga begs the questions,

Who am I?

Why am I here?

What great destiny am I here to fulfill?

Through the practice of Yoga and clearly setting intention, samkalpa, we become who we want to be. It's our choice who we become.

INVENT YOURSELF

You are an inventor, after all. We're inventing our life, one thought at a time.

You are inventing who you want to be, whether it's a physical achievement such as "I am going to be a medalist in the 2012 Olympics", or whether it's a state of mind:

I am generous.

I am thoughtful.

I am loving.

I am kind.

I am grateful.

I am forgiving.

Everyone has been given the gift of imagination. We all have unlimited potential to be, do and to create whatever we want.

Who do you want to be?

What great thing do you want to accomplish?

How do you want to serve the world?

Everyone has a personal ministry. It's through a mindful Yoga practice, paying attention to your thoughts, that you can lay claim to your unique life. Keep the mind on this present moment. In this moment, you have the power to invent yourself.

What are you passionate about?

What excites you?

This is how you will find where your gifts, talents and contributions wait. Your personal ministry is waiting to be discovered.

Yoga is calling all of us to find our service to humanity and the fulfillment of our destiny.

Yoga gives us the opportunity to explore our potential and stretch beyond our self-perceived limitations. Even our limitations help us discover our full potential.

We move from contracted states of fear to expanded states of full expression of our gifts and talents. Yoga teaches us to stretch, to expand into who we're meant to be.

Mary Oliver asked, "What are you going to do with this one wild and precious thing called life?"

It's time each of us become a champion of possibilities and discover our full potential to love and serve.

Yoga is an invitation. It invites you to invent yourself. This is the beautiful and sacred practice of Yoga. This is the promise of Yoga.

Sumya Anani

www.sumya.com

Sumya Anani has been teaching Yoga for 13 years and is RYT 500 through Yoga Alliance. She has studied many styles – Bikram, Ashtanga, Iyengar, Anusara, and sees the beauty in them all. She teaches Vinyasa Flow classes in Kansas City, where she is also a personal trainer and a massage therapist.

Sumya was a professional boxer for 10 years, winning 4 World Championships. She leads "Spiritual Warrior Yoga Retreats" annually to Negril, Jamaica; Lake Atitlan, Guatemala; and Boulder, Colorado. She combines journaling and creative writing exercises to optimize creativity and engage the imagination. Empowering women to discover their own courage and strength is her life mission.

Sumya loves to motivate and inspire others to achieve their best. She speaks for businesses, women's groups, health food stores and schools. She is available for Yoga workshops at your studio, threading the philosophical aspect of Yoga in with the asana.

Sumya created and now hosts a holistic health show, Beat the Health Out of You, on Talk Radio 710am, which can be heard on the internet at www.710kcmo.com (Live, Sundays, 1pm CST). The show highlights 7 habits of health for body, mind and spirit, with each habit relating to a chakra. She's also working on a pilot for a TV show.

LET'S BEGIN WITH POTATOES

JULES WOLF STENZEL

Let's begin with potatoes.

My first kitchen job was as an apprentice, and unhappily, after many hard, long hours, I was laid off. Distraught, I asked the owner for some advice. He told me about his first restaurant job turning potatoes. To turn a potato, you take a paring knife and cut away the peel and any blemishes until the potato is a perfectly smooth ovate shape, then you take the next potato and do the same to it. The hard part is that the second potato should look exactly the same as the first one and so on, potato after potato, pound after pound, day after day, year after year. With time, your skill increases, but you always have to have a certain mindfulness to achieve your goal. He suggested I start at the beginning with a simple job.

Looking back now, with each kitchen job I ever held, there was never any way around those simple, repetitive tasks. They are an essential part of creating something, honing what you know already, learning new tasks, and learning what it is that you don't know.

It is the same way with yoga. We may come to yoga for physical fitness, relief from injury or broken heartedness, or deeper meaning within stressful lives, but there is no way around the repetition. We might not be practicing asanas. We might chant or meditate or pray, but there it is, we roll up our sleeves and begin. Simple, and then do it again. And again.

Why? What happens when we do?

Patanjali described Ha'tha yoga as having eight limbs--among them physical practice, breath practice, moral practice, various states of meditation, and enlightenment. We don't necessarily start with one limb and move to the next when we've mastered that, like climbing a ladder. Instead, as much as we can, we assimilate the skills for each limb simultaneously. Of course, as we become more adept at one limb, we acquire tools to go deeper into the other limbs.

We begin to discover new things through repetition. We start with what condition our bodies are in, what mood our minds are in. We act within the framework of what our day brings us, what environments we're in.

Through mindfulness, we notice how to move certain muscles to achieve sthira sukasanam asanam. We inhale and notice the movement of our bellies and ribs. We reach and enjoy the sensation across the souls of our feet. We can feel how the body and the mind are interconnected, indivisible. At first, we walk deeper into an understanding of ourselves, and then we begin to have a deeper compassion for those around us. Sometimes we feel more connected to them.

The sameness of repetition taps into our originality. The body learns more as we repeat. The quietness of doing something we know draws us inward in a way that we suddenly can look around ourselves and see the world with clearer eyes, a more open heart. We've been walking inward to get out.

After a while, a year, a decade, we might wonder, what does it matter which asanas we use, which chants we sing? We could do anything. The asanas themselves could be any position. Why eagle pose? Why not stick a leg over here, hold your head just so? Why stop at poses? We might build houses for humanity. We might walk the dog, love our families, peel potatoes.

Every moment is a chance to notice ourselves noticing. Any movement is a chance to notice ourselves breathing.

One of my clients held a stressful job. She said she often held her breath while she was working at her desk, and I could see that she also did so as she moved in her yoga practice. I often had to remind her to keep the breath flowing. One day, she bought some fuzzy socks and wore them to work. Having another difficult day, she sat back to take a break from hunching toward the computer. She crossed her ankle over her other knee and noticed that there was something written on the cuff of the new socks. "Just Breathe." Some days we all could use those mindful socks.

Many of my students come to me with neck and back issues. As we tense up or work intensely, we draw our shoulders up and forward. When we hold our shoulders it's hard to breathe. If we don't breathe well, then we're not going to be able to move and think effectively.

At the beginning of a class, I ask my clients to lie back and breathe. We focus on the sensation, the rhythm and pace of the breath. Gradually, I ask my students to notice how they exhale and try to allow their exhales to leave their bodies fully--not through squeezing the tummy muscles, but from letting go, softening. We're good at doing things actively and not so practiced at simply letting things release out of our bodies. Letting the breath dissipate allows the body to start releasing tension right down to the cellular level. We have the skill to hold on to things tightly, and the more we practice, the more we remember how to let go of what we no longer need: carbon dioxide, tension, hesitancy, fear.

Another of my clients was a good yoga student. She wanted to be honest with herself. By trying to admit to her fears and thus live mindfully with them, she thought she could extinguish them. It was constant work, and worn out, she asked me if I thought it was okay to set aside working on her fear for a while so she could breathe again.

We invite our weaknesses, fears, injuries, and habits to be with us so we can scrutinize them, analyze them, and find a road to healing and wholeness. This may make us companions to or guardians of the very things we wish weren't in our lives. It is heavy work. To rid yourself of a trait you must be vigilant. Sometimes we wish we could ignore it rather than sitting with it. The hope is if you study it thoroughly, maybe the fear or habit will dwindle and dissipate like an exhale.

When I was eight, I discovered "Lilias! Yoga and You", the PBS TV program. I loved it. It was so wonderful to be quiet, move, and try to emulate the shapes she created. My favorite pose was lion because on the surface it was so irreverent. Practicing alone, I felt free to be myself. I wasn't very good at gym class or competition, so I was often displaced on the playground by those more assertive. At home, with my yoga, I was able to explore movement and not be in the spotlight. The feeling of being within my body was so interesting, moving, then maybe not moving, holding a pose, and simply existing.

My yoga teacher once said that he spends eighty percent of his teaching time helping people to like their bodies. We spend so much time out of our bodies--in our jobs, taking care of others, in entertainment, pondering--we can lose touch with our physical selves. When we do come back to our bodies, we often don't want to be there. We don't want those injuries. We don't want those patterns and habits. We want to be in "better shape." We feel indifference, anger, or disdain towards our bodies. Our bodies hurt. We want to feel pleasure.

Let's say, instead, with the curious eyes of a child, we hold an asana, or we move through a sequence of asanas. We stay in our bodies and observe. Our bodies become the meditation. We don't need to fix anything. If we can't move into a pose or deeper, we don't. We notice that, and we notice what we are capable of doing at a given moment. We can make note of where we were yesterday and where we are today, not comparing the two. We allow our honest observation to be just that, an observation. Here we are, now.

Now we are getting very close to doing yoga.

I think savasana, corpse pose, is the most difficult pose and possibly the most important.

An old friend once told me he hears music in his head wherever he goes, whatever he's doing. He has a soundtrack to his life. Many of us do have some sort of soundtrack going on. Some of our soundtracks are external -- iPods, radio, noisy households or workplaces. Some of our soundtracks are internal. I have a very chatty mind. It is always talking to me, reminding me of things, worrying, and keeping track of my everyday life. When I lie down at night, sometimes I wish there was an "off" switch.

I end my classes in savasana as many yoga instructors do. I think there is something important in acknowledging that the word "sava" means "corpse." I've heard savasana referred to as resting pose, relaxation pose, or just "lie back" as if calling it by another name will take away any negative associations we have with death, dying, and the undoing of our bodies and minds. Now of course a corpse does "lie back" and that is what we are doing with our bodies, but let's look beyond the obvious.

Remember that Ha'tha refers to union of opposites, sun and moon, and the yoking of that oppositional energy. If that is so and if in using yoga we find honest, breathable existence, then it stands to reason that we must also find the united opposite of that: death. We can look at life and death as flip sides of the same coin.

At the end of our practice, we feel peaceful, whole, ready to rest, so we lie back and then what happens? Too often, like a cosmic joke, the soundtrack switches on, the background music to our life blares. Our plans, judgments, worries, the itches on our skin, the uncomfortable feeling in our lower back starts up at such a high decibel it's a wonder our neighbors in savasana can't hear it too. Sometimes, if we're really wiggling around, they are able to hear it, and we become self-conscious and even less present in our bodies.

We can use that as a gentle reminder and say hello to the noise of our minds and environments, then release it. Over and over again, we let go of distractions, compassionately, and come back into ourselves, breathing, with nothing more to do. I let my students know that this continual process of realizing we've been lured away and coming back *is* the meditation.

The more we practice savasana, the more we are able to use the lessons learned in it as tools for the rest of our yoga practice. Indeed, in our breath explorations, in our prayers and chanting, even in our daily lives, we can release what is not essential and come back to what we were doing.

Here we are doing yoga.

Yoga is a path to honesty and compassion. We try to look at ourselves openly and release our prejudices about what we see, notice and just be ourselves. We breathe and focus. Yoga is a way to be fully present in our physical form without denying the spiritual or emotional aspects of our beings. We seek steadiness and ease but don't deny the wobbles and the pain. Aren't they part of the job of being alive? You get to experience all the moments of your life. Then if you can be here now, truly here, truly present, every moment that you are is an opportunity to become fully enlightened.

Pass the potatoes, please.

Jules Wolf Stenzel

www.yoga-wolf.com

I am a RYT 200 and have been teaching since 2004. In 2005, I founded Yoga Wolf. I teach Vinyasa Flow Yoga, Yogilates, and Mat Pilates. I am training to become a certified Pilates instructor.

I became an instructor because, as my own yoga practice evolved, it seemed natural to share the fabulous things that I've learned with others. I teach full time and wonder why I don't have even more time to teach and do yoga.

In my personal practice I mainly practice pranayama, asanas, and meditate. I am also a poet, dancer, and a mother of two fabulous, dancing daughters.

"Come, come, whoever you are. Wanderer, worshipper, lover of living. It doesn't matter. Ours is not a caravan of despair. Come, even if you have broken your vow a thousand times. Come, yet again, come, come." --Rumi

SNAPSHOTS OF YOGA IN AMERICA

TOBEY GIFFORD

Pausing and taking a mindful breath.... I look around, listen, feel, taste, smell.... and connect. I connect with snapshots, images, sounds, stories and sensations as I have actually seen or experienced.

Yoga is all around us, and I share with you my personal collection of snapshots of Yoga in America:

Yoga in America is being on Facebook, sharing experience and love with other yogis.

Yoga in America is blissfully driving on the snow-covered roads of Vermont, listening to Krishna Das, after a weeklong yoga therapy immersion.

Yoga in America is two children on their yoga mats giggling with each other.

Yoga in America is when one human being remembers how to be present with another.

Yoga in America is a community coming together to purchase beautiful beaded jewelry to support a community in Africa.

Yoga in America is when men in suits take a break from the corporate whir of business and take a yoga class in the cafeteria.

Yoga in America is learning how to live a more simple life.

Yoga in America is people coming together in a time of fear and uncertainty.

Yoga in America is friends shopping together and teaching each other about different Buddhas and Mudras, which they will purchase for their altar.

Yoga in America is a group of yoga teachers working together to learn about themselves and how they might be able to share their learning with others.

Yoga in America is falling and letting go of ego.

Yoga in America is a million dollar business.

Yoga in America is seeing Peace signs everywhere again.

Yoga in America is choosing to go on a healing retreat for vacation this year.

Yoga in America is a mother, a lawyer, a teacher, a student, a dentist, breathing together.

Yoga in America is the silence of a home when a conscious decision is made to turn off the TV.

Yoga in America is a woman with cancer supporting her healing and well-being with breath and compassion.

Yoga in America is children (and adults) dancing and smiling.

Yoga in America is a recovering addict learning how to practice the 11th step ("sought through prayer and meditation to improve our conscious contact with God as we understood him, praying only for knowledge of his will and the power to carry that out.") in his yoga class.

Yoga in America is a group of young people educating others on factory farming at a community college yoga class.

Yoga in America is a housewife learning to love herself, dust bunnies, wrinkles and five extra pounds!

Yoga in America is a fourteen-year-old boy who practices meditation mindfully instead of meeting up with a gang in the neighborhood.

Yoga in America is the smell of Nag Champa in someone's home.

Yoga in America is a senior center with chair yoga, support, and warm smiles.

Yoga in America is visiting someone in a hospital and praying for them.

Yoga in America is coming away from the wall in headstand after five years there, and realizing and trusting that you can stand on your own.

Yoga in America is a small studio trying to follow the yamas and niyamas and survive in corporate America.

Yoga in America is individuals taking yoga to communities and making it affordable/free for them.

Yoga in America is driving through back roads in Upstate NY and seeing cows in a field and feeling an overwhelming sense of joy and appreciation for them.

Yoga in America is yogis joining forces to raise awareness about environmental protection.

Yoga in America is struggling with the competitive mind in an Ashtanga class.

Yoga is releasing that competitiveness and accepting the Self as it is.

Yoga is walking three miles to a yoga class in the snow, because you need to.

Yoga in America is a Vietnam vet finding courage and safety in his own breath and body again with the support of others.

Yoga in America is being totally distracted by the physical benefits you are seeing from the practice.

Yoga in America is deciding to eat healthier to support our body as it carries our Self.

Yoga in America is doing shoulderstand against a gymnasium floor with a bunch of teens being uncomfortable with themselves (and noticing you feel the same way).

Yoga in America is healing this country.

Yoga in America is Sri Dharma Mittra doing headstand on a sewer cap.

Yoga in America is watching your dog perform down dog with much more skill and presence.

Yoga in America is smiling at work and being happy being.

Yoga in America is a couple of friends working together to free a bird stuck in the grid of their jeep.

Yoga in America is a kirtan in Manhattan.

Yoga in America is a cell phone going off in class and hearing "I'm too sexy for my shirt....", and deciding to smile instead of getting agitated.

Yoga in America is Sivananda, Kripalu, Omega and other retreat centers bringing large communities of people together to practice.

Yoga in America is a group of friends cleaning up a park one afternoon.

Yoga in America is a group of people getting together to discuss Patanjali's Yoga Sutras.

Yoga in America is a single mom doing yoga in her living room with her favorite DVD.

Yoga in America is being truly happy for someone else's joy.

Yoga in America is a quieting of a materialistic mind.

Yoga in America is taking a mindful breath when you are losing your job.

Yoga in America is believing in the possibilities.

Yoga in America is a food drive at a yoga studio and people relearning how to care for each other and themselves.

Yoga in America begins as a workout, but one day takes on a deeper meaning, as a heart that was hardened by life begins to feel safe enough to open.

Yoga in America is an opportunity for a family to heal as priorities shift.

Yoga is a young woman supporting a friend by bringing the friend to her first class.

Yoga in America is a woman remembering to breathe as her car is rolling over, avoiding any serious injury to herself, and letting go of her car.

Yoga in America is slowing down to enjoy the moment as your child is holding your hand.

Yoga in America is a couple breathing together even though their marriage is falling apart.

Yoga in America is a woman working to relearn how to feel safe in her body after years of being abused.

Yoga in America is a flower blooming in a store, and our pause to be with it.

Yoga in America is our conscious decision to recycle our materials.

Yoga in America is someone getting excited to "get" a pose.

Yoga in America is a "vacation" from day to day life....or is it?

Yoga in America is a family doing asana in the livingroom.

Yoga in America is a hotel conference room full of hundreds of people in Boston, doing downdog and listening to the teacher with a headset on.

Yoga in America is letting a car go in front of you.

Yoga in America is doing tree pose with a tree.

Yoga in America is deciding not to support unethical businesses.

Yoga in America is an infomercial promising a Yoga Butt!

Yoga in America is thousands of people praying and meditating on World Peace on the same day, connecting with people all over the world.

Yoga in America is falling in front of others, and realizing that it is ok.

Yoga in America is children of all ages in a circle holding hands and speaking about being grateful.

Yoga in America is a group of people in meditation while a loud basketball game is happening in the room above.

Yoga in America is a woman visiting a prison to offer instruction on breath, asana and forgiveness.

Yoga in America is tears of bliss and love taking over as we surrender.

Yoga in America is one human helping another.

Yoga in America is a student bragging about their practice, while another holds the space and tries not to judge.

Yoga in America is a class or book called Yoga for Golfers, Yoga for Skiers, Yoga for Runners, Yoga for Men, Yoga for Pregnancy, Yoga for Dummies, Yoga for the Rest of Us, Yoga for Seniors, Yoga for the Special Child, Yoga for ….you get the idea, and knowing it is all good.

Yoga in America is deciding to go to class, instead of happy hour at your favorite bar.

Yoga in America is four women sitting at a local park on a beautiful sunny day, reading the Bhagavad Gita.

Yoga in America is seeing, being and breathing change.

Yoga in America is a bunch of yoga teachers writing a book together about what yoga is in America.

Tobey Gifford

"Since the mind, body, and spirit are closely connected, by tuning into all aspects of ourselves, we can grow, learn and heal. When we begin to do our work and heal, we begin to heal the planet."

Tobey Gifford is an E-RYT yoga teacher, physical education professor, certified yoga and Thai therapist and Reiki Master. She is co-owner of the Lemon Tree Yoga and Healing Arts Studio in Glens Falls, NY and teaches at various locations in and around the community.

Prior to establishing her life and career in yoga, Tobey spent over 25 years as a competitive gymnastics coach, fitness instructor, recreation administrator and exercise physiologist.

Her yoga background comes from Ashtanga, Dharma Mittra, Phoenix Rising Yoga Therapy, Jivamukti, Vinyasa styles, as well as influences from Kripalu and Iyengar. She is humbly grateful to her teachers who include Dharma Mittra, Pema Chodron, Nancy Gilgoff, Manju Jois, Kathy McNames, Michael Lee and Karen Hasskerl, staff at the Trauma Center in Boston and others including her family and friends, who continue to share their courage, light and love.

GENTLE HATHA YOGA
KEEPING IT SIMPLE

ED & MAUDE VALENTINE

Our classes incorporate a gentle form of the classic Hatha Yoga as taught by Integrative Yoga Therapy. This gentle and slower paced approach makes it more accessible to people of all sizes, ages, and fitness levels. It is non-competitive and most poses are easily modified to fit the individual needs of the student. Yoga has been around for over 5,000 years and has proven itself to be a valuable complimentary approach to healing and nurturing the mind, body and spirit.

Our style of Yoga is not about twisting yourself into a pretzel; it is about gentle, slow-moving poses that bring health, enjoyment, and well-being into your life. We believe that anyone, regardless of their level of physical fitness, can experience the benefits of Yoga. We have taught Chair Yoga to cancer patients and their care givers, private sessions for students with various health issues and group classes. Our students range in age from 13 years old to 76 years young.

We believe that some of the Yoga magazines you see on the shelf do a disservice to the Yoga profession in general. We believe that the young buff bodies you see on the cover of the magazine doing poses that most Yoga teachers can't even do scare a lot of people away from Yoga. Yoga videos that are labeled as "beginning Yoga" are most often more intermediate and can discourage newcomers to Yoga.

Unfortunately some Yoga teachers seem more concerned about showing off what they can do in front of their students rather than guiding the students on their Yoga journey and accommodating their needs according to their level of fitness. Yoga is not about competition, it is about what you can do within your own physical, mental and spiritual makeup and about moving forward on your Yoga journey. We discourage students from watching the person next to them, as their level of ability may not be the same as the person they are watching. Watching someone else may make the student feel like they are doing it wrong.

We emphasize that nothing the student does in class should be painful. Maybe a little uncomfortable, but not painful. If the student is feeling pain we suggest that they back off a little or ask for assistance in modifying the pose. We encourage our students to go to their edge and challenge their bodies; we discourage any poses that cause pain to the student. "Always listen to your body" is a phrase that we use throughout our classes. It is OK to not do a pose. If the teacher is telling you to do one thing and your body is saying "no way", then you always want to listen to your own body. Your body is much wiser than any Yoga teacher you may have.

A typical class with Ed and Maude begins in a seated position with a few moments of centering and letting go of the stresses of the day and week. This is followed by 15 to 20 minutes of gentle warm-ups, 30 to 40 minutes of asanas (poses) followed by a 10 to 15 minute relaxation period called savasana, which often includes guided imagery. We believe that the best classes combine the physical, the mental, and the spiritual aspects of Yoga as well as the breath. The student should walk away from the Yoga class feeling refreshed and relaxed. We design the majority of our classes to be a meditative or prayerful experience. We try to keep class sizes small with no more than 10 students.

Cardio exercises are great. However, we don't believe a Yoga class should be a cardio class. If the student wants cardio, they can always go to the Y and take a Zumba or a cycling class. The ancient Yogi's were most likely very fit by the nature of their life style. For this reason their Yoga was most likely a slow and gentle movement, almost prayerful. They observed the animals in nature and studied their movements and modeled their poses after their teachers, the animals around them. This is why most poses are named after animals.

We don't use the Sanskrit names for the poses in our classes; we use the Americanized or English name for the poses. Newer students are more comfortable in the class when they can understand what the teacher is talking about. If you ask a new student to go from cobra to table to child, he or she will intuitively have a good idea what you are talking about. If you ask the same student to go from bhujangasana to marjariasana to balasana, you most likely will get a blank or frustrated look.

Not to say that Sanskrit has no place in Yoga, just that throwing big words around isn't a very good teaching tool, especially with new students. Many instructors are taught that there is something mystical about using the Sanskrit names for the poses. We don't believe that. We believe that the magic is within the student's own Yoga journey.

Ever since the mid-60's when four young men named John, Paul, George and Ringo, joined up with the world famous Maharishi Mahesh Yogi, a great spiritual leader from India, Americans as a whole have really taken to Yoga and embraced it as their own. There is a Yoga style for everyone, and of course we feel, as I'm sure instructors of other schools do, that Gentle Hatha Yoga is the most beneficial.

Ed and Maude Valentine

www.YogaValentine.com

Ed and Maude Valentine, teach a very gentle form of Hatha Yoga as taught by Integrative Yoga Therapy. They studied with Joseph and Lillian Le Page at Enchanted Mountain in Garapoba, Brazil.

The Valentines have been involved in Yoga for several years and are registered through Yoga Alliance. Both teach group classes and private classes at various locations, as well as at their in-home studio in Tacoma, Washington.

Maude is a registered nurse working in a hospital setting and Ed is a retired IT professional. Both are Reiki practitioners and certified Clinical Hypnotherapists.

THE ANCIENT ROOTS OF MODERN YOGA

TONY CRISCUOLO

After thirty years of teaching yoga all over the U.S. I have come across pretty much every imaginable way of approaching this deceptively simple discipline, as well as seeing a wide variety of competence in teachers. Sad to say, many do not have the proper foundation in wisdom and experience.

Aside from knowledge in teaching the postures and breathing methods, I believe it is crucial to have an understanding of the historical and philosophical roots for what we do on the mat. The ancient texts, principally found in the Vedic wisdom of India, but including the later "Yoga Sutras", are very clear on the direction of yoga practice as leading to a conscious connection with The Divine Energy, whether in a personal or impersonal form.

This is not to say that every practitioner will have this as a goal; certainly there is nothing wrong in applying the more mundane benefits of yoga that include improving health and vitality, creating a flexible, strong and balanced body, and expanding the focus and abilities of the mind. But in our Western zeal to package and popularize yoga (especially in America) rarely is there sufficient attention given to the ancients and their awareness of the transcendental possibilities inherent in a dedicated approach to yoga: freedom from the bondage of the material world and the joys of a conscious connection with The Divine.

There are two foundational texts: "The Yoga Sutras" which describe the way the mind is constructed to process information and the application of this knowledge in our quest for spiritual freedom; and "The Bhagavad Gita", which basically lays out the organization of the world, our place in it, and describes how to be in harmony with The Divine. Let's take a look at what these ancient texts have to say about yoga, beginning with "The Yoga Sutras".

Even a casual reading of this text, particularly the section which describes the Ashtanga Yoga System, makes it clear that whatever yoga is, it has little to do with the physical body, beyond maintaining a healthy, strong vehicle for the journey of the spirit. Within the eight limbs of yoga, in Sanskrit 'Ashtanga', the yamas and niyamas present us with a guide to leading an ethical and moral life, with rules of conduct meant to help us avoid the pitfalls of material existence and improve our relations with all beings.

Asanas (postures) and pranayama (breathwork and maintaining life force) assure the health of the physical body and allow a stilling of the mind that can, at least momentarily, free us from the pull of material desires. It then becomes possible to turn the senses inward (pratyahara) and really begin the investigation of consciousness, which makes up the final three limbs (dharana, dhyana and samadhi) of the Ashtanga Yoga System.

This is the methodology for freeing the restless mind from thought based on a temporary view of life and describes how to create will, the essential ingredient for any development, by disciplining the body, mind and emotions. As a personalist, I would say that the ultimate goal as outlined in "The Yoga Sutras" is the linking of our little will with the Will of God. An impersonalist might say something like uniting with the creative energy of the universe or cosmic consciousness.

By the way, none of this has anything to do with what we customarily think of as religion; this methodology applies inside or outside of any cultural or religious context. We could call the process the science of the soul. And the freedom referred to is based on the experience of a disciplined practice of yoga, not mere intellectual knowledge, which can impede the actual practice of yoga if not fully understood.

So "The Yoga Sutras" are mainly concerned with the psychological aspects of yoga. It is an instruction manual that describes the inner workings of the mind and how to apply our inner awareness while practicing yoga, no matter what the form.

What is real and what is illusion? How should our individual consciousness relate to this reality in a way that leads to pleasure and happiness? After all, we are all seeking joy in life. And what about the Divine and our relationship to the Divine? For these answers let's turn to the primary text on yoga in the ancient Vedic tradition of India, The Bhagavad Gita.

The larger context of The Bhagavad Gita is worth mentioning. As an episode in the great historical work, The Mahabharata, it is nothing more (or less) than a conversation between The Supreme Lord, Krishna, and His devoted disciple, Arjuna.

Arjuna is about to face an epic war between his family, the Pandavas, and their relatives in the Kuru dynasty. Realizing that he is about to kill some of his dearest relatives, Arjuna, the greatest of the warriors, loses his taste for the battle; he lays down his bow and turns to Lord Krishna for advice. The ensuing conversation is basically the Vedic answer to "What is Yoga?"

The essential aspects of yoga start with the understanding that our situation in the material world is temporary, and that within the body an eternal soul is entangled. Krishna tells Arjuna that he need not be concerned about killing his kinsmen:

Never was there a time when I did not exist, nor you, nor all these kings; nor in the future shall any of us cease to be. (BG 2.12)[1]

And soon after, Krishna makes a key statement that gives a signpost to us as to the path of a yogi:

Oh best among men (Arjuna), the person who is not disturbed by happiness and distress and is steady in both is certain eligible for liberation. (BG 2.16)

Equanimity gives us the composure to see things clearly and not be tossed around by emotional states. Later in the second chapter (BG 2.31) Krishna mentions that there is no better engagement in life than to serve dharma. This is a complex concept that is the primary stepping stone toward spiritual understanding and a key to the ethical teachings of The Bhagavad Gita.

Dharma encompasses universal harmony, being in tune with the reality of creation, as well as a description of our connection to our essential being. It is through the service of dharma that we fulfill our highest potential, transcendental consciousness.

This sounds pretty esoteric, but it simply means that by service to The Lord and His creation we discover our essential being, which has been covered over by our interactions and attachments (karma) to the material world. Through the recognition of the sacred quality of all life, we move toward spiritual understanding by accomplishing our work in the world and accepting our responsibilities as a sacred task.

It makes no difference what our position is, but the attitude with which we do our work and how we do it makes all the difference.

Another way of looking at this is to not serve the lower self, feeding the senses and accumulating more and more karmic reactions, but to turn our attention inward and discover our essential nature (the higher Self). This realization helps us to direct our energies out into the world and perform our duties in family life or whatever they are with an eye toward helping others to follow their dharma.

Finally it is essential to act without attachment to the result, as to do this simply creates more karmic reactions. Perhaps this is what Lao

Tsu meant when he said that the Great Way is not difficult for those who have no preferences.

Following the second chapter summary of The Bhagavad Gita is a complete description of the forms of yoga, the nature of reality, and a beautiful portrait of The Absolute and our relationship to all of this. The last verse of chapter six sums up Lord Krishna's message for yogis:

And of all yogis, the one with great faith who always abides in Me, thinks of Me within himself, and renders transcendental loving service to Me-- he is the most intimately united with Me in yoga and is the highest of all. That is My opinion. (BG 6.47)

Despite the ancient historical and cultural context of this wonderful book, which makes its study difficult for us in the so called modern world, the struggle to understand its message is one of the greatest paths to transcendental consciousness available, even today.

On a more personal note, as we all know, it is not so easy to live without attachment to material desires. It can be quite discouraging to even make the attempt. Further, it has been my experience that most people who show up in my yoga classes are not so philosophically inclined to study these sacred texts. They just want to feel better.

So in my yoga classes I teach the foundation of postures and breath awareness and just mention in passing these higher "spiritual" goals. Experience has taught me that the entry point in yoga is to work on creating a healthy body, maintain the energy required for full participation in life, and improve the ability to perceive clearly.

So I tell students that a higher purpose of yoga exercise is to create a mental state which is clear, alert and able to focus for extended periods of time. And then I ask them to pay close attention to their inner states and to life itself whenever possible and be completely honest with themselves.

I have full confidence that if we do this life will be the greatest teaching and the lessons learned will lead us to an awareness of our inherent spiritual nature in a way that best fits our particular life circumstances.

I love to discuss and share the philosophical and psychological principles behind my teaching but rarely do so in classes, simply dropping hints and suggestions on how to follow up if a student is so inclined. In a sense I offer my services as a spiritual guide and leave the individual free to follow up or not.

After so many years of teaching I realize that most people are up to their necks in material entanglements and it is counterproductive to wave any ultimate goals of life in front of them. I love teaching and connecting with students in whatever way is possible, and believe that one of my tasks as a teacher is to be sensitive to the needs of each student and available to elevate the conversation whenever appropriate.

But I do not see it as my place to define the purpose of life for anyone. I have complete trust in the process of paying close attention to life and practicing the physical aspects of yoga.

FOOTNOTE

[1]There are so many English translations and commentaries on The Bhagavad Gita, and each one to some extent reflects the framework of the translator. I am working primarily from Bhagavad-Gita: As It Is, written by Bhaktivedanti Swami Prabhupada, because it gives word for word and narrative translations of the original Sanskrit text, as well as extensive commentaries. For someone without a working knowledge of Sanskrit (like me) I recommend this translation.

BIBLIOGRAPHY

Davis, Roy Eugene, "The Eternal Way: The Inner Meaning of the Bhagavad Gita". (Lakemont, Georgia; CSA Press, 1996).

Feuerstein, George, "Introduction to the Bhagavad Gita: Its Philosophy and Cultural Setting". (London; Rider Press, 1964).

Miller, Barbara Stoller, "Yoga: Discipline of Freedom". (Berkeley, California; University of California Press, 1995).

Prabhupada, Bhaktivedanta Swami, "The Bhagavad-Gita As It Is". (Los Angeles, California; 1983).

Tony Criscuolo

In 30 years of teaching Tony has led programs all over the country, worked with collegiate and professional athletes, business people, children and families, as well as students in traditional Western yoga settings.

Tony's educational experiences include 12 years of intensive studies with a Sufi Master, a lengthy trip to India with a Jain monk, intensive studies with Iyengar, Kundalini and Ashtanga yoga teachers, and directing a yoga center for five years.

Tony's lifelong calling has been to be a teacher, starting with basketball camps as a collegiate athlete, then as a flight instructor in the air force, college psychology teaching, and finally as a yoga teacher.

He took up yoga as a graduate student because of his disappointment that the field of Western psychology offered nothing for the body. As an athlete he knew that exercise affected the mind and emotions as well as the body; so when he came upon yoga it was a perfect fit that went all the way back to his childhood as an altar boy.

Tony lives and teaches in San Luis Obispo, California. His personal practice involves daily teaching and practice of yoga postures and following the whole of the traditional Ashtanga Yoga System as best he can.

Tony can be reached at yogitony@juno.com.

REFLECTIONS UPON CHOOSING AN ICE CREAM FLAVOR

AMY NOBLES DOLAN

Not too long ago my husband and I took our three kids to Baskin Robbins. When I ordered (as I often do) Rocky Road, my youngest daughter asked me why I chose that flavor. Hmm. I actually can't think of a single reason not to order Rocky Road! But trying to explain to my daughter why this flavor beat out the other thirty left me tongue-tied. Where to start? The creamy chocolate ice cream? The delicate swirl of marshmallow? The chocolate covered nuts that add a perfect textural balance? I had no idea there were so many reasons I love this flavor! Not wanting my scrumptious scoop to melt while I crafted my response, I bailed out of the question with a wholly unsatisfying "Because I like it," leaving her to make her own choice without my input.

Shortly after this incident, a curious student asked me why I had chosen yoga. Perhaps because yoga is a lot more important to me than Rocky Road ice cream, the retort "Because I like it" felt even more like a cop-out than it did in the ice cream parlor. And, perhaps because yoga doesn't melt, I was more willing to take the time to put my thoughts into words. I'd love to be able to say that I stood in front of the ice-cream-case of life and selected yoga for myself. But I can't. It was pure providence that led me to my first yoga class – an Ashtanga class. I shudder to imagine my life without this sustaining daily practice. You see, throughout the years, Ashtanga yoga has always been a perfect match for me. And, I suspect that over the years, it will continue to be.

In the beginning, I was searching for a way to regain my body after years of sharing it with babies. I craved the physical. I needed the endorphin high of a good work-out to carry me through the grueling day ahead filled with diapers, bottles, heavy car-seats and temper tantrums. I yearned to look good again. Heck, I yearned to simply feel good. Ask and ye shall receive. Ashtanga yoga fulfilled all these desires and then some. The challenging asanas toned and strengthened my body. The vigorous, at times speedy, flow steadily increased my stamina and endurance. The stronger and fitter I became, the better I felt. My regular Ashtanga yoga practice was completely revamping my physical body.

Time passed (as it does) and I changed (as we do). My babies got bigger and the challenges that filled my days changed. The demands I faced were no longer as physical. Now I needed the wherewithal to focus on thirteen things at once – imagine three simultaneous requests for help with math homework while cooking dinner, folding a load of laundry and developing a marketing plan for my new yoga studio! I needed the self-awareness to understand that my short temper had more to do with an over-abundance of commitments than with my husband and children. I needed the prescience to see past the scowling face and rude demeanor to sense that something had happened at school to upset my child.

Again, yoga met my needs. The Ashtanga series requires high levels of concentration and focus. As my abilities to focus on one thing at a time and to stay present in the current moment developed, I found myself better able to deal with the multiple demands for my attention one at a time. As I was learning to be curious and aware of myself – my feelings, my fears, my reactions, my ego – on my mat, I became more tuned in to what was behind my feelings off my mat. This awareness also resulted in a heightened sensitivity to the feelings and needs of the people in my life. My regular (now daily) yoga practice was transforming my relationships – with myself, with my family and with my friends.

With time, discipline and dedication, my practice continued to deepen. During my times on my mat I became more inwardly focused. As I became stronger and more flexible, I began to be able to relax into the postures. The more comfortable I was in the asanas, the less mental energy was required of me to stay in them. I could now sink below thoughts of alignment and balance into the quiet of moving meditation. As my physical practice matured, I began to work more diligently with my breath. Yoga's ujjayi breathing became a point of meditation for me, taking me even deeper into a meditative state. And, as meditation became more natural for me, my rests in savasana at the end of my practices became richer and more rewarding. Day after day while I practiced, I drew closer to the divine spark of life and love that is at my core. Day after day, I recognized that same spark in the people I met after I rolled up my mat and moved on into my day. My daily yoga practice was transforming and expanding my spirituality.

And this is what yoga really is. Through our yoga, we hope to create a seamless blend of the sacred and the everyday in the moments, hours, and days of our lives. We spend hours on our mats practicing skills and techniques, meditating on concepts and ideas, quieting our minds so we can tune into the spiritual which moves throughout every aspect of our lives. Our hope is that all this practice will eventually pay off as yoga's skills begin to seep into our lives and activities off our mats. As this happens, we realize that every moment in our lives (even the most mundane) is sacred. Every act we take, every moment we ARE, is a chance to practice yoga.

Yoga teaches us that there is no better time than right now to embrace the gift of our lives. There is no more fitting way to practice spirituality – whatever our chosen faith – than by working to live fully and meaningfully. There is no reason to believe we must step out of the swirl of the everyday in order to connect with God. We can combine the sacred and the everyday. We can live our lives in ways that draw us ever closer to the divine. We do this by focusing on each and every precious moment. We do this by employing the skills we learn on our mats as we move through the activities that fill our moments, hours and days.

Why do I choose to practice yoga? For the same reason I choose Rocky Road ice cream! Because I can't think of a single reason not to! Why do I choose Ashtanga yoga? Because through all the years and all the changes, just like Rocky Road ice cream, it still suits me perfectly! What is it about yoga that brings me to choose it day after day after day? As I said before, I shudder to imagine my life without it. Physically, mentally and spiritually, the practice is transformative – and as wholly satisfying as a scoop of ice cream. Just as Rocky Road ice cream is the perfect flavor for me, Ashtanga yoga is the perfect yoga for me. What about you? What do you choose?

POSTSCRIPT

In late 2005, I was asked to teach yoga one evening at a Mother's Group meeting at our church. That single class stirred up enough interest that the church asked if I would offer an 8-week "Introduction to Yoga" class. Eight weeks later, Yoga With Spirit was born and I was living proof that when you're ready to teach the students will appear.

Since that night, Yoga With Spirit has grown from a single class, one night a week, to a full schedule of adult and children's classes, periodic retreats and workshops. I have found myself surrounded by a wonderful, diverse community of yoga students ranging in age from 5-75. I wake up every morning dazzled that I've received the chance to do this.

Our lives today move so quickly and are so full of activity that we need yoga more than ever. We need to set aside time to be still. We need to set aside the time to reconnect with ourselves -- our minds, our bodies and our spirits. When we set aside the time for our yoga practice, in some amazing way we are always able to find the time for everything and everyone else in our lives. Yoga is truly a gift that gives back -- to you and to all the people who fill your life.

My fundamental teaching philosophy is that yoga works for everyone. We are each formed by our individual life experiences. We each have a different mix of strengths and limitations. Each posture is infinitely modifiable for every body. No matter our age, our gender, or our body type, yoga is for us!

Amy Nobles Dolan

www.yogawithspirit.com

I practice and teach Ashtanga-based yoga. My special focus on the practice is on finding yoga's gifts off the mat and in our lives. I teach workshops on the spirituality of yoga and offer retreats focusing on the intersections of yoga's spirituality and the Christian faith.

I am also a writer. Each week I publish an email meditation called "Yoga Thoughts." These essays are reflections on one regular life (mine) as seen through the lens of yoga. My intention for them is to bring a little of yoga's ancient wisdom sharply into modern focus.

I am honored to serve as community leader for the Therapeutic Yoga, Yoga for Teens and Yoga for Christians groups within the Yoga Journal Community. This is a rich, rewarding place to share and grow.

My teachers have been Sharon Hickey, Amy Gordon, David Keil, and Christine Hoar.

BIKRAM YOGA
YOGA FOR HEALING, YOGA FOR ALL

DIANE DUCHARME

Life can change in an instant, especially when you don't see it coming. I stepped off the top of a six foot ladder into mid air and landed on my heel with a loud crack. The doctor said because of who I was – someone who took responsibility for her own health – and because of what I did for a living – teach yoga – the good news was that he would not mend the broken bone and fractured ankle with surgery. The bad news was that I couldn't put any weight on my right foot for three months. Already practiced in the art of balancing on one leg, my yoga history made standing on one leg in the shower, doing the dishes, and of course, continuing my yoga, possible. It was my yoga practice – doing it and teaching it – that kept me sane during those three months.

Yoga is a tool to keep yourself centered and focused. It's a way to love your body and make peace in your mind. Yoga is many things to many people. For one person, it is the medicine for grief, a broken heart, a broken foot, or depression. For others it's the only way they can continue to enjoy sports or running.

I began sharing Bikram yoga with everyone I knew when I discovered it at the age of twenty-seven. After my very first class, I knew in the depths of my being that I would do this yoga for the rest of my life, and that I would teach it to others. Bikram Choudhury, the founder of this amazing routine of hatha yoga postures, certified me to teach his Beginning Yoga Series in March 1995. I opened the first Massachusetts Bikram Yoga Studio in October 1995.

Bikram promises a better quality of life if you do the yoga as prescribed – 26 postures and 2 breathing exercises in a precise order in a hot room. Since beginning my Bikram yoga practice 23 years ago, I have witnessed countless miracles. I call it "The Healing Yoga."

There is something unique about this series of yoga postures where one person who has practiced for more than two decades and one person who is a first time yoga practitioner are both getting extraordinary results from the practice at the same time in the same class. At this critical time in our economy, people are investing more in themselves – in their "human capital" – and Bikram yoga is giving them the biggest return on their investment. These yoga postures, used in India as prescriptions for health and healing, are unlike our Western pharmaceutical prescriptions, in that yoga has no bad side effects.

Several years ago I received this testimonial from Karen (not her real name).

"I began yoga as a means of helping me cope with the death of my son Ryan. He was born prematurely, and I was never able to take him home from the hospital. Because of the pain and anxiety this caused me, I was having difficulty becoming pregnant again. Each month my heart sank lower and lower. Yoga healed my body and soul. First it calmed me down and let me sleep well at night. The classes left me energized, yet calm, gave me a sense of well-being, and made me physically and mentally stronger. After 3 months of practicing Bikram yoga regularly, I became pregnant. Although my pregnancy was considered high risk, my doctors allowed me to continue yoga. I practiced yoga right up until my delivery date, and I had an easy delivery and a perfect baby girl. Afterwards, getting back in shape was very easy because by practicing yoga until delivery, I never got out of shape. I hope to be doing yoga into my 80's with my daughter by my side."

Angela, a young woman, who suffered severe trauma to her lower leg in a bus accident in South America, used my studio and Bikram Yoga as rehab, working her mind and her body until she could walk again.

"Bikram yoga cured my imbalanced posture, relaxed my tense back, and gave me once again a healthy leg. Even though the doctor predicted it would be a year before I could run or hike again, I went for a run 6 months after the injury and climbed Mt. Washington in the seventh month. Bikram yoga has calmed my nerves, improved my sleep, and sharpened my focus. I am eternally grateful to all of the teachers at Yoga for You for giving me back my pre-accident level of functioning."

Christine, a long time student, sent me this email.

"Recently, I had laparoscopic surgery. Recovery time was estimated to be three days. When I awoke from the surgery however, my left arm didn't work from the shoulder down due to a "positional neuropathy." As a result of this injury, all the muscles on my left side were tired and tight. I couldn't sleep more than 3 hours at a time and in the words of my physical therapist, 'walked with the posture of pain.' Afraid to move for fear that I would hurt myself more, I continued like this for more than three weeks. As a previous student at Yoga for You for about six years, I knew the benefits of yoga and decided to return to class. Three breaths into the first breathing exercise, I was ready to throw in the towel. I couldn't lift my arm and felt ridiculous. Years of yoga had worked their magic, however, and that little voice in my head said, 'Just do what you can do.' I stayed for the whole class and left feeling so rejuvenated that the next day I went back for more and continued to attend classes for most of the month. It's been four weeks since that first class back and I am pain-free and have most of the motion back in my arm."

People who practice over a long period of time, even if they stay away for awhile, remember the value of yoga as a tool for healing whatever ails them. They return to it when physical, mental, emotional and spiritual needs arise. One of my favorite questions to ask is "What benefits are you getting from the yoga?" I hear from students about increased bone density, their ability to quit smoking without gaining weight, their ability to loose or gain weight when medically necessary. They tell me they have normal menses again, reduced symptoms of PMS, fewer mood swings, and that they have been able to get pregnant or stay pregnant. They have healed torn rotator cuffs and frozen shoulders. They have improved the functioning of their damaged knees, elbows, ankles, wrists, spines, and necks.

Students may come in for one reason and then discover that yoga has given them so much more. In 2002, Bill (not his real name) wrote,

"I have a hereditary disease called hemochromatosis – a known genetic defect that causes excess iron in my blood. Over time, excess iron is deposited in the liver and other major organs, which slowly destroys them. The only treatment for the disease is to donate blood which initially causes anemia and eventually a reduction of iron in the blood. This common genetic disease afflicts one out of every 100 people in the U.S. Although easily detectable via a blood test, most people don't know they have it until it's too late. Since I started taking Bikram yoga classes four months ago, the level of iron in my blood has dropped dramatically. Although it was slowly coming down over the past 5 years through normal treatment, the level dropped much faster since starting yoga. My doctor, who is a hematologist, was amazed at how quickly my iron level dropped to normal without giving blood. I no longer need to give blood and my doctor believes I will not have to do so again if my iron levels remain where they are now."

Judith holds a special place in my heart because she is such a beautiful spirit and she really needed to love herself more and embrace all life had to offer. She was in her mid 50's when she started yoga and had suffered with bulimia for decades. She wrote to me after practicing Bikram yoga for 14 months.

"The healing that has occurred in this length of time has been truly amazing. Bikram yoga continues to be on my pathway and a road to a new freedom. It has enhanced the quality of my life on all levels. I had the following ailments when I entered my first class – depression, bulimia, fatigue, food cravings, Reynard's Phenomenon (reduced circulation in the small arteries to the

hands and feet), and constipation. I have sought help for many years from all kinds of professionals, both traditional and non-traditional. I could barely walk when I entered my first class as I had ulcerated wounds on my feet. I remember the excitement after my first class because I was sweating for the first time, my depression lifted, and I felt high. I have experienced a gradual and miraculous healing. The Reynard's has completely disappeared in my feet. My hands are a lot better. My depression, which has been a problem for most of my life, disappeared. I have had no bulimia symptoms or binge eating for 7 months. It became difficult to continue to practice yoga when I was hurting myself with food. I finally choose to take care of myself and do yoga instead of hurting myself. Thanks to the loving environment where there is no judgment and there is a total acceptance, I was able to show up for my practice no matter where I was or how I was feeling. I always left class feeling lifted, and I learned to love myself even with my imperfections. I was brought to a place where I had a deeper understanding of my food sensitivities and with that new understanding I have found true peace and freedom around my body and food. I have more energy now than I ever had before."

One of the basic principles of Bikram yoga is "try the right way" and even if you can do only one percent of the posture, you will get one hundred percent of the benefit. I think the following testimonial from a middle-aged student highlights that teaching.

"I started going to yoga because I have not felt well for some time. I have gained weight, I feel quite stiff, and I am on thyroid medication for an under-active thyroid. I have been on antidepressants. From time to time, I have pain in my neck that my physician diagnosed as a pinched nerve. I try to go at least twice a week, and never less than once a week. Since starting, I feel refreshed, renewed, and better able to concentrate; I have a more positive outlook. I can't explain why something that is so difficult to do, in a very hot room, can become addictive in a way. I can't explain why a class where the postures never vary can present more challenges as time goes on. The pinched nerve sensations have not returned since I started. I am experimenting with reducing the thyroid medication, and I hope to get off it completely. I have been off antidepressants for months now, and I feel better *in general. These classes have strengthened my will and determination. I am also surprised that a practice that is focused on the physical, so down to earth, with no spiritual teachings, can have so many intangible benefits. The teachers are always supportive. I really like the non-competitive atmosphere. I can't do many of the things fully, but I don't care. I keep coming back."*

Susan is a long time practitioner and sent me this testimonial recently.

"I started practicing Bikram yoga in June, 2000, after years of struggling with lower back pain. The back pain, as it turned out, was more stress related than physical. As I became more familiar with the 90 minute routine and as I chose to practice regularly, the back pain all but disappeared. My practice was interrupted in March, 2007 when I slipped on a patch of ice and totally tore all four tendons off my right rotator cuff. The surgeon was a bit skeptical about my recovery, as the tendons were shredded and I was 59 years old – somewhat of a bleak prognosis. Being determined to fully recover, I followed doctor's orders to a T, loyally did physical therapy and 6 months after the surgery began to do the yoga again with Diane, a true hero to me. October of 2008, the surgeon gave me a clean bill of health. I have 100% range of motion and almost full strength in my shoulder – something no one can believe, given the extent of the injury. I attribute my almost miraculous recovery to Bikram yoga and the teachers who guided me through the practice as I healed and regained strength and flexibility. Bikram yoga is both physically and mindfully challenging. The practice requires 100% effort. Listening carefully to the dialogue and staying present in the space is not for everyone. Yet, for me, it's a time to use the mind/body connection to its fullest. I am one of the older people in the classes that I take and the benefits extend far beyond the 90 minute sessions. This yoga is a positive addiction. Now, I plan my days around my practices."

I have watched as cross sections of America, as well as students from around the world, pass through my studio doors and gain balance, confidence, and healing. Firemen, police officers, lawyers, professors, school teachers, physical therapists, nurses and doctors, amputees, war veterans, professional athletes, stay-at-home moms, stay-at-home dads, contractors, the self-employed, the unemployed, musicians, singers, and dancers, young and old—all with varying degrees of flexibility and strength – have stories to tell. I never turn students away even if they cannot afford it. They all get benefits from yoga.

There is something, too, about the group energy; the group dynamic itself creates a healthy culture for men, woman, and even families. They bond with each other, knowing everyone in the room supports their passion for this yoga and understands what it's like to arrange your life in order to get to a yoga class (like Susan). And they keep coming back day after day, week after week, month after month, and year after year. Each of us is committed to a lifetime of practice, working with the body we woke up with today, accepting it, and moving forward from there.

We can take a Bikram yoga class and do the same 26 postures and 2 breathing exercises as prescribed in the series in hundreds of studios across this country and throughout the world. The community of yoga practitioners is always growing. It's a family of people who share a passion for using Bikram yoga as a tool for self-examination. We don't even have to know the language to do the Bikram yoga beginning series because it is always the same. The group dynamic creates an international community that helps us to enjoy our bodies, connect with our minds, and communicate with our spirits.

In spite of the power of the group and the accessibility of so many Bikram yoga studios today, students need to own their own practice and internalize it. Yoga in America is portable. You can learn the Bikram series, take it with you, and practice it wherever you are. A consistent yoga practice has the power to shape people's lives and make our planet a safer, more peaceful place. It helps create more peace and comfort within ourselves by healing whatever ails us. When we are more comfortable in our own bodies and more centered and calm in our minds, we can reach out and connect to each other more openly.

Each time someone finds this yoga and discovers it as a tool for healing, Bikram gets closer to his goal of everyone doing yoga. Bikram has dedicated his life to yoga, and his vision of spreading studios throughout the world includes getting yoga into the Olympics – "to increase yoga's popularity. We can make this world heaven if every child does yoga." Adults who practice yoga always say, "I wish I found this when I was a kid." They are making sure their children know and use this tool we call yoga. Children are discovering it all over the world – in schools, in play gyms, in community centers, and in neighborhoods. And I've seen it start in my yoga studio in West Roxbury with mothers and sons, fathers and daughters practicing together.

Diane Ducharme

Certified March 1995 by Bikram Choudhury to teach the Bikram Beginning Yoga Series.

Practicing Bikram yoga since 1985, sharing it with everyone I know. My passion for this yoga grows more and more as time goes on. I assist in the training of new teachers, and the mentoring process is the most rewarding part of what I do. I have a (nearly) daily, life-time practice.

I manage Yoga for You in West Roxbury, a Bikram yoga studio, where I teach and mentor. I am authorized by Bikram to conduct seminars and workshops worldwide.

"In my yoga studio – as in life – just breathe, everything else is optional"
Diane Ducharme

I AM NEVER DOING YOGA AGAIN!

DANIELLE HOPE HIER

I am only half-joking when I tell people that I am the world's most unlikely of yoga teachers. Born with scoliosis, a reversed C-curve in my neck, and a host of related flexibility challenges, bronchial complications and ear infections because of it, I was not the healthiest of children. I'd have asthma-like attacks when I exercised, so I simply avoided it, and like most kids, sugary sweets and cheeseburgers were always preferable to whole grains and vegetables. Couple that with an aversion to religion (after a strict upbringing), and I was sworn off all things spiritual. I remember feeling like an ugly duckling in the one yoga class I tried in New York, at a friend's suggestion. They were swans, and I was ugly. I left there with a bruised ego and proclaimed to the Universe, "I am *never* doing yoga again!"

I have been a teacher of yoga for more than eight years now.

You see, the funny thing about yoga is, you do not select it, and it does not choose you. Instead, it offers a gentle invitation to explore, but holds no blame if you politely decline. "If not this lifetime," it says, "Perhaps the next one."

I am fortunate that it extended its invitation more than once.

A person's relationship with yoga is a collaborative effort. It will give back what you put into it...and then some. There is no question that yoga form in America differs greatly from yoga in India, China or elsewhere, because the mindset we bring to our practice is unique. As a whole, we as Americans are more inclined to explore the "package" that is yoga and adapt it to our needs (vs. conforming to tradition), because we have grown up in a culture that encourages new ideas and new approaches. Therefore, collectively, we are free to question, to experience and to change.

Admittedly, in my own relationship with yoga, I did not begin with all the pieces fitting together in a perfect puzzle with my hatha practice here, my meditation over there, and my purification processes neatly tucked somewhere in the middle. No, I began with what I understood yoga to be at that time…physical exercise for strength and flexibility, and breathing for health and relaxation.

Over time, my body felt healthier, and I wanted to stay that way.

My emotions became more balanced, and I wanted to stay that way too.

With my newfound health, came body awareness, to the point where – without even trying – foods naturally became distinctly good or bad. "Live" foods like fresh spinach, sprouts and vegetables gave me energy, and made me happier. Too many "dead" foods like fermented cheeses, wines and meats made me sluggish and periodically sad.

This process continued into my relationships with people, where I could begin to empathically feel who was a negative energy drain and who sustained or enhanced my well-being, and thus began the process of distinguishing those who were on the same path as me, and those who were not.

For my spiritual development, I credit my very first martial arts teacher, who I began studying with just two days prior to my 21st birthday. He would write meaningful quotes from the Tao Te Ching and teach me – the one unable to keep body or mind still for more than 30 seconds – Tai Chi Yang Short Form, which became my moving meditation before Bagua Zhang, Vinyasa , Restorative yoga, and eventually long periods of stillness.

I learned how to meditate and still my body and mind.

Whatever the world may believe or disbelieve about America, there is one thing I can tell you for certain. By virtue of having been born here, I was given the unique opportunity to explore every spiritual, metaphysical, and religious practice I chose, and my previous aversion to all things spiritual, turned into an indescribable desire for truth. While there may have been people telling me I *shouldn't*, never did any authority tell me I *couldn't*.

Presently, I understand the overlap of the classical philosophy of Patanjali, outlined in the Yoga Sutras as it relates to other belief systems, just as I am able to integrate knowledge from an Ayurvedic diet with a Superfood approach to eating. I see how the movement of chi in Bagua relates to the Serpent Spine energy of Kundalini.

I learned how to yoke many ideas into one unified whole. This became my truth.

But do not mistake my seemingly "hodge-podge" fascination with learning different physical, dietary and spiritual practices with a lack of direction. It is through exploration that I found my personal path and soul's purpose. Though, to avoid fluttering in the wind, I often recommend that new students try a variety of different classes, find the one that they feel most drawn too, and develop a root (or foundation) in that system, before building upon it.

At no time during my process, did I set out to become a yogi. I set out for *answers*. Everything that followed happened naturally.

So, I've told you about my personal process, including physical practice, diet, mindfulness, and spirituality; but still I have not answered the daunting question, "What is Yoga?"

Yes, I know it is the Sanskrit word "to yoke" and that "hatha" translates as sun and moon; but not what the literal word "means", but what it "is".

Very simply, Yoga is your Path. In Taoism it is the Way.

Your path will be different from mine, as each Soul's journey differs with each lifetime. This is why yoga cannot be packaged, contained or easily defined, because its meaning changes with each storyteller and practitioner.

What is Yoga in America? Well, it is the most liberating brand of yoga there is (and isn't yoga about liberation?), because if yoga is the *path,* America is the land of opportunity to *find* that path. It is the freedom of self-expression, evolution and the discovery of personal Truth.

Danielle Hope Hier

www.birdlandyoga.com

A graduate of *New York University* with a BS in *Mass Media and Global Communications* (with emphasis *on theater & voice)*, certified initially through the *International Sports Medicine Association (ISMA/AAAI)*, and a member of the *International Association of Yoga Therapists* (IAYT), Danielle has been studying yoga, the martial arts, and alternative healing for over fifteen years.

In this time, she's had the opportunity to work with extraordinary teachers of Taoist, Kundalini, Integral, Iyengar, Kripalu, Hatha, Isha, Trikona, and Ashtanga Yoga, and has been a teacher of Vinyasa, Hatha, Restorative and Therapeutic Yoga for over eight years.

Currently, Danielle is a full time writer and web content developer (whose affiliations include Metromix/Tampa Bay 10, Positive Change Magazine, National Examiner Online & The Garden Now), and is author of the upcoming *Acting Out Yoga* series for both instructors and children. In addition to conducting hybrid writing and yoga workshops designed to release emotions, while promoting joy and self-confidence through creative expression, she is also pursuing her Masters Degree in *Professional and Technical Writing*, as well as her lifelong study of Yoga.

YOGA: INDIA AND AMERICA

NINA MOLIVER

I am a yoga teacher and a mental health counselor. I am also a doctoral student in psychology. For my dissertation, I am investigating the long-term benefits of a yoga practice.

As I do my research, I am struck by the differences between the way yoga is understood in India and how it is understood here in America. In India, the term *yoga* is as likely to refer to meditation, pranayama, and devotional chanting as to postures. What we would call a meditation center in the United States is called a yoga center in India. A yoga session in India may include posture practice, or it may not. Postures are one part of the yoga experience, on a par with breathing, meditation, hymns, and selfless service.

Hindu gods and Sanskrit prayers, celibate meditators and devotional chants: For many people who grew up in India, these things came along with mother's milk. Yoga is one of a person's own personal roots, even if the person has never done a posture.

But we Americans do not share the same set of cultural assumptions and practices that people from India do. For Americans, yoga has long been part of an alternative lifestyle, hovering at the margins of mainstream healthcare practices and mainstream religion. When we embrace the symbols of yoga, we are not enmeshing ourselves in the ways of our ancestors. On the contrary, we are usually veering away into the other direction, into the strange and the unknown.

As yoga puts down roots here, it is adapting to its new home. It is changing to fit the needs of American culture. For one thing, Americans are highly sedentary. We sit on chairs, rarely on floors. We eat a lot of meat, junk food, processed food, and high-glycemic food. At the end of a workday, our joints feel creaky and we are desperate to discharge toxins and revitalize our stiffened bodies. We want to move; we want the gifts of Hatha yoga, of asana.

Many of us enjoy a few minutes of weekly chanting at our yoga classes, or perhaps a beginning and ending *OM*. But for most American yogis and yoginis, it's the postures that make the yoga class. Busy mothers with frantic schedules will carve out an hour of yoga per week for their sanity, but without posture work, they might not make that commitment.

What are the most popular forms of yoga in America today? Iyengar, which emphasizes postural precision, and its offshoots, such as Anusara; heated, power, and flow yoga; Ashtanga and Bikram yoga. Yoga in fitness clubs. Yoga done to rap music and R & B. Yoga to move the body and to work out.

Some yoga teachers are uneasy about the change from the way yoga is done in India, with its heavy doses of chanting, *pranayama*, and devotional hymns. I am not. Yoga in America is becoming what it needs to be in its new home. Americans are not dragging yoga down; on the contrary, yoga is bringing our exercise practices up. Yoga is teaching us that exercise is not always about pumping the body; that we need to become mindful and tend to the breath when we move; that we need to find the stillness in the middle of our hard work. That we need to turn our exercises into a form of prayer.

For Americans, yoga is not a step backward from a wealth of devotional, meditational, and breathing practices. We cannot step backward from those ways of doing things, because we never had them to begin with. For us, yoga is a step forward, a step away from the mindless, pounding intensity of mainstream aerobic exercise, the kind that shortens the breath, tightens the spine, builds a competitive ego, and "treats the body like a racehorse," as yoga master B. K. S. Iyengar has put it.

The American yogi or yogini has a different starting point: an American starting point. S/he is learning to work the body, to exercise and move, in a different way: with mindfulness, with an open breath, with patience, self-love, and nonviolence.

Nina Moliver

Nina Moliver, MA, M.Sc.(A), RYT, is a certified yoga teacher and a mental health clinician. Her yoga teaching style is safe, supportive, and joyful. Nina uses her profound understanding of the body to help her students align themselves comfortably, prevent and heal from injury, and deepen their self-discovery. Her classes are slow-paced and heart-centered.

Since taking her first yoga classes in 1968, Nina has studied in the Integral, Kripalu, Svaroopa, Bikram, Iyengar and Anusara traditions. Nina was certified in Iyengar-style Hatha Yoga in early 2004 under the guidance of Eileen Muir. After that, she continued to study with some of the world's greatest yoga masters. Her travels have led her to Anusara Yoga, which is currently the major influence in her teaching. She is also certified to teach yoga to elders.

Nina offers private yoga therapy sessions, psychotherapy, life coaching, and whole-foods counseling. She also tutors statistics and coaches doctoral students in writing their dissertations. Her own doctoral dissertation focuses on the long-term benefits of a yoga practice.

Nina, an alumna and learner at Northcentral University, can be reached at yoganina@alum.barnard.edu.

THE MELTING POT OF AMERICAN YOGA

HANNAH SCHOEN CARATTI

Mr. Iyengar sat on the back of a student who was in the sitting forward bend, paschimottanasana. That wasn't what enthralled me about yoga, though it was a powerful approach. What drew me were the weekly three-hour yoga classes with Iyengar's student, Barbara Linderman, at the University of Michigan in Ann Arbor.

The classes were filled with a sense of community, communion, yoga poses (asanas), breathing exercises, long relaxation sessions (shavasana), chanting, meditation, and sacred readings. Our first assignment was *Patanjali's Yoga Sutras*.

That was 1974. Linderman encouraged us to continue our daily one-hour asana practice sessions and engage in regular meditation. She enticed us to attend weekend retreats where the immersion in that yogic lifestyle of chanting, meditation, sacred talks and asana practice did indeed enthrall me. The chanting especially ignited a fire of joy within me that continues to glow.

YOGA

The word yoga means "to join, to unite." It is a joining and aligning of body, mind and soul. There are many ways to do this, by following the four paths of yoga: the path of Bhakti, or Devotion; the path of Jnana, or Knowledge; the path of Karma, or Dedicated Action; and Raja Yoga, the path of Discipline, which includes Meditation

(Dhyana), Yoga Postures (Asana), Breathing Exercises (Pranayama), and more.

The practice of Yoga is one of the greatest joys and passions of my life, and I have been blessed to share it with thousands of yoga students on the East Coast, West Coast and in Hawaii since I began teaching yoga professionally in 1976. More recently, I have enjoyed offering devotional music for retreats and workshops led by my mentor and friend, Richard Miller, Ph.D.

YOGA IN AMERICA

Yoga in America has changed significantly during the past three decades. I learned Iyengar Yoga from Iyengar's students Barbara Linderman and Karin Stephan, and from Mr. Iyengar himself on occasion. In those days, there were no certification programs. We simply dedicated ourselves to the daily practice of yoga, with a 3-hour group class once per week, for two years without a break. Then our teacher encouraged a few of us to start teaching.

I subsequently trained with Sita Frenkel, Lilias Folan's teacher, in Sivananda Yoga for one year as an apprentice at her yoga studio. Thus far, each teacher I had worked with incorporated postures, breathing exercises, relaxation, meditation, and chanting in their yoga practice.

I finally trained in the healing, flowing style of Synergy Yoga as taught by Charmaine Lee, based on Randolph Stone's Polarity Therapy. This did not incorporate meditation or chanting, but was based on a healing modality that promotes physical and emotional health and well-being.

Yoga in America reflects the melting pot that America is. Many American yogis have trained with Indian yogis, or the students of Indian yogis (or the students of the students...), and they have taken the treasures of the ancient teachings and presented them in their own way. Thus instead of the five primary 'schools of yoga' that I recall from years ago, now we have possibly fifteen or twenty primary "schools of yoga," each one with a different focus, perspective, approach, and gift. I used to teach workshops describing the different 'styles' of yoga. I've given that up since there are more new styles now than I could ever keep up with!

One other big change in the field of yoga in America is related to certification and registration. Yoga has become more professional, with the registration of certified yoga instructors with Yoga Alliance and other similar organizations, and clear guidelines for the skills, knowledge and background needed in order to teach yoga.

WHAT IS YOGA?

Here's a glimpse of the four paths of yoga, just to share a deeper understanding of what yoga is, from the perspectives I have learned as a student and teacher of Iyengar, Sivananda, and Synergy Yoga over the years. I have also studied Vedanta Philosophy as described by Swami Vivekananda, and Mindfulness Meditation, as taught by Thich Nhat Hanh, Sylvia Boorstein, and Jack Kornfield. These approaches are an integral part of the yoga classes that I teach at health clubs, spas and community centers. It is the energy, the chi, the 'prana,' the 'life-force' that we share as yoga teachers that is the primary element, and that comes from our own depths, the essence of the ancient teachings that we have gleaned from all we have learned.

BHAKTI YOGA, THE YOGA OF DEVOTION

This is the path of Love, the path of the heart, in which the yogi, or 'devotee,' calls upon Spirit by chanting the holy names, offering flowers, food and gifts to the Eternal, reading sacred songs, and conversing with friends about their eternal Beloved...or Friend, Child, Mother or Father. Spirit is considered to be near and dear to the devotee, who speaks to the Eternal one with a chosen 'bhava' or devotional mood, and interacts constantly in communion with that Light and Love, the Indweller within all beings. To learn more about this path, you can read the Narada Bhakti Sutras, an ancient yogic text describing Bhakti Yoga, the path of Love. The idea is: if we are going to love, then love the highest, the Spirit that dwells within all hearts.

We are so fortunate to live in this time when Krishna Das, Deva Premal, Jai Uttal and others have rocked the musical world and the yogic community with their devotional music. If you haven't heard their chants, you are in for such a treat! And if you have, then I'm guessing you know what I mean. Not since Mirabai during the 1500s in India, and Chaitanya long before her, have so many people been swept away in the ocean of devotion that is 'sacred chant.' Robert Gass has explained it well in his book, *Chanting: Discovering Spirit in Sound*.

JNANA (GEE-ANA) YOGA, THE YOGA OF WISDOM, AND TRUTH THAT SETS US FREE

This is the path of the intellect. Yogis who are drawn to this path use their mind, their awareness, to cut through the many aspects of the self to arrive at the radiant inner Self that is the peaceful witness of all that happens to the body, mind, ego and emotions. From this perspective, the real Self that you are is more than your body, your thoughts and your emotions; it is united with the infinite ocean of Spirit and non-separate from Spirit. It cannot be hurt, killed, or destroyed in any way whatsoever. This inner Self is powerful, peaceful, and imperturbable. It is free from the struggles, ups and downs that constantly occur at the level of body, mind and emotions. This path is beautifully described in the *Bhagavad Gita* and in all of the *Upanishads*, the ancient Indian texts focusing on Jnana Yoga, the Yoga of Wisdom.

KARMA YOGA, THE YOGA OF DEDICATED ACTION

"Whatever I do with my body, speech, mind and senses; by my intellect, self or nature; all this I offer unto Thee…" "Kayena Vacha Manasindriyairva…" This is the creed of the Karma Yogi. Every action and effort is dedicated to the Source, the results are offered to that universal energy, without being attached to the outcome of one's efforts. Yes, easier said than done! But karma yogis keep on dedicating their actions and efforts, and continue to let go of the results as a lifelong practice, so that hopefully, just like meditation and yoga postures (asanas), the process becomes easier over time. It is similar to the Buddhist notion of non-attachment to desires and results….the karma yogi continues to act, surrendering the outcome. Again, the *Bhagavad Gita* describes this approach very well. Swami Vivekananda also wrote beautifully on the topic of Karma Yoga and Raja Yoga…

RAJA YOGA, THE PATH OF DISCIPLINE

The word 'Raja' means King, as it is the 'Royal Road' to Nirvana or Samadhi, the ultimate goal of all yogis. This path, so wonderfully described by Patanjali in his *Yoga Sutras*, includes:

the Yamas (non-violence, truth, not coveting, purity of mind and body, non-possessiveness);

the Niyamas (cleanliness, contentment, discipline, study of scriptures, surrender to Spirit);

Postures or Asanas done consistently to keep the body well, preserving prana, the life force. These poses can help calm the whole body and the nervous system, preparing the mind for concentration and meditation.

Pranayama or Breathing Exercises are beneficial to overall health, calm the mind and the nervous system, preparing the yogi for concentration and meditation.

Pratyahara, withdrawing the senses from their external objects. We do this as a matter of course during many yoga classes, ideally becoming more indrawn during the session, to taste the nectar of the inner Self.

Dharana, concentrating awareness on an object such as a flame, the mid-point of the eyebrows, or the image of a deity.

Dhyana, steadfast meditation, the undisturbed flow of awareness toward the object of meditation. The meditator remains separate from the object of meditation.

Samadhi, oneness with the object of meditation. This is achieved by constant, uninterrupted meditation on the object of meditation, which is eternal, free, powerful, and blissful by nature.

WHAT IS YOGA IN AMERICA?

From the perspective of Swami Vivekananda, Sri Ramakrisha's foremost student, what the East needs is more of the West's business acumen, efficiency and technical capability, and what the West needs is more of the wisdom, spirituality, faith, freedom and bliss that are inherent parts of the ancient teachings of the yogis of the East.

This exchange between East and West that Vivekananda presaged in 1900 at the Parliament of World Religions in Chicago is happening now, and has been happening more and more during these past three decades.

Yes, incorporate yoga into the fiber of our American society! This will be to the benefit of our lives, physically, emotionally and spiritually. Yes, continue to make it available in every town, every neighborhood, in schools, health clubs, churches and hotels! It is beneficial and has been sorely needed since the industrial revolution stole away some of the spirituality that had been at the foundation of our American society in the days of our founding fathers....and mothers...

Yes, bring in the Goddess/matriarchal element, in the chants, the readings, the t-shirts, and let it balance out the patriarchal elements of our society, so that men and women become equally cared for, remunerated, and respected. And speaking of patriarchy, it truly is, of course, as sacred as matriarchy, even though the Goddess has been highlighted here in our yogic culture quite a bit recently. For how can a bird fly on one wing? And where there is nurturing, love, kindness, compassion, and flexibility, there is also a need for strength, clarity, boundaries and guidelines. Still the Goddess energy needs to be clear, strong and supported, because it is only now in this new millennium that the balancing of yin and yang (or Shiva and Shakti in yogic terms) is beginning to be achieved.

BACK TO BUSINESS...

In the American way, yoga has become big business. This is a good thing! Yoga has become more available, and the sharing of information and training has been greatly facilitated by regular professional conferences within the yoga community. I must admit, as a life-long mystic and one who loves silence and solitude, I have only attended a couple of yoga conferences and a handful of yoga retreats in recent years. As part of my training during my 20s, I did spend nine years at a meditation center in upstate New York with more than two hours of daily meditation and chanting, in addition to monthly weekend retreats and a 10-day summer retreat each year. We also traveled to India several times on pilgrimage during those years.

I have been so immersed in offering my own classes and workshops (and taking local classes) that I rarely venture out to the larger gatherings. Whenever I do attend workshops and conferences, I greatly enjoy them and am delighted to learn from wonderful and experienced yogis and yoginis; yet in the midst of the crowds and the marketplace, my soul hearkens back to those pilgrimages in India, as we chanted our way by bus, plane, and horseback to the shrines and temples from Rishikesh and Haridwar in the North, to Vivekananda Rock at the southern-most tip of India.

As the saying goes, though, great yogis can bring the stillness and peace of the meditation cave to any city or marketplace. The stillness and peace are always there, within us. Namaste.

Hannah Schoen Caratti

www.yogahealingarts.net

Hannah Schoen Caratti, MFTI, E-RYT teaches yoga in Sonoma County, California.

Her *Gentle Yoga* DVD, and CDs *Mother's Heart, Walk with the Angels, Peace Chants,* and *True Self* are available at the web site above. To download the CDs, you are welcome to visit www.cdbaby.com, and search for Hannah & Friends.

Hannah offers counseling for yogis in the private psychotherapy practice of her supervisor, Winnie Piccolo, MFT.

THE ANCIENT WISDOM OF KRIYA YOGA IS ALIVE AND WELL IN AMERICA

CAMELLA NAIR

"Teach them want they want to learn", were the parting words of my Paramguru as I graduated the Hatha teacher training program with the Temple of Kriya Yoga in Chicago. He added jokingly, "If they want big boobs, help them achieve that". Then he added, with a serious look on his face, "Then help to give them what they need".

The path of Kriya Yoga is for the householder. That means the average person on the street. It does not require you to become a bramacharya (abstain from sex) or to fast to great lengths or do anything in fact to the extreme. Learning how to live a life of balance and contentment is the path that Patanjali outlined in his pithy four books of Yoga Sutras.

I remember that when my mother first introduced me to yoga some 30 years ago, my father complained half jokingly that she was a "yogi bore". What he meant was that she was starting to preach to him how to live, and that is something that as yogis we should never do. The work that needs to be done is on our self, and if there is a barometer for spiritual improvement, it is that we should able to get along with other people better than before.

There is only one type of yoga that Patanjali mentions in his Yoga Sutras, which were short terse sayings about the science of yoga eventually written down about 200 yrs. B.C. That is Kriya Yoga. Kriya can be generally translated as "action". What is the right action? What needs to be done at this moment to yield a certain outcome. It is enmeshed with the doctrine of cause and effect that is widely known as karma. That which we think, say and do has an effect somewhere in the future.

There are three facets that make up this science called Kriya Yoga. The first element is Svadhyaya, or Self-Study. We need to be mature enough to be able to take a good long look in the mirror and see where we need to make some adjustments in our lives, balancing our ego personality in the process.

It does help to know some very basic terms in astrology and have a copy of your natal chart because the writing really is "on the wall", so to speak. The chart will tell us what type of personality we will tend to have, what is important to us, how we want people to treat us, and how we treat them. The most important factor is that it will indicate where the "red button" is for us, or the triggers that cause us to become emotional.

Why is this so valuable? Because if we know where we are likely to become emotional, we have some idea of where the personal sadhana (effort) needs to take place. As humans we have a lifetime of experiences that are pretty cyclical. That means that an event happens, say we get married to a rat fink. We get divorced and then proceed to move onto husband no. 2 and the pattern begins all over again. He's also a rat fink! Learning from the experience is crucial and so we need very broad shoulders if we are serious about the path to enlightenment.

Discernment is key, and for that we need to be able to understand the personality that we have wrapped around ourselves and recognize that we are not that personality at all. It is only a manifestation of the memory tracks of the past, or samskaras, that, as my guru explains, just want to keep asserting themselves.

Now, there are quite a few branches of the Kriya Yoga tradition that are alive and well today both in the East and the West. Parmahansa Yogananda, who wrote the mystical book "Autobiography of a Yogi" (which seems to inspire many people, but for the wrong reasons) came to America on the advice of his guru in the 1920's to share the ancient wisdom of the Kriya Tradition.

He had many devotees and a few disciples and there is a distinct difference between the two. The devotee is not necessarily expected to be diligent in study and practice, whereas the initiated disciple is expected to exercise great self-awareness at all times.

Contrary to some branches of Kriya Yoga that claim Yogananda is their guru, if you have not been initiated by a physically incarnated soul, your guru, you are not a disciple. The flame of the Kriya lineage is passed on in the oral tradition and is a direct transmission of consciousness that is passed on from one living being to another.

Part of the reason for this is that we need a physical body to be able to achieve enlightenment. It is for this that we took form. The guru initiates us and links our memory tracks and our physical body to his astral (spiritual) body. That way when he or she passes (or we do before him) the link is still there and the teachings go on in the spiritual realm.

When we incarnate the next time, we pick up the teachings again and continue on our spiritual path. Any effort on this spiritual path is not wasted, so even if we don't become enlightened in this lifetime, it will be part of our experiences, or samskaras, that will have sewn seeds for future experiences on the spiritual path.

I mentioned that there are many branches of the Kriya lineage alive today. They all have one thing in common and that is sharing techniques that have been passed on from Yogananda. If one does not want to become a disciple (initiated by a living flame in the tradition), then one can take Kriya initiation after some period of study and practice.

The school that I have been initiated into is probably the most mystical of all of the schools known in the West today. The student is encouraged to study some astrology and follow the path of wisdom rather than bhakti, or devotion. There is an emphasis on attunement to one's chosen form of the sacred.

The second element of Kriya Yoga is Tapas, or Self-Discipline. It is often referred to as heat. The process of "softening the hardened hearts of mankind", as my paramguru teaches, is an alchemical process that involves melting and remolding our habits in the same way that gold is purified by the heating process. This can be done through asana, pranayama, fasting, mantra, etc., and is specific to each individual. The guru or teacher will help the student find the correct approach here.

As a yoga teacher, my intense physical practice needs to be balanced out with times of resting the physical body, and I love to take short naps when I can. Getting up anywhere from 4-6 am in the morning to meditate and then teaching hatha and rushing around after two teenage boys is demanding and I need to make sure that I don't burn myself out.

I also practice mouna, or silence, which is terribly important since, as teachers, we speak so much. Most of my free time is spent studying or writing for my next book, which will be on the more mystical aspects of being pregnant and not just Prenatal Yoga. I love to chant and have produced two CD's to help the student focus while practicing hatha or meditation.

I spend as much time as possible on retreat with my guru (Swami Enoch Dasa Giri) and paramguru (Goswami Kriyananda, not Swami Kriyananda). Actually they are intense study courses rather than relaxing retreats. One takes from them what is important as an individual and then incorporates it into one's daily life.

The third element in Kriya Yoga is Ishva Pranidhana, or Attunement to One's Chosen Form. It is vital that we can step beyond our ego personality, and for that we need to have a "bridge", something that has a name and form, because it is so very difficult for most of us to conceptualize something that is beyond name and form.

God consciousness or Self Revelation is a long journey, and help in the form of a guru is critical. The guru will point out our shortcomings, if we are strong enough to take it, and this keeps us on track. Many souls leave the path simply because their ego cannot take it.

No matter. When the time is right, they will pick up the teachings again.

As a yoga teacher, I teach many different students on land, and in the water as well, as this is a wonderful medium to experience yoga in. We are, after all, made up of more that 70% water. I try and share the wisdom of the Kriya lineage with my students so they can take yoga off the mat and into their lives.

Once a month I host a sutra study group and also a women's spiritual support group. As a priest or swami, I occasionally get to perform a wedding or baby blessing, too, and these are very enjoyable to do.

Most of my inspiration has come from the branch of Kriya Yoga that stemmed from Shelly Trimmer, who was a direct disciple of Yogananda. From what I gather the two of them shared a common interest in magic and the more esoteric elements of yoga that are only practiced by a few advanced souls.

I have a great respect for all other traditions and try to learn from as many of them as possible. I was taught that I would meet many more fools than saints and so to "make everyone you meet your teacher".

Camella Nair

www.camellayoga.org

Camella Nair (Swami Nibhrtananda) -- Registered and Certified Yoga Instructor and Priest in the Kriya Yoga and Ayurvedic tradition.

Author of "Aqua Kriya Yoga".

Trainer of certification in Aqua Kriya Yoga as a continuing education module.

Runs several retreats through the year in Northern California.

"Aum Hatha Sadhana" CD for hatha practice available from Cdbaby.com.

THE PATH OF THE URBAN MYSTIC

DARREN MAIN

"Those who aspire to the state of yoga should seek the self in inner solitude."

— *The Bhagavad Gita, 6:10*

At 5:30 each morning, my stereo is programmed to wake me up. This morning I woke up to the soft sound of Krishna Das chanting his "Devi Puja." As the deep, rich sound of Krishna Das' voice coaxed me out of a dream I can't quite remember and into a waking state, I considered going back to sleep and skipping my morning practice altogether. Yet something deep within pulled me out of bed.

This morning was not much different from other mornings. I put on some water for tea, then lit a few candles and an aromatherapy lamp. My small bedroom was magically transformed into a sacred temple. It was chilly, so I turned on the heat and sipped on some hot herbal tea while I washed my face, brushed my teeth and slipped into the loose-fitting, white cotton clothes that I reserve for my spiritual practice. Finally, I rolled out my yoga mat and began.

I started my practice by bowing my head to the earth in surrender and chanting a devotional prayer, followed by the sound of "Om." I then entered into some yogic breathing techniques. My mind and body began to wake up. Before long I was in downward-dog pose. I have done this pose a few thousand times, yet still my body resisted it. Again I considered going back to bed, but instead chose to breathe more deeply.

After a few more yoga poses, my body and mind began to melt into the practice. My resistance faded, and I felt my whole being entering into an effortless rhythm, holding some poses and flowing through others – each pose bringing me deeper and deeper into the practice. I moved from downward-dog to upward-dog and then hopped through to assume triangle pose.

My breath was shallow at times, and when I realized this I allowed it to deepen, filling my entire body. I finished my asana (poses) practice by moving through a series of floor poses that included the camel, the cobra and the posterior stretch. After doing several rounds of the "breath of fire," I took a seat on my meditation cushion, wrapped myself in a white blanket, and closed my eyes. Now my breath was deep, but unregulated. I felt my mind resting on the breath, but often drifting into plans for my day. Each time I noticed myself playing this familiar game, I smiled and returned my mind to the gentle flow of my breath. I sat for what felt like both an eternity and a few short moments. I opened my eyes softly and concluded my morning practice with a brief reading from the *Upanishads* and then chanted the sound of "Om."

As I rose from my meditation cushion I could feel a quiet calm. I showered, dressed, and walked down to Courtney's, a small corner market that is famous in San Francisco. My goal was simple – to buy some fresh fruit and yogurt for breakfast. As I waited for the light to change, I took a few deep breaths. Children were showing up at the grade school across from my home. I felt as though nothing could shake my peace of mind. . . but in the moment that followed that thought, I stepped out into the street, only to hear the blare of a car horn. A woman in a tiny car ran the red light and nearly knocked me over. To add insult to injury, she gave me the finger.

I was flustered, but continued across the street to the market, only to find that they were out of yogurt. I begrudgingly settled for some granola and rice milk. On the way home I picked up the morning paper and began to read the headlines as I walked. I read that the economy was still showing signs of slowing, and that another teen had shot his classmates somewhere near San Diego.

By the time I got home again, less than one city block, I could feel stress consuming my body and mind. As I walked by my bedroom door I caught the scent of lavender from my aromatherapy lamp. I had to laugh! Not more than an hour earlier, I was sitting in peace, and here I was now, in the middle of a drama that my ego and the environment had conspired to create.

This, of course, is the difficulty in trying to live a deeply spiritual and centered life. It is why most people who really want to cultivate a life that is devoted to and guided by Spirit consider renouncing the world to find a quiet little cave or monastery. The world we have created is not one that encourages a spiritual life. Therefore, it is challenging to try to live as an *urban mystic*. Nothing short of a deeply held commitment will suffice. That is what this book is all about.

I use the term *urban mystic* because it describes a great many of us. A mystic is a person, from any spiritual tradition, who seeks an intimate relationship with Spirit. A mystic may or not be a religious person, but he or she is committed to turning his or her mind over to the guidance of Spirit. A mystic seeks a direct experience of the Divine, but mysticism is not to be confused with religion, for religions seek to explain what cannot be explained, and a mystic seeks to know through experience.

In the past, people who wanted to practice mysticism would go off to a hermitage or join a religious order. Some were revered, others seen as fools. In either case they did not fit into the worldly life. They saw things through very different eyes, and as a result they did not have a home in the urban world.

This is all starting to change. People from all walks of life are developing a deeper connection to Spirit and living in the world at the same time. They are meditating on their lunch breaks and practicing Tai Chi before the kids get up. These *urban mystics* are filling yoga classes and studying Kabala. There is a movement underway, and it is much more than a flaky New Age fad. People are looking for something more than a good job, a sexy spouse and some over-inflated stock options.

Sitting next to my computer is a statue of the Buddha. He has a shaved head and is wrapped in a saffron robe. His legs wind gently into a lotus pose and his eyes are softly closed in meditation. In one hand he holds a cellular phone and in the other a cup of coffee.

I keep this little statue by my computer because it reminds me so much of the spiritual path I am on. Like many others, I am called, or so it would seem, to walk between two worlds. I am torn between living a deeply contemplative life and being a full-fledged member of my secular community.

There are a growing number of people in our western culture and around the globe who are torn between two worlds. On the one hand we strive to grow spiritually and to seek the deeper meaning of life. We yearn to know the secrets of Spirit, and we know what needs to be done to make the earth a peaceful place. On the other hand, we feel a need to live in communities and contribute to society.

The problem is not in our commitment, for that is very strong. The problem is that we are torn. Many spiritual techniques, yoga included, were developed by and for people who had renounced the world. Rather than form families, build homes and live in the community, the mystics responsible for such techniques as yoga and Kabala left the material world and went to live as monks or nuns.

There are great spiritual lessons to be learned from living in a cloistered setting and stepping outside the basic chores of day-to-day life. Yet there are an equal number, and some would argue more, spiritual benefits and lessons to be gleaned from a secular life. As we begin to walk with one foot on the path of the renunciant and the other on the path of the householder, difficulties arise, and there are not, as yet, mechanisms in place to guide us along. Humanity is evolving into a new level of spiritual awareness, and we are blazing new trails even as I write these words.

Darren Main

www.darrenmain.com

This essay is an excerpt from Darren's book, "Yoga and the Path of the Urban Mystic".

Darren Main is a yoga and meditation instructor and author. His other books include 'Spiritual Journeys along the Yellow Brick Road", "The Findhorn Book of Meditation", and "Hearts and Minds: Talking to Christians about Homosexuality".

In addition to his writing, he facilitates workshops and gives talks on yoga and modern spirituality throughout the United States and abroad and is the director of the Yoga Tree Teacher Training Program. He currently lives in San Francisco.

ALPHABET YOGA

GINGER GARNER

Trying to answer this question of "what is yoga in America" could (and should possibly) yield as many answers as there are yoga practitioners in the United States. Quite often, when we seek a single answer to a question, we should consider there are many answers, all of which can be valid and meaningful, and that there is no one single answer to this question. Perhaps all answers to this question, when answered with a pure heart, can contain Truth.

Yoga is **A**cceptance – It is not what, who, or whom we exclude, in the words of the screenplay from the movie, *Chocolat*, but instead – what, who, or whom we include in our lives. Too much of the world is plagued with violence because one group excludes another group, for whatever reason. We should strive for inclusion, to wrap our arms around others, with compassion and love.

Yoga is **B**alance – If we are honest with ourselves, we know we are not perfect. If we are honest with ourselves, we know we can be better. Being better, however, does not always mean doing more. Sometimes being better means doing less. Time in earnest, spent on the mat in meditation, whether in seated or in the midst of asana, can reveal to you the equation of balance for which we all strive and yearn, If – we listen.

Yoga is **C**hange – Only when we consent to change, will we begin the transformation toward personal evolution. All the facets of the body, mind, and spirit – physical, energetic, mental and emotional, intellectual, and spiritual hold fast to one Truth – gaining true wisdom requires surrender. We cannot become a creature improved, renewed and a better version of our old Self, without first letting go of the old Self – old habits, activities and people that do not nurture the body, mind, and spirit.

Yoga is **D**iversity - To each individual yoga is different, just like America began and still is a beautiful melting pot of cultures from all over the world. Yoga is a proverbial melting pot in America today. There are many different disciplines of yoga, and each passing season brings new lineages in yoga. I may perhaps be the youngest and most recent yogi to have created a new lineage of medical yoga therapy, for example, in PYT™. Yoga is beautiful in all its forms, just like there is beauty in all creatures.

Yoga is **E**ducation – We should all seek to be lifelong learners. The education and enlightenment process never ends in yoga, as in life. We should continue to learn until we take our last breath.

Yoga is **F**reedom – Liberation for the mind, body, and soul. I came to yoga for liberation of the body and mind. Through its practices combined with my own spiritual belief system, I found living liberation for the soul through the vibrant dance of yoga.

Yoga is **G**ratitude – Each day and each moment spent on the mat, through injury, hurt, pain, pregnancy, post-partum, post surgical, and on even those ordinary days where no trauma clouds the day – I am grateful for my body and how I can watch it change and grow through the years, evolving with my mind and spirit in contentment.

Yoga is **H**umility – Ahhh – the great lesson that both God and yoga brings – to not think of oneself too highly that ego and pride cause one to stumble. Scriptures in many spiritual disciplines teach that pride comes before the fall. Humility though, is not just about a lack of pride or dampening our ever present ego, but humility is about appreciation for other creatures. Humility allows us to hear others, to appreciate their contributions, and to realize that we would all fare better to speak less and listen more.

Yoga is Integration – When the body, mind, and spirit are disconnected – through trauma or complacency – we suffer. Whether we experience trauma or apathy in a social, psychological, emotional, spiritual, physical, or energetic sense – when one part of the "body" does not communicate with another – pain ensues in some form – not always physical. Yoga teaches us to integrate and "re"integrate all of these sheaths of the body – so that we have complete health – physically, energetically, psycho-emotionally, socially, intellectually, and spiritually.

Yoga is Joy – Pure joy. Joy is a function of immense acceptance. We all want to feel accepted and loved. When we do, there is true joy. Yoga teaches us to love others and to follow our own spiritual roots to discover what the ancient scriptures say about love, unconditional and eternal.

Yoga is Kindness – Practicing "ahimsa", or non-violence, is paramount in the 8-limbed practice of yoga. The opposite of violence could be described as kindness or compassion. Yoga teaches us to seek the face of the Divine in every living creature, so that we treat everyone like the fragile being that we are. Fragile and delicate is humanity – fragile and delicate are we, and every living creature on this planet. We should proceed to interact with each other based on this Truth of creation.

Yoga is Love – There is no greater emotion written about or sought after in all of time and history. Everyone seeks to love and be loved. Why then, should so much suffering exist in the world? We should seek to take the pain of others as our own, others tears as our own – to share in each other's sufferings so that we may ease one another's burdens and sorrow. Sometimes it takes experiencing pain first hand before we can begin to understand others' pain and have empathy for them. However, yoga teaches us the way to love through selflessness.

Through ahimsa, or non-violence, through the yoga of action, or karma yoga – working without seeking the fruits of work. A wise person once said that a man's true character can be known by how he treats someone who can do nothing for him. Yoga teaches selfless action and devotion to Higher purpose….all in pursuit of perfect Love and Truth.

Yoga is a **Marriage** – For me, modern yoga is not just the yoga of the ancient. Yoga has been present in the United States for decades now. As each art, like music, should grow and change, breaking down barriers, breaking oppressive rules and coloring outside the lines - so should yoga. If yoga stands still and does not evolve with new discoveries, it will not grow. If a thing does not grow, it dies. If yoga will grow, it can become more relevant, safer, progressive, and effective for everyone, regardless of their cause of suffering.

Yoga is **N**on-dogmatic – In my personal and professional practice, the PYT™ method is non-dogmatic – yoga should not lead one away from their own spiritual roots but it should deepen their own spiritual devotion and personal faith. Yoga is not a religion – it is, in the words of Rumi – "Not Christian or Jew or Muslim, not Hindu Buddhist, Sufi, or Zen. Not any religion or cultural system. I am not from the East or the West, not out of the ocean or up first, last, outer, inner, only that breath breathing human being."

Yoga is an **O**vercoming – Through diligence and the pursuit of "tapas", or burning effort to accomplish something despite circumstances, we can overcome. The practice of yoga and "tapas" helps us learn to persist on the mat, so that we can persist off the mat as well. In the societal climate we live in today, a spirit of courage to overcome circumstance is more important than ever.

Yoga is **P**atience – A quality not often revered in today's society. Yoga teaches patience, most obviously and grossly through the practice of asana and pranayama, but more subtly and finely through control of the mind and thoughts.

Yoga is **S**haring – Share in one another's sorrows, grief, and tears – and yoga teaches we will know the Self better. It is in serving others that we can also best work through our own pain and suffering.

Yoga is **T**herapeutic – All yoga is therapeutic, but only if taught with safe and biomechanically correct methodology. The yoga of the past, like any other art or science, should evolve. The yoga of tomorrow should utilize the discoveries and science of western medicine, the miracles of modern medicine, in order to remain relevant.

Yoga is **U**nity – History repeats itself. There has been a continuous, unbroken line of oppression and violence through all of time, with mankind suffering at each other's hands. Have we not yet learned that we are all connected? As John Donne, the English poet born in 1624 wrote, "no man is an island...do not think for whom the bell tolls, the bell tolls for thee." And, in the words of Martin Luther King Jr., in a letter written from Birmingham jail on April 16, 1963, "In a real sense all life is inter-related. All persons are caught in an inescapable network of mutuality, tied in a single garment of destiny. Whatever affects one directly affects all indirectly. I can never be what I ought to be until you are what you ought to be, and you can never be what you ought to be until I am what I ought to be." Yoga teaches unity, if it teaches nothing else. Yoga teaches us the rule of karma, as the Bible teaches the Golden Rule. We are to treat others as we wish to be treated, and to do unto others as we would have unto us.

Yoga is **V**alor – Act honorably, act with courage, act with awareness. Practicing even the most seemingly simple pose in yoga is to realize that this is perhaps the most difficult pose of all. Yoga teaches us to finely tune our senses in order to increase our sensitivity to the world around us, and to our inner world. Yoga teaches us to act and take responsibility for our action – through karma and dharma. Martin Luther King Jr. wrote, "truth pressed to the earth, will always rise". When we act with honor, courage, and awareness – with valor – no matter how misunderstood we are, internally or externally, inside ourselves or those around us, Truth will rise – eventually, and for eternity. Then we will finally know, our Self, and God.

Yoga is **Wisdom** – What is wisdom? I once read an author who said sometimes wisdom is knowing what to ignore. It is the same as saying in some sense, "choose your battles". Said yet another way, it could mean knowing how to discern what is important in life, and what is not. The Sutras tell us not to confuse the impermanent with the permanent or the painful for the pleasurable. It is asking us to attain wisdom through knowing the Self, which is to say – we cannot attain wisdom without first knowing our own body, our own mind, and our own spirit; without first conquering the weaknesses of the flesh, weaknesses of our own mind, and weaknesses of our own spirit. So in the practice of yoga, we do have to learn what to ignore.

Yoga is **X** –Yoga = X because it is often that missing variable in the proverbial mathematical equation wherein if we practice X, knowledge will come. If we practice X, we can learn volumes about our nature, and learn to overcome pain and difficulty. Yoga, the missing X in the equation then, can equal transformation and bring ultimate knowledge about our Self.

Yoga is **Y** – Yoga is yin/yang. To borrow the term from Traditional Chinese Medicine, yoga means balance, it means a union of a pair of opposites (Hatha Yoga), it means moving in opposite directions simultaneously, it means moving past the simple five senses to know the soul. In TCM, yin and yang represent opposites, and strive to reach a balance between the two. So for yoga, the discipline strives to teach its student that one must always strive to strike a balance.

Yoga is **Zeal** – Enthusiasm, joy, courage, dedication, discipline, flowing breath and uninterrupted focus – yoga is all of these things, and in America today – this is what yoga means, and can be for everyone. Just like the individual, yoga must be carefully and cautiously tailored for each person, each human being – in order to give them the best chance for a rich quality of life.

Ginger Garner

www.proyogatherapy.com

Ginger Garner, MPT, ATC, ERYT, is the founder of PYTS (Professional Yoga Therapy Studies) and developer of the PYT™ (Professional Yoga Therapy™) lineage of yoga therapy which uniquely combines elements of western rehabilitation and science, western medical research, western psychology, and other elements of western medicine with yoga and Ayurveda.

Ginger earned her Master of Physical Therapy from The University of North Carolina at Chapel Hill, her undergraduate degree in Athletic Training, and has completed studies in The School of Public Health at UNC-Chapel Hill and in music therapy, Ayurveda, Yoga, and Yoga Therapy.

Ginger has also written 6 training textbooks for PYTS, including the new "Childbirth Educator" course and text, "Yoga Therapy for Motherhood and Beyond". Ginger is also the author of the "Advanced Dialogues in Spinal and Lumbopelvic Yoga Therapy" course and textbook. Ginger has produced and is featured in her DVD for chronic pain, "Ancient Yoga, New You", shot on location on the coastal outer banks of North Carolina in Emerald Isle.

HOW PATANJALI COMES ALIVE IN MY CLASSES AND MY LIFE

KERRY MCCLURE

Yoga is creating the space for the Voice to be heard. It is a process of connection. A conversation that remembers, reacquaints, reestablishes and reintegrates the body, the mind and the spirit. It is a balance of the soul enabling one to look at life from all sides. Yoga is a non-sectarian, non-denominational, non-dogmatic spiritual discovery back to one's Self. It is recognition that each person enters into a practice whole. They are not in need of "fixing".

We are all blessed with a unique set of talents and gifts that we bring into this world. As we practice yoga, we are able to use these in ways that honor our limitations and incorporate our totality. From the air as it touches our skin to the core of our being when we feel the beauty of a sunset in our soul, each of us has the intuitive knowledge of the intrinsic nature of the Source energy.

Unfortunately, in today's world, we allow our daily lives and challenges to take us away from that knowledge. Yoga is the journey we can take to connect our body, mind, and spirit and realign with that intrinsic nature of the Source energy. It is a tool to enable a more meaningful and fulfilling life, while celebrating our creativity. It enables us to invest in and reinvent ourselves. Yoga is about connecting with the breath, deepening awareness, finding compassion, enabling balance, and creating space.

I was first introduced to yoga through my mom who, actually, has never taken a public yoga class. Her belief is that yoga is a very personal and private journey and so she happily and contently practices in the sanctity of her own home. She has been practicing yoga most of my life. I "dabbled" in yoga throughout my teens and young adulthood but did not find "satisfaction, nor contentment" with my practice until 1999 when I moved to the coast.

The first week in my new home I took a walk around the neighborhood to get my bearings and learn about the area. What caught my eye was an unusual looking building overlooking the ocean. So curiosity got the better of me and I went inside. It turned out to be a beautiful, quaint, eclectic yoga studio and the rest, as they say, is history! I fell in love. It wasn't long after that discovery that a teacher told me "you don't find yoga, yoga finds you."

I remember taking my first public yoga class. It was an Ashtanga yoga class at this beautiful, quaint studio I had discovered. The teacher asked the class to notice, of all things, the curtains. The owner of the studio had lovingly stitched Patanjali's Eight Limbs of Yoga onto the curtains. At first I was confused and didn't understand the relevance or importance of the Eight Limbs of Yoga. I was still trying to get used to being in a public yoga class! As my practice evolved so too did my understanding and love of Patanjali's Yoga system. Patanjali's Yamas and Niyamas were of particular interest to me and became guidelines and tools for self-understanding.

From a physical standpoint, I have been an athlete all my life. My athletic experience includes body conditioning; aerobics; 10K's; triathlons; 100-, 200-, and 300-mile cycling events; and hiking. Basically, anything with physical challenge and endurance, count me in! Like many people, I was originally drawn to yoga for the external, physical aspects. I felt I needed to add something to my life that lengthened out all my tight, short, bulky muscles.

From a career perspective, I spent most of my adult life in the "Corporate" world working my way up the ladder, achieving, striving, and accumulating money, a home, a car and for what? Each day I would come home completely depleted emotionally, mentally, and physically and wonder what I had accomplished in my day. My days were filled from 4:30am till 11:00pm, sometimes midnight, everyday. I was busy being busy! I felt deep down inside that something was missing. I felt spiritually empty, physically depleted, and disconnected.

I have discovered that my life experiences both in the athletic world and "Corporate" world have brought me to a place of compassion and understanding of the students walking through the door looking for a little piece of sanity and connection. I could identify with their tired, stressed, over-worked, and spiritually undernourished bodies. I have been in their shoes.

I hear oftentimes from new or potential new students that they can't do yoga because they are not flexible. My comment back to them is to remind them that the only thing they need to bring to their yoga practice is a flexible mind – be with what is and let the possibilities unfold. As compassionately as I can, I try to explain to them that we are not here to do gymnastics or acrobatics. We are here to open the body from the inside out. Creating space for the energy to flow and reconnect to their inner Voice. This usually puts them at ease especially when I tell them my own journey of opening a tight athletic body.

As my practice has deepened over the years I have incorporated both a meditation and pranayama practice, which has helped tremendously in helping me move from an "external" to an "internal" practice. At the time I began this yogic journey no one could have prepared me for what would happen since that fateful day walking into a yoga studio in my new surroundings. My yoga practice has not only given me a longer, leaner, more flexible body but the gift of truly discovering who I am and reconnecting with my spirit. Yoga has provided me a framework to work with my emotions, resolve them, and move on instead of staying in the emotions and stagnating. It has taught me how to respond rather than react to situations and circumstances. It has opened my body from the inside out.

Patanjali's Yamas and Niyamas have become tools for me to use in my everyday life. I find everything I experience about myself on my yoga mat translates into my daily life. I was so excited about what I discovered in my yoga practice that I wanted to shout it from the rooftops but I knew that would not be appropriate. We all learn in different ways and at different speeds. Just as I wouldn't have listened or understood when I first started on the yogic path so it might be the same for others. Following are some examples of how I have incorporated the Yamas and Niyamas into my daily life:

YAMAS	Applied In My Personal Life
Ahimsa (nonharming)	Being mindful of treating everyone as I want to be treated
	I eat a vegetarian – mostly vegan diet
	Respectful of others' beliefs, lifestyles, space
	Respectful of myself
Satya (truthfulness)	Truthful with others without being harmful (ahimsa)
	Learning to separate my judgments from my observations
	Truthful with myself as to how I want to live my life from a perspective of leaving the "Corporate" world and choosing a lifestyle more consistent with my spiritual path
	Truthful about my yoga practice, not forcing postures, backing out of injuries and honoring my body where it is in this moment

YAMAS	Applied In My Personal Life
Asteya (nonstealing)	Try to be mindful of others' space, energy, time, ideas Give credit to those that have been my teachers, mentors, guides
Brahmacarya (chastity)	Try to live life more in balance Mindful of not overindulging in any one thing like food, work, activities, myself, etc!
Aparigraha (noncoveting)	Mindful of what I have, letting go of things I don't "need" or "want" Minimizing life Left "Corporate" world for more simple, meaningful life. Not that you can't find that there but it just was not working for me anymore…if it ever did!

NIYAMAS	Applied In My Personal Life
Sauca (purity)	Try to have purity of mind. I try not to think ill thoughts. A significant example of this was my thoughts towards those that caused the devastation on 9/11. I try to remove the anger long enough to understand I teach yoga classes regularly and am mindful of my own personal hygiene and thoughts towards others as I am in close contact with people all the time Participate in food cleanses twice a year
Samtosa (contentment)	Try not to dwell on what did/did not happen in the past or what might/might not happen in the future (very challenging!) Try to be happy in the present moment as this is truly all we have

NIYAMAS	Applied In My Personal Life
Tapas (austerity)	Very disciplined with my yoga practice and all other aspects of my life I choose to engage in. If it is worth doing it's worth doing to the best of my ability I hold the intention of doing everything with intention. Some people accuse me of being "intense"...I do live life with fullness
Svadhyaya (study)	I make time to read every day. I always have at least two or three books going at any given time Spend time talking and sharing with others my experiences/thoughts/ideas about the subject I am studying at the moment
Isvara-pranidhana (devotion to the Lord)	I have two altars in my home specifically for daily ritual and meditation practice I believe in a spirit higher than myself

Years ago, I remember teaching a private Yoga class and my client made a comment to me that she was starting to feel different and things were starting to "bubble up" for her and she didn't know what to do or understand what was going on. So we talked for a while and she said, "how come you didn't tell me this was going to happen?" My response to her was that she needed to discover this for herself. If I had tried to explain it to her before she was ready then she would have missed the pot of gold inside (her spirit). First, she needed to find the house (herself physically).

In my public classes I am mindful as to how and how much I share with students about spiritual and other information about yoga. Not everyone is in class for the same reasons. Even for those who are there for something more, I don't want to infringe on their space because they may not be ready, etc. I save those times for specific workshop topics. The following illustrates some examples of how I subtly share the Yamas and Niyamas with my students:

YAMAS	How I Share the Yamas with My Students
Ahimsa (nonharming)	Individually greet everyone that comes to class and provide a comfortable, safe environment for students to practice Create safe, inviting, open atmosphere for all to practice individually with the benefit of group energy Ask students to take awareness inward creating privacy for themselves as well as creating privacy for those around them
Satya (truthfulness)	Encourage students not to push beyond their edge and many times to pull back from their edge Take several moments throughout the class to check in and notice "what is true" for them in their practice in that given moment Encourage each person to set an intention for their practice
Asteya (nonstealing)	Respecting others' space, not walking on others' mats Keeping room/props neat and tidy Allowing others' space to discover what comes up for them in their practice
Brahmacarya (chastity)	Find balance in a pose between strength and flexibility; firmness and softness; opposing forces of energy Not "overdoing" in a poses
Aparigraha (noncoveting)	Practice in a modest space

Not being attached to a goal

NIYAMAS	How I Share the Niyamas with My Students
Sauca (purity)	Are you thinking impure thoughts about yourself/others in your practice? Am I doing this "right?" They look better than me. I don't like what they are wearing, etc. Keep space they are practicing in neat and tidy
Samtosa (contentment)	Be happy where you are in your practice at this very moment, our bodies change every minute of everyday Stay in the moment and welcome the "what is" of the moment
Tapas (austerity)	Stay focused, breathe, be diligent and mindful Encourage students to develop a personal practice
Svadhyaya (study)	I always share a reading at the beginning or end of a practice Whatever I am reading or studying at the time is usually what I share with my students I always try to share something that is either relevant to the class, current news, etc.
Isvara-pranidhana (devotion to the Lord)	OM together at the end of practice Sit in silent meditation at the beginning and end of practice for a few minutes Connect with something beyond the Self, whatever that may be for you

One of the more valuable things I have learned through my yoga practice is to listen to and trust in the intelligence of the body. After all, the human body is an ancient system, which gives it seniority to tradition. When I have been riding my bike, lifting weights, running or hiking or doing a lot of physical work around my house I adjust my practice to a softer practice, balancing the more rigorous activities of my day.

If my body has been more sedentary from sitting at the computer or driving, I find that a more flowing, vigorous practice seems to unfold. There can be many ways to practice. For example, there are the vigorous, soft, flowing, rhythmic, therapeutic and technical styles of yoga. I am grateful to have had the opportunity to learn many approaches and variations so that "my body can choose" what is needed in the moment. I have also noticed that when we have rigid practices and beliefs our yoga often loses its joy, flow and creativity. When we are open to keeping joy and aliveness in our yoga practice we no longer have to force ourselves to do it. It becomes a gift to one's Self.

I feel incredibly humbled and profoundly grateful to be able to practice and teach yoga. I am deeply indebted to all my yoga teachers, mentors, guides, and yoga's sacred texts for giving me wings to delve deeper into my personal practice and to help me to share this wonderful modality we call Yoga.

I am guided through life by Gandhi's quote, "We must be the change we wish to see in the world." Change begins within each one of us. For me, the yoga path is what guides me to and through those changes.

Kerry McClure

Kerry is a life-long student of yoga. Her primary influences have been Paul Reynolds, Ganga White, Tracey Rich, Sarah Powers, Paul Grilley, and Maritza.

The style of yoga Kerry teaches is considered an "eclectic vinyasa flow" style thanks to the diverse backgrounds of the yoga teachers she has studied with.

She blends aspects of Ashtanga, Vinyasa Flow, Iyengar, Yin, and Anusara Yoga styles with an emphasis on mindfulness, breath and heart combining a flow-style with alignment details.

Kerry is the owner of HeartLight Yoga. Kerry is a Registered Yoga Teacher (RYT) with the Yoga Alliance. She is currently enrolled in a Masters/PhD program in Holistic Nutrition.

Kerry can be reached at HeartLightKerry@gmail.com.

JUST ME AND MY MAT

LYNDA SANDORA HOFFARTH

It doesn't care about the rush of traffic on my way to teach,
or those thoughts to myself, "do I practice what I preach?"

It overlooks my unwashed face
and the graying hair that's out of place.
It's only happy I have chosen the time
as I begin my practice with an intent and a chime.

What once was just a rubber mat
is a hallowed place that I look at.
As I step upon its cushioned feel
beneath my feet it seems surreal.

Like a long lost love or friend to me
reconnects me to my heart you see!
It soothes my troubles, fears and woes.
I wonder how? Do you suppose?
It's made of magic, even though
some see a mat and nothing more.
For some it's merely just a chore.

But as for me, it's comforting
unloading my problems that I bring
to sit or stand within my space
takes me to another place
where I can self examine me
in stillness pausing mindfully.

Lynda Sandora Hoffarth

Lynda has trained with a variety of master teachers, including: Integral Yoga, workshops with Ester Myers, Gary Kraftsow and Kam Thye Chow, Certified Structural Yoga Therapist and with Mukunda Stiles.

She also works with healing modalities such as, Reiki, Thai Yoga Massage, Triom Touch Healing, and Lynda is a personal fitness trainer.

In my personal yoga practice I put on an inspiring piece of music and let my body find the way it needs to move. I use countertops, doorways, and stairs to work on a variety of things that include balance, strength, flexibility and breath work.

NOT JUST A T-SHIRT SLOGAN

SHANA MEYERSON

Yoga is life.

I don't say this as a clever tee shirt slogan or even as the words of a fanatic yogini. I say this because yoga practice is life practice. Like life, yoga can only be practiced, but never perfected. It is a never-ending exploration and discovery of self that begs contentment over complacency.

In America, the practice of yoga is mostly a function of asana—asana being the name that designates each yoga posture. Distilled down to its physical essence, to translate the word "asana" to mean "pose" or "posture" is both a misnomer and a disservice. In fact, the word "asana" means "to sit still or quietly." Asana is much less about the physical movement than it is about the stillness of mind that accompanies movement of the body.

Shavasana, lying still in corpse, is the most important of the postures, as within it is contained the essence of all yoga. To have five or ten minutes of absolute physical and mental stillness is nurturing for the soul. Once that is mastered, though, the real work is learning to carry that quiet energy through the entire practice. A calm, still, open mind as you sweat, struggle, and even fall. Then, more importantly, a yogi/ni can maintain that stillness all the way out the yoga studio door and into life. We all waste so much energy on negative and useless thoughts. If we can learn to control that and become less reactive, we can all become yogi/nis.

Release is what it is all about. It is interesting that we have a tendency in the Western World to cling tightly to the things that hurt us, and release easily those that heal. In a nation plagued with clinical depression and anxiety, where are the statistics on clinical elation? As we learn to let go of the stuff that holds us back in life and hold on to that which helps us grow, our yoga truly becomes transformational because, honestly, no one on earth actually leads a stressful life. Stress is not something that happens to us, it is something that we create. We cannot usually control the circumstances of our lives, but we can always choose to control our reactions to those circumstances.

The person who comes to yoga practice and gets worked up over some posture that they cannot master is, most likely, also creating significant amounts of undue stress in his or her daily life. When you boil it down, doing a handstand is never really going to change your life, but learning to stay calm while you are falling out of one will.

It is ironic that people come to yoga all stressed out, stress out during yoga, then have a few minutes of relaxation in shavasana at the end of the practice, and go out into the world claiming yoga relaxes them so much…just to recreate the cycle of stress all over again.

Someday, a yoga practice is not just bookended by calmness, but is a continuum thereof. And then, some day, a yoga practice is not just bookending a day with calmness, but is a continuum of a calm and controlled life.

Yoga isn't about learning to stand on your hands, but on your own two feet. It's about accepting that there will be things that you can do and things that you can't, but they are all worth the pursuit. And it's about believing that you can do anything that you set your mind to. There is no muscle more powerful than the mind.

Literally, translated, "yoga" means "yoke," to yoke together mind, body, and spirit. Too often, people break themselves down into just mind, just body or just spirit. Maybe they are so intellectual that they cannot conceive of spirit. Or perhaps they exist on such a spiritual plane that they feel no need for this physical existence. More often than not, they are just so grounded in the physical that they cannot understand anything bigger or more profound than self.

I don't think that any one of these is better (or worse) than the other. Is the pursuit of the spirit inherently more righteous than that of the body, for example? No. Each human being was blessed with a sacred triumvirate of energies. Without a corporeal body, we literally cannot exist on this plane. Without a mind, we would not be able to function. And without a spirit, we would be nothing more than flesh and bones. Body, mind, and spirit need each other. And yoga is the practice that brings them all together.

The misinterpretation of the word "asana" reminds me of another common misinterpretation: that of the word "shalom." As any Hebrew School graduate will tell you, the word "shalom" means "hello," "goodbye," or "peace." But that's not true. The word "shalom" comes from the root shin-lamed-mem, or "to complete." Basically, "shalom" means "you complete me." It is used in both salutation and parting, and it is used to convey a sentiment of peace, but really it means so much more than that. There can be no me without you and vice versa...just as there cannot be mind without body or body without spirit. It's all about completion. Yoga is a book that is often skimmed, but rarely read. Our job, as American yogis and yoginis, is to carry a torch that is not limited to the simplistic interpretations of movements, but the moving interpretations of simplicity.

Yoga understands that even simplicity can be profound. It's when we stop paying attention to the details that we miss the beauty. When you start to pay attention to the unobvious, you start to get a more complete understanding of the world.

Think about pranayama. Luckily, our bodies will breathe on their own, whether we think about it or not. But instead, we choose in our practice to pay attention, thereby transforming simple sustenance into true meditation.

You cannot achieve yoga without paying attention to the details. If you want to do a complicated arm balance, you can't just focus on the arms. You can't just focus on the movement and positioning of the legs. You can't just focus on the engagement of the core. Instead, you need to look beyond the gross movement and into the finite. Again, yoking together a whole body and mind full of energies and bringing them together to a common end. That includes arms and legs and core and mind…as well as fingers, tailbones, neck, gaze…it all fits in the mix. Every part, no matter how small, plays a role. It's in that appreciation that one can begin to master some of the postures that, from the outside or superficial level, may seem virtually impossible.

That being said, the practice of yoga doesn't have to involve Warrior Poses, Headstands, or even stretches. Yoga can be baseball, art, a relationship. Any time that a person's combined energies are devoted to the same task, s/he is practicing yoga. Likewise, no matter how aesthetically pleasing a person's physical practice is, s/he is not a yogi/ni until s/he has mastered the urges of the body and the motivations of the spirit.

Perhaps the most beautiful aspect of an asana practice is that it is pretty much the only place on earth where the best you can do is just perfect. In a way, yoga can be the spark that ignites world peace. Though it sounds dramatic, if a practitioner can learn to accept that, despite Yogi Berra's quote to the contrary ("Baseball is ninety percent mental and the other half is physical"), all that you can give is 100%, you must accept that—falling or not—you, too, are giving 100%. Even on an off-day when you know you can do better, on that day, in those circumstances, perhaps 60% is all you have to give. Which even makes 60%, 100%. And if you can accept that in yourself, then you have no choice but to accept that in others. We are all in this together and we are all giving things the best shot we know how to with the tools we've been given. Yoga is about accepting the inherent perfection of all human beings—even in light of all of our (sometimes drastic) mistakes—and refraining from judging others, just as we learn to stop judging ourselves.

Yoga doesn't care if you fall. It only cares if you get back up. It doesn't care if you succeed. It only cares that you try. And then try again.

Take Thomas Edison. A yogi. Who also happened to invent the light bulb. Mr. Edison, considered by most to be one of the most important inventors of modern times, and certainly one of the greatest intellects, made *ten thousand* attempts at the light bulb before he found one that worked. And one, purportedly, was even made out of peanut butter. Peanut Butter. When he finally created a light bulb filament that provided consistent, sustainable light, he remarked, "I have not failed 10,000 times, but rather have successfully found 10,000 ways that will not work."

That's yoga.

It's the knowledge that there is always a way that will work. But you may have to plod through 10,000 others before you find it. Tread 9,999 steps and you won't find it. You have to follow through that last step.

While the number of people who go to yoga classes in America has exploded in the past decade, the number of yogis and yoginis sadly hasn't. So many people come into yoga classes with a competitive spirit or inextricable ego. They get proud. They get frustrated. They get attached. They get a fix…like it's a drug instead of a practice.

Ego, I believe, is yoga's nemesis and it can work in a number of ways.

Sometimes an overactive ego will push people into poses that they are not ready for, so they can easily injure themselves…or, even worse, their egos. Problem is, when a yoga practitioner becomes too attached to the physical results of his or her practice, there is a tendency to recede into a comfort zone. Yoga is not about comfort zones. It is about pushing the boundaries. Not being confined by the shell, but finding the world your oyster.

The only way to grow in life is to take risks. If you do the same thing every day, you are destined to sameness. When egotistic attachment leads to frustration, people shy away from trying new postures. There is no longer growth within the practice, just stagnation.

In fact, many people's egos get so involved that instead of getting frustrated, they get paralyzed. Those who don't try, never look foolish. And so, again, there is an unwillingness to try, to be surprised.

Your yoga practice is a microcosm of your life. What you bring to your mat, you bring to the world around you. When a challenge presents itself, do you run up to it or run away? Do you see it as an obstacle or an opportunity? When you fall, do you get frustrated or more determined? Are you busy comparing yourself to others or just looking for your personal best? Are you focused or scattered? Conscious or unconscious?

Yoga can be an extraordinary and life-changing practice. Or it can just be a workout. America is still in the process of figuring that out.

In a tough and competitive world, sometimes the hardest thing you can do is take a good, honest look at yourself. Confronting one's own fallibility can be painful or even frightening. And yet, it is our inherent imperfection that makes us human. The world has yet to see a single perfect human being tread upon it. And yet, we hold ourselves up to this unforgiving standard that is both unrealistic and, in fact, damaging to the very fabric of our existence.

Ultimately, if we can sit down, in stillness, in quietness, look inside, and be at peace with what we see, we will know that we have found our divine yogi nature.

POSTSCRIPT

I grew up a very intense athlete. I played the Junior USTA tennis circuit in high school, later trained for the Race Across America (bike riding 100 miles a day), and worked out like a fiend (three hours a day) all through my 20s.

One day I was walking around my apartment, ran into my CD cabinet, and broke my pinky toe. I think if most people were asked what one part of their body they need the least, they would say pinky toe. Well, for me, it meant that I couldn't walk on it or put a shoe on it, much less run the stairs, spin, play tennis or any other activity that I was obsessed with doing every day of my life up until that point.

As it was healing, still too tough to put in a shoe, but gaining usability, I remembered that there was a guy at the gym who, for years, told me that I had to try this yoga class in Santa Monica on Sunday mornings. And for years I told him, "Yoga? Yeah, right." Well…it was time to try yoga.

I dragged my sister and close friend over to Bryan Kest's Sunday morning class in hopes of moving something around a little bit, maybe getting a little exercise in. And, boy, was I in for the surprise of my life. My whole life changed that day.

Turns out that yoga was everything I ever needed: mind, body, spirit, intensity in a way I never got at the gym. From the first day I walked into class, I knew that this was it.

Up until that point, I worked in the real world. Started at ICM, moved on into screenplay development, went from there to work for Microsoft and then helped build a number of Internet companies. When I discovered Bryan, I was also getting my MBA at UCLA.

Within weeks of starting yoga, I began ditching work and school to get to yoga classes. I couldn't get enough. And one day I told Bryan that all I wanted to do was yoga all day. And he replied "Well, why don't you?"

Why don't I? But I'm in Business School. I have an Ivy League undergraduate degree. I earn a ton of money. What am I supposed to do? Drop everything and become a yoga instructor??!?!?!

Yes.

That day my wheels started spinning. And a few months later, I withdrew from UCLA, left my job, and put out my new shingle: Shana Meyerson, Yoga Instructor.

It was a tremendous leap of faith for me. Leaving Business School was harder for me than getting in. I am not from among the quitters in this world, to say the least. But I did what I felt I needed to do. Up until the day I healed my broken pinky toe, I'd have told you the last thing on earth I could ever see myself doing would be teaching yoga. Now I do it and love it with every ounce of my being.

My students see my passion for the practice when they work with me. They learn, they grow, and they evolve. That's what yoga does. It changes lives.

Shana Meyerson

www.YOGAthletica.com

www.miniyogis.com

I have been teaching full-time for seven years, both in the context of power yoga as well as working with children. My yoga program for kids—mini yogis—has afforded me the wonderful experience of teaching teachers and children all around the world.

My personal practice is a daily exploration of anything new and different. I specialize in arm balances and inversions, as I love the mental and physical challenges these postures present.

HEALING THROUGH THE
SACRED REALM OF EMOTIONS

SANDRA CARDEN

SACRED SPACE

The alive and vibratory echoes of our drums reverberated through our fingers, arms, bellies, and chests. As I gazed across the drumming circle, my eyes met clearly with each person's eyes. Bright eyes, happy eyes, alive and vibrant eyes. No one here looked ill or unhappy or scared or even distant. The healing percussive tones thundered through our bodies, stilled our minds, and lifted our hearts as the rhythms rose and swelled, twirled and danced. There was only the sound, the essence of the vibration, the intense energy, the moment. No one was concerned with cancer. In that culminating moment, no one even remembered cancer.

The weeklong retreat for cancer patients had been nurturing and healing for participants and practitioners alike. As in the manner first pioneered by Commonweal, we had created a program of optimal healing. We had shared stories, silent walks, and artful creative expressions of our own very personal experience. We had luxuriated in somatic therapies, Yoga, and massage. Our hearts and minds were open. This was the final evening of our retreat.

I knew Ken had received a massage that afternoon, but it wasn't until my eyes met all those around the circle that I realized he was missing now. I leaned toward my colleague and whispered, "Where's Ken?"

She whispered back beneath the percussive fullness, "He went to his room." My eyes met hers with questioning, wondering if he felt all right. "Why don't you go look in after him? Maybe offer him Yoga therapy?" I immediately left the circle and made my way up the stairs. I knocked, and Ken's hushed voice invited me in. He was alone, sitting on an overstuffed chair, wrapped in a blanket and looking small, yet wide-eyed. Clearly something was bothering him. I asked if he'd like me to sit with him awhile, and he nodded in agreement. I sat on the floor and asked Ken to tell me what was happening.

Ken said he was not feeling well and did not feel up to being part of the drumming circle. I asked him to tell me more about not feeling well, and he went on. He said his tummy felt fluttery and his chest and shoulders ached. The words spilled out as he hugged the blanket closer around his shoulders. Ken said ever since his massage in the afternoon he had felt out of sorts, upset, emotional, and vulnerable. He talked for a while longer and I listened. He said he felt like something was wrong, felt that he was going to explode. He did not feel like himself, and did not know what to do with himself.

My sense was that Ken's energy body was opened as a result of the support he had felt all week long, and it was taken to the edge of release during his massage. Now might be a very good time to introduce Ken to Phoenix Rising Yoga Therapy (PRYT). Through its nondirective approach, Ken might feel safe enough to let go.

After explaining the why and how of PRYT, Ken decided he would like to open himself to the process. "Why not? Maybe it will help, and if you think it will, I'm willing to go there," he said. Just with expressing this desire to go deeper, he began to feel calmer. He hoped the experience might be relaxing enough to allow him to sleep.

THE VESSEL OF PRESENCE

I made an impromptu "Yoga therapy mat" on the floor and asked Ken to lie comfortably on his back. I positioned pillows under his knees, adjusted his neck and shoulders, and then checked in with Ken about position and comfort. He was ready to begin.

We started with a simple Yoga breathing technique, which Ken learned easily. With his breath to guide him, his body settled and his mind became emptier. After leading him in a brief body scan designed to give a baseline reading of his physical and emotional status, I asked Ken what he would like to receive from Yoga therapy. Ken stated his intention, "To let go."

After a few more minutes of breathwork and then some minor adjustments designed to release stress to the shoulders, neck, and hips, I moved to Ken's feet. I knelt to hold each of his ankles in my hands. I told Ken I would be lifting each of his legs slowly, with the rhythm of his breath. I asked him to tell me which leg should go first. "The right."

Breath by breath, micro-inch by micro-inch, I began to lift Ken's right leg, supporting his knee joint, using his breath to guide me, feeling for any hesitation or stickiness in the joint. After a few minutes I asked Ken what was happening.

Ken said, "I hear those drums. It feels like . . . reminds me . . ." Then he cried out, "Oh!" Ken's entire body jumped and tensed. I continued to breathe evenly, gently supporting his ankle. After letting Ken know that I was there, and listening, he refocused, and went on, "My leg! My leg! Oh...it hurts so bad." I had lifted Ken's foot and leg about eight inches from the floor and could feel no resistance. I backed off just a bit, feeling no change, and inviting him to tell me everything about the ache in his legs. He started to weep, choking back tears.

"My legs hurt. They both hurt so badly. They are so tired. They ache . . . everywhere . . . so tired."

Ken's breath was short and shallow. I coached him to notice his breathing, and it gradually slowed and deepened. I told Ken what I had heard him say and asked him to tell me more about the tiredness, and the ache in his legs. His story began to unfold. Ken's body-mind took him back to a vivid memory.

IN UP AND OUT

Ken was again a soldier in Vietnam, a captain in charge of a battalion conducting ground reconnaissance. It was a beautiful morning in the native jungle village where he spent much of his free time. He was alone in the small hut he shared with his lover, a beautiful young Vietnamese woman named Kwan-yi. She was giving him a massage. He was lying on his stomach looking down at her sweet small brown feet. He could see the sun's filtering light through the open window and feel its warmth on his back. The air was full of the scent of heavy flowers and the sweet and pungent cooking smells wafting from the village fires. He could see the tiny hairs on her soft leg and could smell the fresh scent of her sheer white cotton dress, could smell the fragrance of her skin and her hair as he felt her hands magically release the knots in his back. No one could give a massage like Kwan-yi. All was perfect. For a moment time stood still, and there was only love.

The next image that came to Ken was of running. As I listened, I continued to slowly lift his right leg. Ken's breath quickened and his legs and arms twitched. "Tell me more about running."

Ken had been away from the village for several days, out on a mission with his men, and he longed for rest and the comfort of Kwan-yi's arms. He trotted swiftly ahead of his men, anxious to reach the village, but before he reached its edge he was met on the path by a staggering and severely injured old man, an elder from the village whom he recognized immediately. The man was tortured, crying and wailing, stumbling, reaching out to Ken, uttering some horrible indiscernible words. Something was terribly wrong. Something unspeakable had happened. A deep and ancient fear clenched his gut.

Ken roared past the old man, racing toward the village. The stench of fire and ashes and death hit him before he saw what was left of the cluster of small huts, burned to the ground. Everyone was gone. Instantly Ken realized that everyone had been murdered, by hand, violently. He barely saw the blood-caked and twisted bodies, men and women, children and old ones, lying where they fell, as he raced through the village. These people he had known and loved . . . all gone. Ken flew into the charred remains of their hut and found Kwan-yi's body, crumpled and covered with dried blood. He scooped her into his arms.

All he could think was, "This is not right. She's all dirty. I need to wash her off. I need to take her to the river." With Kwan-yi in his arms like a child, he began to run. He ran through the forested jungle. He ran for miles. His legs and arms and neck and back screamed, and still he ran. Finally, after what seemed like an eternity, he came to the river. He knelt down and gently laid her body at its bank and washed the eternally lovely Kwan-yi.

I lowered Ken's right leg.

Ken's breath softened. He relaxed. After a time, I began to raise Ken's left leg on slow exhalations, breath by breath, bit by bit. His eyes moved rapidly under his closed lids. I invited Ken to tell me what was happening.

Ken saw Kwan-yi's face, just as she was the last time he had seen her alive, the morning of the massage in the hut.

Her face is shining, she is young and brown, fresh and unspoiled — beautiful. Her long black hair glistens and her soft eyes fill with love as she looks into his eyes. "She is here, now, he whispers."

"Tell me more."

Ken says he hears her voice. Kwan-yi tells him she loves him and is proud of him and what he has done with his life. She says she is always with him. She tells him she is his angel. Then, she is gone.

Ken relaxed more deeply. He suddenly says he has known that Kwan-yi has always protected him. After she died, he was reckless. He'd walk through minefields and take ridiculous risks. With this uncanny ability to know—without knowing—exactly where to safely tread, his men came to trust that he was somehow "golden" and could not be harmed. They came to trust themselves to walk only in his very footsteps to avoid danger. It was as if he had an angel.

At the end of his session Ken told me that in all the years since he had not told the story to anyone but his dearest friend. He had come home from the war a hero. He did his best to put the past behind him. In time, Ken fell in love, married, raised a family, and become contentedly integrated into his loving community.

Ken knew in his bones that Kwan-yi had been with him the whole time, and was to this day. His sense was that everything was exactly as it should be. He knew that she was pleased that his life was rich and full of love, family, and friends. She was happy, at peace, whole and well. And most certainly, she was always meant to be his angel.

To integrate further, Ken looked back and named the Yoga therapy experience. His intention had been to "let go," but he had not been consciously aware of what had been held for so long. The name Ken gave to his Yoga therapy session was "accepting my angel." In letting go of the buried memory and accepting the experience he had tried so long and hard to bury, his body was suddenly free of tension and pain. He felt light and alive, and truly healed. Ken affirmed himself with the words, "Now I am free."

FREEDOM FROM SUFFERING

Yoga therapy did not cure Ken's brain cancer, but it did help to heal a deep and old wound. Before he passed on some six months later, Ken emailed me and told me he felt at peace and was no longer afraid of dying. He felt enormous love for his wife and children, a vast appreciation for the many blessings in his life, and an ease that he would be shepherded beyond, by one meant to guide him home.

Ken's story, while unique, is not unusual. Yoga has a very positive and powerful affect on the body, mind, and spirit, even amid great adversity and discomfort. Research from the National Institutes of Health (NIH) suggests that almost all medically treated illnesses have a psychological component[1]. Some forward thinking medical professionals believe that "virtually all illness, if not psychosomatic in foundation, has a definite psychosomatic component.[2]"

It is too bad the word "psychosomatic" has gotten such a bad rap. The Latin roots "psyche," meaning soul and/or mind, and "soma," meaning body, have long ago come together to express a union that science seems to regard as a threat to the authenticity of any given illness.

Yoga therapy, particularly Phoenix Rising Yoga Therapy (PRYT)[3], creates a true psychosomatic response, bringing to play all elements of the physio-psycho-spiritual human being in a perfect gestalt of personal inquiry and inner wisdom. While the PRYT process is client-driven, the practitioner acts as a "witness," affecting the outcome of the session by holding the intention that all is exactly as it should be.

MODERN RECOGNITION TO ANCIENT TRUTH

A new and subtle shift to a quantum-relativistic–based understanding of the phenomenal world, much more aligned with Eastern philosophy, has begun to emerge since the mid-twentieth century. In fact, the "Cartesian division" has actually helped to bring about a greater understanding of emotions as being the body-mind connection. This has been established through the scientific ability to examine the molecular link between physiology and psychology, psyche and soma.

The microscopic observations of the new physics now recognize all things as interrelated aspects of the ultimate and same reality. In this more Eastern view, not only are all things—including consciousness—interrelated, but all things are fluid, dynamic, and changing, with something akin to Divinity as an intrinsic guiding element from within.

This means that we, as mere "observers" of the phenomenal world, are affected by, and actually affect the world by our observation. Dr. Fritjof Capra wrote, decades ago, in Tao of Physics,

> "In Eastern mysticism this universal interwovenness always includes the human observer and his or her consciousness, and this is also true in atomic physics. . . . In atomic physics, then, the scientist cannot play the role of detached objective observer, but becomes involved in the world he observes to the extent that he influences the properties of the observed objects."

This idea, from quantum physics, of the "observer" affecting the outcome, plays an important role in understanding why Yoga therapy is so effective in creating an immediate and lasting sense of well-being on the part of the "receiver."

Science has studied the body's response to stress since the 1940s, but it was not until the 1970s that research conducted by Dr. Herbert Benson proved the mind's ability to shift the nervous system from sympathetic to parasympathetic dominance. His book The Relaxation Response set the stage for the acceptance of Yoga and meditation as popular and scientifically condoned antidotes to stress, but we still did not understand why it worked.

In the 1970s the biochemical link between consciousness, mind, and body was proven with the work of NIH research neuroscientist Candace Pert, Ph.D., thus paving the way for understanding the body-mind connection and opening up a whole new field of medicine: psychoneuroimmunology.

SCIENCE AFFIRMS BODY/MIND

Dr. Pert has long had a fascination with consciousness and how the body responds to signals from the mind, and vice versa. As a scientist, she devoted her talents to uncovering why certain drugs like morphine and heroin create a sense of well-being—even euphoria— despite great pain. She was also interested in how the human body-mind naturally creates its own pain-relieving opiates. Dr. Pert's research led her to the discovery of the opiate receptor in 1972, for which she and her colleagues were nominated for the 1979 Nobel Prize in Medicine.

As Dr. Pert explains it, the body and mind converse with each other through the emotions. This highly elegant communication system is a demonstration of the body-mind's innate intelligence, seeking well-being through instructing virtually every system in our body.

The first component of the "molecules of emotion" is the receptor, lying on the surface of cells throughout the brain and body. The receptor is only one molecule, made of proteins. The average host cell it rests upon might have millions of other receptors on its surface. Each receptor acts as a pulsating scanner—vibrating, dancing, and jiggling to attract other information chemicals toward it with a mysterious and powerfully attractive force.

When the right chemical (a ligand) comes along, it dances a bit with the receptor, making sure they speak the same language. Then it "mounts" the receptor in a process called binding. (Sounds sexy, doesn't it? Molecular sex!) The instant the receptor and ligand bind there is a shimmying and morphing that changes the shape of the molecule, and the "message" brought by the ligand enters the molecule. Presto! Instant change.

For instance, on the surface of cells is an opiate receptor (among many kinds of receptors), which attracts only the opiate chemical group, like endorphins morphine and heroin. When that chemical is diffused throughout the system, whether administered externally or naturally produced internally, the proper ligand enters and binds to the molecule's receptor and the good feeling of well-being associated with opiates is almost immediately felt.

It has long been suspected that depression and stress can suppress the immune system, inviting disease. Aristotle is credited with saying, "Soul and body, I suggest, react sympathetically upon one another." When we are happy, we are less prone to illness.

One possible explanation for this is that certain illness-related chemicals, such as those that cause the viral cold, use the same receptor as norepinephrine, which is an informational substance associated with free-flowing feelings of happiness. This "happy" chemical is created internally when you experience "doing what you love." Since they both use the same port, if that opiate receptor is already occupied, the "bad cold" chemical cannot enter. Sounds like a good excuse for a vacation to me.

So, what we know about these informational chemicals is that we can create them with our minds to affect our bodies, or our bodies can create them to affect our mind. In fact, it is a two way street—the body can affect the mind as well as the mind can affect the body.

CREATION AND EVOLUTION OF SELF

This is where Yoga and meditation come in. We know that through meditation and somatic practices such as Yoga and bodywork we create our own natural morphine-like chemicals and other molecules of emotion that give us a sense of connectedness and trust in the world. We know that having a "witness" affects the outcome. We know that through breath awareness and intention we harness the mind into the safety of the present moment, where long-held emotions may be revealed, explored, and released.

This release of emotions is tantamount to the process of evolution. When emotions are held back or not felt, the chemical markers that hold the emotional charge are stored within the body. Too much holding creates stagnation. Stagnation leads to an interruption of the flow of prâna, or "vital life force."

Charles Darwin, in *Expression of the Emotions in Man and Animals*, first postulated that the emotions, shown universally in all humans and some animal species, are key to the survival of the life force. Emotions include not only expression of joy, fear, sadness, rage, etc., but also basic sensations including hunger and thirst, pleasure and pain, and even more subjective human experiences such as spiritual inspiration, love, and awe.

Dr. Pert's expanded research in the 1980s proved that the limbic brain, long associated with emotion, contained 85-95% of the neuropeptide receptors associated with emotions. Not only were these peptides found in three-trillion-celled humans, but they also were discovered in the most primitive one-celled creature. This supports Darwin's theory that the physiological basis for the emotions most needed for survival would be "conserved" throughout various evolutionary stages.

And, even more startling, Dr. Pert's research indicated that these communication peptides, the molecules of emotion, exist not only in the brain but also throughout the entire organism, with the greatest concentrations in the regions traditionally associated with the chakras of Yoga and Ayurveda.

What this means to us, as practitioners of Yoga and Yoga therapy, is that we can instantaneously alter the way we feel though our practice, and we can assist others in finding their own way toward happiness and contentment. For people who are in pain, be it emotional or physical (as the body reads pain as pain, no matter what kind), there is a way out.

TO FEEL IS TO LIVE

The Buddha said the most outstanding characteristic of the human condition is dukha, or "life is painful." We fail to grasp the transitory nature of the universe, and with that comes frustration. "All things arise and pass away," said the Buddha. As long as we do not understand the impermanence underlying all creation, we will inescapably experience physical discomfort and emotional upheaval.

Buddha's teachings go on to explain that the cause of our suffering is trishnâ, or "attachment" (lit., "thirst"). Attachment takes its form in desire and aversion. We want things to be how we want them to be, and if they turn out differently, we have a hard time. Even though things will be painful, however, the Buddha said we need not suffer. The Buddha did not say, "Don't feel."

The Yoga-Sûtras state this teaching another way: heyam dukham anagatam. "Suffering as a result of mind-projection is avoidable." The real lesson is to allow the feelings to flow through without clinging or "stuckness" to a certain idea, concept, or belief. The key to the end of suffering is the freedom to see what is behind the suffering, to express that, and to let it go.

Both Yoga practice and Yoga therapy require attention and intention. Attention to body, breath, and mind, and the intention to stay present and watch what happens, to act as a witness and observe the emotional quality. The shift from normal waking consciousness to a mindful and choiceless awareness shifts both body chemistry and the resultant tensile quality.

FREEDOM

When introducing a student to Yoga, I remember that my purpose is to create a safe place in which to explore the secrets of the body-mind connection, and through that insight to release from habitual holdings toward true freedom. Many patients I see are close to the end of their time on Earth. Facing the very real disintegration of the self, they often embrace a greater Self, unknown before their relationship with disease. As one beamed just this morning, "I'm not Tracy-with-cancer, I'm me! Tracy!"

----

[1]University of Texas at Austin, Health Psychology Dept., URL: http://homepage.psyc.utexas.edu/homepage/deptarea/Social/Health.htm; BodyMindNews Archives, URL: http://www.body-wisdom.com/bodymindnews_991015.htm.

[2]Pert, Candace B. *Molecules of Emotion*. New York: Scribner, 1997, p. 18.

[3]Phoenix Rising Yoga therapy, West Stockbridge, Mass.

Sandra Carden

www.unionyoga.com

Sandra Carden, C.Y.T., ERYT 500, is a Certified Yoga Therapist and Registered 500-Hour Yoga Instructor who has taught Yoga since the 1970's.

Sandra's studio, UNION/YOGA llc, in Leelanau County, Michigan, was established in 1989.

She offers Yoga instruction, Yoga Alliance approved Yoga Teacher Certification, retreats, and private Yoga therapy.

IF I WERE A WILD HORSE, I'D THROW YOU OFF MY BACK

SUZANN BAIN

I am blessed to have a wonderful and healthy friend who is obsessed with all things medical and is easily panicked. Should her intestinal area become loosened or irregular in any way, she is overwhelmed with anxiety and panic and immediately rushes to the conclusion that Death's creepy hand is already knocking on the front door of her existence. Should her heart rate increase unexpectedly, she is automatically convinced that her inner electrical system has hit an irreversible glitch and, instantly clutching her chest, she will sit down in an attempt to make her transition into the otherworld more peaceful. These panic attacks are so sudden that she will not leave her house without a pill in her pocket "just in case."

This kind of experience is very real for many people. When it comes to this way of negative thinking, one of the biggest enablers is the Internet. If I perform an Internet search for a common medical condition, the following possible causes begin to haunt me: 1. bacterial infections; 2. viral infections; 3. food intolerances; 4. parasites; 5. reaction to medicines; and 6. intestinal diseases. You will quickly note the words infections, parasites, and diseases. How can we keep from panicking with so much doom and gloom cavalierly splashed across the computer screen that we rely on so heavily each and every day in this country?

Prior to the advent of the Internet, some of us had mothers who filled our heads with pessimistic thoughts. My own mother, well-meaning as she was, would not allow me to play softball with my cousins when I was younger. She was afraid that, since I wore post earrings in my ears, the ball would strike me in the ear thereby shoving the end of the post into my carotid artery, killing me horribly within seconds. Never mind that the earrings most certainly could have been removed prior to me playing the game. Although this would seem to be a reasonable alternative, I knew at a young age not to push the issue as, had I offered this solution, she would have concocted an even more twisted scenario leading to my inevitable demise. When she taught me how to shave my legs, she repeatedly warned me not to push down too hard behind my knee as I could cut myself and bleed to death. Her preference, she recommended to me, was to just not even shave that area at all and avoid the danger altogether.

This kind of pessimistic thinking is contagious and, once it takes root, it spreads and can follow us through life. In my early 20's, I visited my brother in Coral Gables a few times. During one of these stays, I awoke in the middle of the night to find myself lying in a pool of sweat, my head aching, and a profound feeling of heat penetrating my body. I was so hot and so sweaty that I, of course, concluded that I must be moments away from death via a brain tumor (since my head was hurting). I managed, however, to make it through the night.

The next morning, I said to my brother, "Oh my gosh, last night I woke up and I was so hot! I think I got your sheets really dirty because I couldn't stop sweating. I was so scared because I thought I had a brain tumor!"

"No way!" he exclaimed, "Me too! I woke up hot and sweating and thought that I must have a brain tumor too!"

"I wanted to come and find you but I was so fatigued I thought I should conserve my energy so I just lay there all night thinking it might be my last," I shouted.

"Me too!" he yelled.

"Well, what was it then? Are we both dying?" I asked.

"No," he laughed, "I checked the air conditioner this morning when I got up and it's broken." We realized we were definitely raised in the same household and laughed until our eyes almost popped out of our heads.

Negative thinking manifests in other ways too. Maybe you're driving down the street and you think, "At any minute, the ladder could fly off of that truck, crash through my windshield, and kill me." Or, maybe you are sitting outside one day and your mind suggests, "You know, a meteorite could hit the earth at any given moment and destroy all life forms." Some lucky folks never have these thoughts at all. What about the rest of us though? Are we destined to forever carry a pill in our pockets "just in case?"

Negative thoughts are so difficult to still, especially with the horrible images and stories we are bombarded with on a daily basis. I find it very hard to tolerate the news sometimes. Yet, on the other hand, I want to be an informed citizen of the world. There seems to be a fine line between viewing and observing the news and allowing ourselves to be affected unnecessarily by it. Sometimes, we can be affected by bad news in very positive ways. Negative images and situations can provide an incredible impetus for change. Look at the sit-ins and civil rights marches of the 60's. Other times, we allow ourselves to become invaded by negativity and project problems into our lives that don't even exist. The reality of it is, there are millions of sick people in the world dealing with real life or death situations every single day. Likewise, there are millions of healthy people torturing themselves with the thought that they might or could get sick on any given day.

For a diagnosed illness, there is typically a treatment plan to follow. When it comes to negative thoughts, we're on our own.

What can we do to calm our minds and get rid of, or at least minimize, our negative thinking? According to yogic philosophy, our minds are like monkeys. Wild and unpredictable. I like to think of the mind as a wild horse. Wild horses, by nature, are like monkeys. Given the chance, a wild horse will certainly choose to throw a person off rather than be ridden. I know I would if I were a horse! In order to tame a horse, it must be broken. In other words, the nature of the horse is to be wild until someone takes the time to tame it. This takes tremendous time, dedication, and effort. The mind is like a wild horse. The nature of the mind is to be wild until we tame it. Now, our other organs don't have to be tamed ordinarily. Unless we are born with a genetic defect, the heart beats as it should, the bladder does what it's meant to, the stomach digests without direction, etc. The mind is very different and must be trained. We actually have to use the mind to tell the mind what we want it to do and not do.

The question then becomes, how do we train the mind? If we want to train a wild horse, we can easily find manuals, books, and articles devoted to this practice. We can easily find manuals, books, and articles devoted to training the mind as well. However, I would argue that training the mind isn't something to be studied or summarized in an article, but something that should be practiced over and over again. In my humble opinion, the best way to train the mind is through yoga and meditation. Some people, however, are turned off by this idea. I overheard someone say recently, "I can't meditate. I just can't sit still long enough." I cannot think of a more fitting candidate for meditation than someone who feels unable to sit still. Sitting still is a challenge because, in our culture, we are so focused on "doing," rather than "being."

For people who find it difficult to sit still and meditate, I think the best approach is to begin with a chanting meditation that involves a mudra and possibly a visualization as well. The mantra is crucial because it redirects our thinking. Since it is virtually impossible for most of us to just sit down and clear our thoughts entirely, the mantra gives us something positive to think about and concentrate on. The mudra also gives us something to think about and focus on. In other words, we have something to "do" while we're meditating. This is a terrific way to ease into a meditation practice and become accustomed to sitting still. The next step, of course, is to attempt to wean yourself off of the mantra and eventually become comfortable with sitting in silence and stillness for prolonged periods of time.

This can be an arduous process. When I am meditating and my mind starts to wander, I visualize my mind as a horse and I remind myself that, even though the horse is allowing me to ride it, I still have to constantly maintain control over its movements. Everyone who has ever been horseback riding knows that, if you ease up on the reins for an instant, the horse will lower its head to eat the grass on the ground or wander off aimlessly on its own course, most likely, in the direction of the stable. So, like the mind, once the horse is tamed, it still has to be guided and controlled. If I begin to lose focus while meditating, I imagine myself tightening the reins, picking the horse's head back up, and leading the way. I focus on the sound of my own breath and bring myself back to the present moment. I remind myself that my mind, like the horse, isn't good or bad, it just needs my constant guidance. It is just wild by nature and needs to be tamed.

This is what yoga and meditation do. They help us to tame and control the wild horse of our mind. Over time, a yoga and meditation practice should extend beyond the four corners of our sticky mats and influence each and every aspect of our lives. We become more able to see, focus, and think clearly so that we can slow down and, eventually, rid ourselves of negative thinking. When we can have a better grasp of how we allow our thoughts to pollute our minds, we become happier and healthier individuals who are better able to serve others. Yoga helps us to feel centered when the pressures and demands of society cause us to feel an unraveling. Yoga calms us when we allow outside influences to plant seeds of negativity and doubt in us. Yoga reassures us that we need look no further than our own breath for the ability to deal with life's many challenges. A spiritual technology to still the wild horse of the mind – this is what yoga is to me.

Suzann Bain

www.suzannbain.com

Suzann holds a bachelor's degree in English from the University of Central Florida and a juris doctorate degree from Nova Southeastern University Shepard Broad Law School.

As a Yogi, she completed a 7-month teacher training at The Kundalini Yoga Center in Altamonte Springs, Florida and was certified by the Kundalini Research Institute to teach Kundalini yoga. She currently incorporates long deep yogic breathing into a "Negotiation and Deal Making" class that she teaches at a university in Orlando.

A musician (guitarist and songwriter) since she was 15 years old, Bain produces music for yoga and the genre of mind/body. She co-produced the successful "Ajani" series of yoga CDs for Muscle Mixes Music and recently released a yoga CD entitled, "Honey Onyx: Volume I" with Fitness Initiatives, LLC. Bain also produced songs for "Final Cuts 5" on the Muscle Mixes label for high-energy workouts. "Ajani" has been featured in Body + Soul Magazine, YOGA Magazine, Enlightened Practice Magazine, and IDEA Fitness Journal.

Passionate about the relationship between yoga and music, she is the Group Leader of the Yoga and Music group for the Yoga Journal Community. Bain's article, "A Little Too Much Happiness?" was featured on www.ecolifenews.org.

SELF CARE YOGA

KATE FOREST

I took my first yoga and mindfulness class ten years ago. It was a full day workshop with yoga in the form of postures, breathing techniques, conscious listening exercises, mindful eating, walking meditation, and sitting meditation.

Parts of the day were very challenging for me, especially the stillness and the quiet. I wasn't used to being still or even slowing down. But that night I noticed a shift in the way I was used to feeling. The underlying anxiety I often experienced was gone. I felt calm and at ease with myself, and my body didn't ache.

Prior to discovering yoga, I had tried many ways to lower my stress level, but nothing came close to the peaceful feeling I was experiencing after just one day of yoga. I knew that night that I had found a way to live with greater depth and joy. What I didn't know at the time was that this peaceful feeling I was experiencing would affect my life on so many levels, and that this new self-awareness was the first step to positive changes in my body, my mind, and my life.

As a continuing student of yoga and mindfulness, I am reminded that when I practice self-care I am better able to support and care for those around me, with greater love, patience, and compassion. I also remember that when I didn't practice self-care I was more impatient, frustrated, tired and overwhelmed. When I'm more conscious, more present with and connected to myself, I am more present and connected with others. Because of this, I enjoy my moments more, and I laugh so much more.

Over the years my teachings have evolved into what I now call Self Care Yoga.

I encourage students to explore their needs by paying attention to what their bodies are asking of them. In class we move very slowly and mindfully into and out of each posture. We explore our edges and respect our current limitations.

I ask students not to compare themselves with others, reminding them to accept their bodies as they are this week, in this moment. I ask them to release rush-mode and give themselves permission to slow down. I remind them again and again to reconnect and bring their wandering minds back into their bodies.

I remind them that this is their time. Their time to reconnect, and replenish, and practice self-care. I have come to know that practicing self-care is a form of self-love. I don't mean self-care in a selfish or narcissistic way, but self-care in a nurturing and replenishing way.

I have a series of yoga postures and other mindful movements I do when I work at my desk, when I do my dishes, as I blow-dry my hair, even as I vacuum my house and weed my garden. I use conscious breathing and mindful movements throughout my day to keep tension from creeping into my body or my mind. In these ways, in these small moments of mindfulness, I am able to fit self-care into even my busiest days. These techniques help me to release stress and stay focused, they also help me to feel more connected with myself and those around me. I encourage all students of yoga to do this in addition to their regular practice.

I believe that self-awareness, observing our behavior, is the first step to realizing we do have a choice in how we react to stressful and challenging situations. The next step is teaching ourselves to change. This is not always easy, but it is possible.

What follows are a few of the core concepts of my personal practice and my teachings at this point in my life.

CORE CONCEPTS OF SELF CARE YOGA

Move, breathe, and think mindfully as you go through your day.

Support yourself so you are better able to support others.

Observe your behavior. Notice your reaction to stressful situations and breathe through them.

Treat yourself and others with loving-kindness and respect.

Practice mindful breathing techniques throughout your day to improve your physical and emotional health.

Challenge yourself, step through your edges, and practice self-care at the same time.

Incorporate moments of mindfulness into each day.

NINE WAYS TO INTEGRATE THESE CONCEPTS INTO YOUR LIFE

Below are just a few of the many ways that I keep myself connected to the moment and release tension from my body and mind using yoga postures and other mindfulness based techniques. Before you practice any of the yoga postures below, please speak with a qualified yoga teacher for proper instruction. Remember to move slowly and mindfully, and to stay connected mind, body, breath, and moment.

In the morning before you get out of bed bring your knees to your chest and hold them for a few long easy breaths, then do a gentle twist on each side. This morning routine will only take a few moments and will help you to ease morning tightness and quiet your mind before you rush into your day.

When you get in your car, as you put the key in the ignition take a long slow breath and relax your muscles as you lean back into the seat. Take this connection and this self-awareness with you into your driving experience.

As you sit at your desk, keep your body from tightening up by doing a few gentle cat and cow tilts, or neck stretches, or a seated twist. Or stand up and stretch your arms over your head for a few long slow breaths. This will help to ease tension from your back and shoulders, and to keep you awake and focused.

Engage your senses. Pause before your first sip of morning coffee or tea. Feel the warmth of the mug in your hands, breathe in the aroma and relax your shoulders as you exhale.

Ask yourself powerful questions such as: "What is one thing I can do to simplify my life?" Or, "What is one character trait I'd like to further develop in myself ?"

If you're having trouble falling asleep at night, place your hands on your belly or sides and notice how the breath is moving your body each time you breathe. Focus on slowing down the breath and letting it fill you slightly deeper than is normal for you in that moment. Each time you exhale focus on the slow release of air as you let your muscles relax into the bed. This will give your mind other thoughts to focus on besides the ones keeping you awake.

As you sit down to dinner, pause for a breath. This will help you to leave the stress of your day behind and be present with yourself, your loved ones, and your food. It can also help you to slow down and to be more mindful of how you are eating.

Notice your reaction to distraction and reconnect mind, body, and breath as a way to ease your tension and bring yourself back to the present moment.

Bring the mind, body, breath connection with you into your other exercise routines.

HOW MY PERSONAL PRACTICE AND STUDY OF THE TEACHINGS OF YOGA HAVE HELPED ME

To grow into a kinder and more compassionate human being.

To acknowledge my mistakes, learn their lessons, forgive myself, and grow forward.

To cultivate a deep sense of gratitude for the many gifts in this life.

To speak less and listen more.

To know that every time I hug a loved one goodbye could be the last time.

To be comfortable with quiet and stillness.

To acknowledge when I need help and ask for help when I need it.

To think for myself.

To overcome many self-limiting beliefs.

To disagree out loud.

To strengthen many relationships in my life and release others.

To realize that I always have a choice, and that with every decision I make I am either moving closer to, or farther away from physical health, emotional balance, and spiritual well-being.

To be present in this moment. Not worried about the past or anxious about the future. Not living in my head, but present in my body. Right here. Right now.

To acknowledge my strengths and to help others to acknowledge theirs.

As a teacher and student, I am grateful to see the practice of yoga becoming more widely accepted and understood in America today. I see physicians and therapists referring their patients to yoga, and teachers and children in school systems in many parts of our country are practicing yoga. More people are seeing yoga as a tool for stress release, physical rehabilitation, and emotional balance, as well as a source of community, and an important part of their lives.

There are all kinds of teachers with all kinds of personalities, philosophies, and trainings. Each one is in some way unique. All teachers and styles of yoga are beneficial to some, but you must find the yoga that feels right to your body, to your heart, and to your beliefs. Keep searching until you find the right fit for you at this point in your life.

And whatever style speaks to you, it is essential that you learn to listen to your body and honor your needs in yoga class. Also, know that your needs will likely change over the years and be willing to explore these changes as your practice evolves.

"Be the change you are seeking in the world." ~ Mahatma Ghandi

Kate Forest

www.kateforest.com

In my nine years of teaching yoga and mindfulness based stress reduction techniques I have taught thousands of yoga classes. For nearly six years I owned and operated a yoga center in my hometown of Wilbraham, MA. I now teach onsite yoga classes in gymnasiums, conference rooms, senior centers, and wellness centers, teaching to students of all ages and abilities.

My trainings and personal practice include yoga, meditation, non-violent communication, stress reduction, and self-care. I am a Registered Yoga Teacher with the Yoga Alliance as an RYT 500, with over one thousand hours of yoga teacher training. My teachings and personal practice have evolved into what I call *Self Care Yoga*, a healing style of yoga with emphasis on the mind, body, breath connection, and on bringing this connection into everyday life.

My intention as a yoga instructor is to share the benefits I have gained from my personal practice with others. In addition to the practice of yoga, I offer students mindful living techniques to practice outside of class, which help them to integrate self-care into their busy lives. This benefits not only the students, but those around them as well.

Kate is a Mindful Living Consultant & Author.

THE ZEN OF YOGA:
HAPPY, HEALTHY, AND ALIVE
FINDING YOUR SPIRITUAL ESSENCE

AARON HOOPES

Everyone has had moments in life when everything became bright, clear and alive – everything was perfect. There was a glimpse of pure awareness, when past and future no longer existed and total attention was focused on the moment.

At that one point in time you were aware of your spirit. Your aches and pains vanished. Your worries and problems faded away. All of your wants, needs, and desires disappeared. For that moment you weren't just experiencing life – you *were* the experience. Your body and mind were in perfect coordination, and you were completely open to your spiritual essence.

It is easy to define the body. It is your physical presence. You can see it when you look in the mirror. The mind is not as tangible but it is also ever present. It is the conscious essence in your head that defines who you are in the physical world. The spirit, however, is more elusive. It is not easy to put your finger on because it is much more than the in-the-world entity you define yourself as. Your spirit is connected to the infinite essence of the universe, and trying to restrict it and define it is as futile as trying to grasp water. The harder you try to hold it, the faster it slips through your fingers. When you look for it, it is not there, yet at the same time it is everywhere. It is your true being. If you try to define it, categorize it, or put it under a microscope to study, it will still remain beyond your reach.

So how do we discuss the spirit without being able to discuss it? We do it by concentrating on the parts of ourselves we *are* able to discuss and allow the spirit to arise of its own accord. A healthy, happy and energized body and a calm, clear, quiet mind offer fertile ground for the spirit to grow and flourish. By combining body awareness with mind awareness we can cultivate a state of being that is in the highest degree receptive to the spirit and capable of experiencing the ultimate fullness of existence.

BODY AWARENESS

The body can go for days, even weeks without food. It fails after two or three days without water. But it is virtually impossible to go without breathing for more than a few minutes. Without fresh oxygen to the brain the bodily systems quickly shut down and we die. Breathing is a natural and automatic function. The body works efficiently without us having to pay attention to our breathing. This normal, everyday breathing can be defined as unconscious breathing. It brings just enough oxygen into the body to keep it working. Unconscious breathing, though meager, is adequate as long as the body is healthy and active. But what happens if there is an accident, sickness, or trauma? Without an excess of stored energy, there are no reserves to tap into when needed. It becomes difficult for the body to repair itself.

Conscious breathing is the process of modifying the body's breathing rhythm to maximize energy intake. Nearly four thousand years ago in ancient China and India people understood that becoming conscious of the body as it is breathing is the key to a long, healthy life. Just the action of noticing the breath brings our awareness to it and increases its quality. One of the most common themes in the teachings offered by spiritual leaders is the principle of internal cleansing, getting rid of that which is old, worn out, and stale, and exchanging it for what is new, fresh, and energized. That, of course, is the central principle of conscious breathing as well. During inhalation we are bringing in fresh oxygen, nutrients, and vital energy. During exhalation we are expelling carbon dioxide and other toxins and poisons that we produce or collect in our daily living.

The deep rhythmic respiration of the abdominal cavity during breathing exercises brings another, more hidden benefit. The vigorous expansion and contraction of the diaphragm acts as an internal massage of the stomach, liver, kidneys, spleen, and intestines. This passive massage strengthens and energizes the internal organs, making them less susceptible to disease and degeneration.

The change from unconscious to conscious breathing is accomplished by becoming more aware of your breathing and your body. Most of our behavior is unconscious. We walk around in our bodies rarely noticing how they feel, unless there is pain. Seldom do we consciously think of the body as feeling good, but feeling good shouldn't be an absence of pain. It should be an invigorated, energetic state where we are comfortable and happy in our bodies. Becoming aware of our breath is a way to reach that feeling. Expanding our breathing ability is a way of extending that feeling. The key, however, is not to force it, just slow down, relax and breathe.

MIND AWARENESS

Rows of skinny, bald monks sit in a cold, empty room and chant hour after hour, stopping just long enough to eat a bowl of dry rice. For many people that is the first image that comes to mind when they hear the word "meditation." In reality, that is only one extreme of what meditation truly is. At its core, meditation is simply seeking peace within. It is about seeking calmness within the mind.

Have you ever stood still and calmly watched a sunrise or sunset? Have you ever sat in a peaceful setting by a stream or waterfall, or on a windy hill, or deep in the woods and simply listened intently? Have you ever allowed yourself to become so immersed in something that the outside world disappeared, leaving you existing in that solitary moment? If so, you have already experienced meditation. At its most basic, meditation is the practice of existing in a quiet place, turning the attention inwards, and following a pattern of breathing that helps both still the body and calm the mind. By concentrating on your breathing and letting your thoughts flow of their own accord, you open yourself to finding a deep inner stillness and contentment that can help you deal with the stresses and tensions of life. This kind of meditation is easily accessible to everyone.

Usually the mind is so preoccupied with ordinary day-to-day distractions and the relentless flood of information the world drowns us in, that it flounders and fails to connect with the true reality of existence. The mind has been swept up in a never-ending stream of consciousness that prevents us from taking a moment to ask ourselves if that is really how we want to think or the way we want to feel.

The stream of thought that rushes through your mind all day is like static that obscures the peace and tranquility of the spirit. The calmer the mind, the longer the spaces between thoughts and the more peaceful you become.

The measured lifestyle and close contact with nature that characterizes more traditional societies is being lost. People today gobble up experiences, swallow them whole, and then stuff more in. As these undigested experiences accumulate, existence becomes more superficial. Watching television has become a substitute for real experience and even that rarely holds our attention for long – we click to the next channel. Vicariously living through the stimulus overload has dulled the senses to the magic of real life. The rapid pace of technological advances creates a sense of urgency while the high-speed transfer of data through the Internet and telephone systems brings an immediacy to everything. When we finally do go out and do something, we often feel driven by an ego-based urge to get through it as fast as possible.

In contrast to this, you need to find a state of pure calmness unfazed by the pace of the world around you and the myriad of unbidden thoughts that vie for attention in your mind, a state of peace and tranquility that enables you to relax and enjoy the sense of your inner and outer selves being in tune with each other. The mind is not turned off. Instead, it is slowed down and sufficiently quieted so you can clearly envision and capture the essence of self. Once you reach this state your mind has been freed of its habitual thought patterns. You can begin to open up to all the possibilities of existence and experience because a simple, quiet calmness pervades your being. And you will begin to understand what meditation means. At its most basic level, meditation involves simply sitting quietly and breathing deeply. Keep that in mind as you begin the process.

THE ZEN OF YOGA

Awareness is at the heart of all breathing, stretching, movement and meditation exercises. It is the pathway to putting your mind in tune with your body. Body and mind reflect each other. As one calms, the other relaxes and vice versa.

The combination of Zen and Yoga blends together the different philosophies of various Eastern health and fitness traditions. The philosophy of Zen, as embodied in the graceful movements of Tai Chi, the energized breathing of Qigong, and the calm serenity of Zen Meditation presents a beautiful contrast to the peaceful stretching and breathing exercises of traditional Indian Yoga. It is a holistic exploration of living in the present moment and being fully alive.

Let's begin with Zen. What is Zen?

Well, Zen is... Sorry, it's not that easy. As anyone who has looked into Zen knows, attempting to define Zen is like trying to catch a fish with your bare hands. It immediately wriggles between your fingers and slips away. The more you seek it, the harder it is to find. For starters let's just say that Zen is conscious awareness of this present moment of existence. The roots of Zen are based in ancient Chinese philosophy that was concerned with the integration of the disparate aspects of the self into one complete and divine being.

Zen was eventually brought to Japan where it became the foundation of the Bushido code, the way of the warrior. The samurai, who lived their lives at the edge of a sword and could die at any moment, were taught to concentrate on and immerse themselves in the here and now in order to connect with the fundamental core of their being. It helped them develop the powers of concentration, self-control, awareness and tranquility. If they approached each battle as if it were their last, they would be able to have every part of their being at their disposal. To practice Zen is to live fully and completely right here and right now.

SO LET'S NOW TURN TO YOGA. WHAT IS YOGA?

Yoga originated in India. The word "Yoga" is derived from the Sanskrit root *yug* meaning to join together and direct one's attention. It is the union of the body and mind with our spiritual nature. It is also the union of the individual with the Universal Spirit. At its most basic, Yoga is any practice that can turn its practitioners inward to find and experience their spiritual essence. When one is able to bring their own body, mind and spirit into health and harmony, then they can bring health and harmony to those around them and even to the world as a whole. Yoga is much more than a physical practice. It teaches us the way to treat the body with reverence in order to give the spirit or soul a special place to reside and flourish. Yoga is mental as well as physical, psychological as well as spiritual. It teaches a way to turn inward and explore the inner core of being.

There are many different methods of practicing Yoga. Some deal mainly with dynamic physical postures, while others concentrate primarily on breathing exercises, chanting or meditation. The underlying philosophy of Yoga is that of wholeness, wholeness within the individual and wholeness in the individual's connection to the world. When there is coordination between the body, mind and spirit, there is a connection to the divine part of us.

So that brings us to Zen Yoga. By putting Zen and Yoga together we get a holistic system that unites all aspects of the human self by meeting the fundamental needs of physical health, mental clarity and spiritual peace. It is a spiritual discipline that is vast and profound. It is both Zen and Yoga. Through the integration of body, mind and spirit Zen Yoga creates flexibility, health, vitality and peace of mind. The pace of modern life is characterized by hectic social and economic activity. We generate stress in our daily lives as our concentration is fractured and our energy is sapped. Exercise is put on the back burner because we are so caught up in all of the other things that are demanding our attention. Zen Yoga seeks to reverse this flow by bringing into balance proper and effective breathing, energizing movement, and deep relaxation practices.

Zen Yoga seeks to challenge you to realize your own potential by stretching, moving, breathing and meditating at your own pace. It is not a competition. It is not a contest. It is simply a way to feel better and better, to be happy and healthy, and to enjoy life to the fullest. Zen Yoga offers the opportunity to become aware of the spiritual essence that exists within us all and give it the nourishment it needs to grow and flourish. Zen Yoga is not about what you can't do. It has been designed to be accessible to anyone regardless of their age, level of fitness, state of health or spiritual development. Most of us are seeking more from life. Unfortunately, life itself often gets in the way of our search. Zen Yoga offers an opportunity to get to know the self...to feel happy, healthy and alive.

CONCLUSION

As we move toward awareness of our spiritual selves, the coordination of body and mind is essential. It may seem impossible at first. The body is tangible. It has shape. The mind has no shape. How can we bring these two opposites together? The answer is that they are already together. It is our natural state to have body and mind functioning in harmony. But the rigors of daily living fracture our attention and disrupt our awareness. Our mind is scattered and our breathing is shallow. Our spiritual nature is blocked and remains unable to develop because body and mind are not coordinated.

Coordination and harmony can be brought about through the principles of Zen Yoga. The calmness of body and serenity of mind that results is wonderful. In doing this we break down the barriers between body and mind and allow them to unite again and form our Spirit. By coordinating the body and the mind we lay the fertile ground for our spiritual nature to grow and develop. Each of us has the potential for spiritual self realization, but without the connection between body and mind it is very difficult to get a clear sense of our spirit.

In the end your spiritual nature is unique and it is up to you to discover it on your own. Getting the body breathing and the mind calm gives you the opportunity to explore that. I offer you many blessings and much peace on your journey.

Aaron Hoopes

www.artofzenyoga.com

Aaron Hoopes has spent over twenty-five years studying Tai Chi, Yoga, Zen Shiatsu and other Eastern healing traditions. He created the practice of Zen Yoga to encompass the wisdom he has gained learning from teachers around the world. He has taught hundreds of classes and workshops in Japan, Australia, Canada and the United States.

He is the author of five books including "ZEN YOGA: A Path to Enlightenment through Breathing Movement and Meditation" and "PERFECTING OURSELVES: Coordinating Body, Mind and Spirit."

His bestselling Smart Living series includes "BREATHE SMART: The Secret to Happiness, Health and Long Life", "EAT SMART: The Zen Anti-Diet", and "LIVE SMART: Staying Balanced in a Changing World" (forthcoming).

He is also the creator of the deep relaxation program "INNER SUNRISE", and the "ZEN YOGA" DVD Series.

BEYOND THE GAME OF LIFE

KINO MACGREGOR

When we begin practicing Yoga the deepest part of our consciousness asks for clarity, awakening and truth. What is sometimes the first step in taking positive steps towards the peace that we all yearn for is a recognition of exactly how deeply we are entrenched within our ways of internal warfare.

Yoga, for example, can sometimes be riddled with fierce competition. You might find yourself competing with a new Yoga practitioner in your daily class who is naturally very flexible. Or you might find yourself competing with yourself and comparing your body in a negative light with the way it was last year, last week or yesterday. Yet still you might be competing with your friends and peers. All of this is totally normal because it is totally and completely part of being human.

Ashtanga Yoga, you could even say, creates a fertile ground for the competitor's mind because the postures are taught sequentially based on proficiency. It is even tempting to judge a person's spiritual development by the level of postures they're doing. Yet the real Yoga happens within. It really does not matter how good your lotus position is, how many handstands you can do, or how deep your backbends are if you're unconscious about the way you treat other people, other living beings, and yourself.

Similarly it is often the insurmountable challenge of the six series of Ashtanga Yoga that teaches the most competitive practitioners a very deep and hard lesson--humility. There will always be someone stronger, more flexible, younger, and more knowledgeable than you. There will always be someone doing more Yoga postures than you. You will never get it done and you will never be the best forever if at all. And that is a good thing because it teaches you to learn that although you bring great gifts to Yoga practice and to life, you are not entitled to set yourself on a pedestal high above, away and apart from your fellow human beings. Paradoxically we are all both absolutely unique and totally equal on some level.

The learning that happens within the field of Yoga asks you to embrace both the part of yourself that has a vital contribution to the flow of life and the part of you that is connected to all sentient beings. If you think you're going to beat one of your fellow teammates at the game of life, think again, because life is not an Olympic sport with gold, silver and bronze metals. There is no judge waiting at the finish line to rate your performance, except maybe yourself. The reason why there can be no competition in the deepest sense of life is because the parameters by which life is truly measured are infinite.

The questions most often asked by people who survive a near death experience at the moment of their passing is whether they had loved enough, whether they had been truly happy, whether they had been able to forgive, whether they shared their true beauty with others, and whether they had known real peace. While career, politics, success, money, shopping, drama, fame and fortune are aspects of life that cannot be avoided and can even be fun and entertaining, they are not the parameter for measuring the deepest experience of life. Instead forgiveness, acceptance, peace, beauty, freedom, joy, happiness, and love are the highest truths of life.

Yoga teaches you to ask whether each and every one of your actions answers to these highest truths. There can be no real competition because time has no real meaning in the field of learning in which Yoga takes place. Yoga itself is eternal and universal.

Yet we live in a temporal world where eternity and peace are often far from our daily reality. We live in the shadow of sensationalism, pop culture, and television's ubiquitous theater. Finding the space to truly delve into the dark caverns of consciousness amidst the dramatic interludes of life can be quite challenging. At its best our drama entertains, teaches, and makes people laugh. At its worst it brings out division, hurtfulness, and hatred. Yet human beings are somewhat enthralled with the ups and downs of their own emotions. You might even venture to say we are addicted to them.

It is all too easy to get dragged down into the habit pattern of the mind's sometimes sordid past when emotions flare and all too hard to choose the higher, more peaceful ground above. There is truth to the notion that our inner world is a kind of jungle in need of healing. Freud and Jung sprouted a whole field of study dedicated to untying the knotty landscape of our inner world.

Yet the choice to practice Yoga is a chance to step outside the realm of our penchant for tears and venom. It is no coincidence that the opening mantra of Ashtanga Yoga includes the invocation of a jungle doctor to clear out the poisons held within the mind. Drama as a permanent state of being can be toxic.

Yoga at its best represents an invitation to live a life of inner peace. In such a world peace and empathy take precedence over drama and grievance. When you learn to maintain your composure even when you feel under attack you have learned one of life's hardest lessons-- that is, that drama cannot be solved with more drama. Instead only a peaceful, caring response heals the wounds of the past. Peace, compassion and wisdom have to supplant righteousness, justification and narcissism as the highest priority in any given situation.

There is a vigilance and due diligence you must learn in order to accept the invitation to life without getting caught in the juiciness of humanity. By training the mind to focus on chosen points of attention you develop the strength of character necessary to break the deepest, most restrictive patterns in your life. In doing so you become a true player in the magical game of life.

Yet be clear in understanding that there is nothing wrong with drama itself. Understood as a play in the field of life it can be entertaining and amusing. When given the full weight and importance of your attention, emotionality is heavy, binding, and tragic. One of the great paradoxes of life is that the muddy waters of human drama contain the seed for ultimate awakening. Never is there a moment when your heart aches for peace more than when you are under emotional or physical attack. Never is there a moment when you yearn for freedom more than when you feel most constricted and bound.

So in a sense the very presence of drama in any form in your life is a request for peace and a signal asking for reconciliation. Every situation, no matter how filled with immaturity or insanity, has the potential to enlighten your consciousness to a new level of being.

Sometimes in moments of great need, intensity, or doubt I feel like the world responds to me with a guidance that I can almost read in everything around me, from plants to clouds to situations, as though all of life really is not separate from me and really conspires to lead me towards new realizations. When time slows down long enough to break the pattern of the past, then clarity, connection, wisdom, and grace arrive to trumpet the dawn of a new day. With daily Yoga practice your inner world relaxes into the beauty of life, whole, complete and totally at peace.

You create your reality by the thoughts that you think. Your attention is itself responsible for your life experience. No matter how awful the traffic jam is, how loud your neighbors are, how inconsiderate people may seem, how delayed the airplane is, you are the one who is in control of your reality.

Regardless of what type of experience finds its way into your life, you always have power over your reaction to reality. In doing so, you are the true master of your own fate. Think that life is awful and it is...for you. Think that people are careless, blind and ignorant and they will be...to you. The power of positive thinking is a common topic of conversation, books and seminars in our post-new age, twenty-first century world. Most of us agree that it's a good idea to concentrate our thoughts towards a positive goal, rather than lull around in the doldrums of complaint and whine. The real question lies not in the debate about whether we can create our own reality or not, but rather in the how.

Enter the five thousand year old tradition of which you take part when you practice Yoga. Yoga is a true science of the mind where you actively practice choosing a peaceful response to distressful situations, thus giving you the tools for creating your reality in each moment. When you practice Yoga, you watch your mind's reaction to touching the borders of your physical reality. Your inner dialogue in postures that seem impossible to you parallels your reaction to life situations that push the boundaries of your comfort. Pushing these limits brings up fear, anger, sadness, frustration, and numerous other emotions.

It is easy to let your mind spin away into these temptations. However, with regular practice, you will have the strength to remain calm, focused and aware. It's like the difference between scratching an itch automatically and feeling the itch, then choosing not to scratch. As you remain calm, you are able to choose a peaceful response to your experience and thereby create your own reality.

Wayne Dyer says that it is always possible to stop any life experience and say to yourself, "I can choose peace over this." Yoga gives you a forum to practice saying to yourself that you actually can choose peace over the patterns that you've practiced in the past. You finally have the strength to stop scratching those pesky itches.

Your thoughts are crystal clear in between your breath, posture, and drishti (point of focus). With no one else to blame, nowhere else to run, nothing left to do, start where you are, in the center of your created life experience and begin the dedicated, devotional path towards creating a peaceful life in the present moment, one breath at a time.

Kino MacGregor

www.dynamicself.com

Kino MacGregor is one of a select group of people to receive the certification to teach Ashtanga Yoga by its founder Sri K. Pattabhi Jois in Mysore, India. The youngest woman to hold this title, she has completed the challenging Third Series and is now learning the Fourth Series with Guruji and Sharath.

Kino and her husband Tim Feldmann are the founders of Miami Life Center, a space for Ashtanga Yoga, holistic health and consciousness on Miami Beach, www.miamilifecenter.com. Both teaching locally on Miami Beach and traveling internationally, you will find Kino leading classes, privates, workshops, Yoga conferences and retreats in traditional Ashtanga Yoga and total life transformation.

As life coach and Ph.D. student in holistic health with a Master's Degree from New York University, Kino integrates her commitment to consciousness and empowerment with her Yoga teaching.

She has been featured in Yoga Journal, Yoga, Mind Body Spirit, Yoga + Joyful Living, Travel & Leisure Magazine, Ocean Drive Magazine, Boca Raton Magazine, Florida Travel & Life Magazine, and Six Degrees Magazine as well as appearing on Miami Beach's Plum TV and the CBS Today Show.

In 2008 she produced two Ashtanga yoga DVDs, "Kino MacGregor - A Journey" and "A Workshop; Ashtanga Yoga Primary Series"), and a yoga practice card and is currently working on her first book, Inner Peace, Irresistible Beauty.

DENYING, BUYING, TRYING, APPLYING
THE FOUR STAGES OF GETTING INTO YOGA

DONNA BROWN

Let's look at the stages one goes through in the process of discovering what yoga is. Just as anyone who is dealing with a chronic illness or is encountering change in their life goes through stages in helping them cope with these changes, there is a similar process involved in accepting and incorporating yoga into your life.

I am not suggesting that yoga be compared to chronic illness. Yet it seems to me that many people do come to yoga when they have health problems, as opposed to when they are healthy.

Here are the stages of yoga practice I have observed over my 12 years of teaching:

DENYING

Whenever confronted with anything new in our lives or something that involves change, we tend to dig our feet in and resist, not knowing what to expect. When you are first introduced to yoga, you are likely to hesitate and counter with, "Who me? I already work out at the gym." Or I have heard people say, "Nah, I'm not flexible enough, and besides don't you have to put your foot behind your head?" Another common retort I often hear is, "I'm too busy." Well, guess what, we are ALL too busy, and that's all the more why we need to do yoga!

I first discovered yoga at the age of 24 while attending a week long yoga retreat in the Bahamas. My reason for being there had more to do with location rather then having an actual interest in yoga. The routine was fairly rigorous: awakening early every morning to attend hour long meditation sessions, followed by 2 hours of vigorous yoga practice until being served a sparse breakfast. An even more invigorating 2 hour afternoon practice followed, until another sparse dinner was served.

I prided myself in the fact that I stayed for the whole week without succumbing to joining my friends at McDonald's, yet had no desire to resume the practice after the retreat. I came away from that experience with the impression that yoga involved more lifestyle changes than I was willing to make at the time. What I didn't realize was that even though I didn't practice for many years after the retreat, yoga had still made an impression on me and was gently leading me back to that experience full circle.

BUYING

Yoga is hard to miss! It's done everywhere, in studios, recreation centers and in the work environment, yet before you "buy it", you need to see how it will benefit you. Perhaps all your friends are doing yoga and have said you should at least "try it". Your curiosity is aroused, yet you're still not convinced it's for you.

Or perhaps your doctor has strongly recommended you lose weight, so you decide to put yoga on your mile-long New Year's resolution list. You know it's supposed to be good for you, yet you're not on your deathbed yet, so you put it off.

In my situation, there were no suggestions from friends or doctors. A very challenging health problem known as tinnitus, or ringing in the ears, hit me hard and fast after undergoing surgery. Frustrated with trying to get answers from the numerous doctors I saw, I turned in desperation to yoga to escape the relentless and hideous clamor I was hearing.

At first, I didn't believe that anything would help, yet after a few months of consistent practice, I found relief and a renewed sense of purpose in my life. I also had less of a need to seek answers to the constant questions of "How did this happen?" and "Why me?" These questions were eventually replaced with, "Hey, this stuff really works! Why did I wait so long?" When I did my practice, yoga became a peaceful place within amidst the chaotic noise, and a powerful method of dealing with stress.

TRYING

So you're finally at a yoga class and actually doing those "pretzel" poses that you could never see yourself doing in a million years, and meditating and feeling calm, peaceful and more relaxed than you've been in ages. You finally admit you need yoga in your life.

When I first started my home practice, I found many poses, such as Downward Dog and Warrior I and II, very challenging and resisted doing them for quite awhile, choosing to do easier poses (like Savasana!). I've always been self-critical, and would chastise myself for not being more flexible or able to hold the poses for any length of time.

As time passed, being in the poses felt more natural. The more I practiced, the more confident I became and the more I enjoyed being in the poses, even the more challenging ones such as Handstand and Shoulderstand.

I vividly recall attempting Handstand for the first time. Of course, I used a convenient corner wall and walked my legs up the wall, flipped them over to the other wall, and after doing this routine at least 10,000 times, finally stayed up in the pose. Feeling jubilant and absolutely exhausted, I tried to cheer, yet it's a bit awkward when you're upside down!

After years of practice, I started noticing that instead of just being in a pose, I felt one with the pose. This can best be described as total surrender, or letting go into the pose, the moment, and feeling at peace with myself and the universe. This to me is yoga.

APPLYING

At this stage, you are most likely attending a class or classes at least 1-2 times per week and/or have established a regular home practice. You have also most likely learned or are still learning about the philosophy of yoga, and are trying to apply at least some of the principles such as non-attachment, contentment with what is, being present in the here and now and living fully in the moment.

For some, this is as far as they want to take their practice, yet others wish to pursue teaching and this is the path I chose.

I was regularly attending yoga classes at an ashram for a number of years in addition to working a full time nursing job that was very stressful. The decision to leave nursing was an option I considered for a number of years, yet leaving a steady income was a hard thing to do.

When it was suggested by a teacher at the ashram that I take their month long teacher training, I nonetheless jumped at the chance. Spending a whole month at the ashram immersed in yogic philosophy, meditation, pranayama and chanting was indeed a life transforming experience. This time I was ready to make and embrace the changes required for a more authentic lifestyle that was congruent with the philosophical concepts I had learned during my training.

By the time I completed the training, I was eager to get out into the real world and share what I had learned with my students, yet I still needed to learn how to impart this information. There is a saying, "teaching is an art," and I truly believe that how you teach is just as instrumental in the learning process as what you teach.

A GREAT NEW INSIGHT

Throughout seven incredible years of teaching, I have learned many things from many different teachers, and one in particular stands out in my mind. A few years ago, during a Yoga Therapy teacher training taught by Kaustaub Desikachar, grandson of yoga master, Krishnamacharya, I learned yet another definition of yoga in spite of what I thought yoga is.

At this point, I had been practicing yoga for 6 years and teaching for over a year. I was curious to find out more about specific poses for specific ailments my students presented me with, and when I asked Kaustaub about this he laughingly replied, "So you think yoga is just about asana?"

Hearing this question blew me away, as most of my practice up to that time was focused on asana, and I was about to experience yet another opportunity for growth and learning. "Apparently not", I faltered, turning redder than the shirt he wore, and he further explained that helping change a client's mindset is a more important tool in healing an illness than using specific asanas. He also added that when a person changes their habits, they heal. He explained the difference between curing and healing, curing as relating to disease and healing as referring to the person.

It was at that moment as he held my gaze that I realized the true meaning of the mind-body connection and the wisdom of what he was saying. In the Western medicine tradition, clients are often viewed as the disease rather than the person underneath the disease. Perhaps our illnesses persist and we don't get "cured" because we lack this vital sense of connection to each other and acceptance of who we truly are as individuals. Yoga will always validate your perception of yourself and this is the essence of what yoga is... healing.

Donna Brown

www.healthfuljourney.com

Teaching experience: 7 years as a yoga teacher, 15 years as a professional pantomime who studied with Marcel Marceau.

Teaching style: Hatha and various blends of styles gathered from numerous phenomenal teachers I studied with.

Inspiration for teaching: My students! I love to share what I've learned with students who are ready and/or curious to know. I taught for a number of years at recreation centers, senior centers, and corporations, and finally got up enough courage to open my own yoga studio a year ago, and this has been a challenging, yet truly rewarding teaching experience.

Personal yoga practice: daily meditation, pranayama and at present am doing mainly restorative poses to enable me to continue teaching 2-3 classes at day at my newly opened studio.

"When the teacher is ready, the student will appear…" Anonymous

REVELATIONS FROM A STRAP

ANN BARROS

"Oh, Wow! That transferred up my whole body and affected my entire alignment!" A student in last week's yoga class was referring to the use of a belt tied tautly around her upper thighs as she approached the ascent into Sirsanana, Headstand.

As we made the necessary body adjustments, the student could feel her body posture transform. Another student shared with me that she has experienced great relief to her tension headaches and cramping in her female organs after regular practice of Setu Bandasana (Supported Bridge Pose) which, with the use of props, elevated her chest and pelvic area, allowing her breath to move more deeply and fully into the lungs as she relaxed her facial muscles and brain, closing her eyes and moving deeply into the pose.

These are wonderful revelations for my students as they grow in understanding of the physiological effects of asanas through the correct alignment of the poses. Each asana is a laboratory for self-exploration, a storehouse of body memory and an opportunity to break old patterns. I believe the asana can become more alive, more open, and more exciting as we hold and grow into the pose. Explore it. Deepen it. Gain insight from it. Asana practice can be a tool for growth, physically, emotionally and psychologically, reflecting the union of body, mind and spirit.

On the emotional and spiritual levels, one set of asana stimulates the 'animus' / male part of our inner being. Another set of asanas open the 'anima' / feminine nature. It is useful to know when to practice which sets of asanas for specific concerns. Of equal importance is sequencing in the practice. Which poses stimulate the Sympathetic nervous system, and therefore uplift us; and which poses stimulate the Parasympathetic nervous system with the result of nourishing the heart area and quieting the brain, and in which order should I design my home practice?

Many and various supported poses are antagonistic to Carpal Tunnel Syndrome in the wrist, Scoliosis (Curvature of the Spine), and Arthritis (inflammation and pain) in the joints. Awareness of correct alignment is invaluable in the practice of curative asanas. In India, under the careful guidance of B.K.S. Iyengar, a woman student with an enlarged ovarian cyst avoided surgery by practicing diligently over a period of months a supported pose which helped to nourish her uterus and ovaries, and in time the cyst dissipated.

In the Iyengar tradition of Yoga, which I have been practicing and teaching for 28 years now, particular attention is paid to alignment. My eyes, though well trained are still learning to "see". As I observe a student practicing the asana, I make adjustments, use props, modify, or challenge the pose according to his/her needs, so that he/she can attain maximum benefit for their unique and individual spinal column and well-being.

I love my work, my practice, my classes. After nearly three decades, there is never a dull moment. I am nourished daily by my practice and enjoy changing my relationship to gravity, and discovering new inner sources of strength to hold myself up on my hands, elbows and forearms, my head, one foot and one hand, etc. I am exploring constantly with new props and new challenges for myself and my students.

I was fortunate to study directly with Shri B.K.S. Iyengar in India in 1976 when I was suffering with Scoliosis, my curvature was approximately 2.5cm to the right in the mid-Thoracic vertebrae.

Under his close scrutiny, I endured an intense re-positioning of the musculature of my back and through long held supported traction, my spine went into vertical and perfect alignment. It was not easy or quick; and sometimes I cried, but the discipline and passion to cure my spine was there. The seed of inspiration was then planted in me and has remained my lifelong passion.

At the end of each class I say "Namaste" which means I honor the Divine in you of Love, of Light, of Truth. I honor that place in you and that place in me where we are One.

Ann Barros

www.baliyoga.com

Ann Barros is a senior Iyengar yoga instructor with over 30 years teaching experience, including 5 years at UCSC, where she introduced the Iyengar tradition to the Santa Cruz, California community. She has led over 40 successful Yoga In Bali tours.

Ann has led workshops both domestically in California and Colorado, and internationally in Singapore, Jamaica, Greece, Mexico, Jakarta, Kuala Lumpur, and China, as well as her beloved Bali, which has become her second home.

Ann first studied with BKS Iyengar in India in 1976. He personally guided her into curing her own Scoliosis. She is certified by the Iyengar Yoga Institute of S.F. since 1980, and later that year, after studying again in India, first came to Bali.

FROM ASANA TO THE INNERMOST PLACES OF MY HEART - YOGA AS LIFE JOURNEY

SUSAN KRANTZ

When I first started taking yoga classes at the age of 17 my quest was a flexible trim body. In a few years time, I lost interest in yoga – the āsanas were too easy. So I moved on to other physical challenges – running and the renovation of our 1890 dilapidated mansard-roofed house. I severely injured my shoulder working on that house. When my physician informed me that I would need surgery to repair my shoulder and that ultimately he could not guarantee 100 % range of motion, maybe I would have 75 % after surgery, I was emotionally devastated. As I was sitting in an ice cream store sugaring my emotions with my husband and lamenting about my pain and options for recovery, a yoga therapist overheard me and handed me her business card.

I returned to yoga, this time for healing. The therapy was challenging and the yoga was very different than attending a group yoga class. The session was focused on my needs, and as we progressed so did the yoga – and not just āsana, but also prāṇāyāma, meditation and yoga nidrā. It took close to two years, working intensively with a yoga therapist and massage therapist. Through this yoga work of physical healing I was introduced to spiritual yoga practice. My teacher encouraged me to study this ancient science/art, first to learn more about myself for myself, and eventually to teach others.

In the evolution of my experience of Svādhyāya (self-study) and teaching, as a witness and observer of my own physical, emotional, and spiritual challenges, I now define yoga as "the relationship one has with one's self--to learn to trust one's intuition and ability to discern what are the right choices for the self". This process of learning about, strengthening, and deepening the relationship with the self takes time and is a continuous journey of the Hṛdaya (heart), Deha (body), Manaha (mind) and Jīva (soul).

To care for one's self – first – places the self in a position of calm strength and allows for the unfolding of an innate direction. We can then care for our families and friends, choose careers that speak to our Dharma, and live a life in harmony with our deepest wishes.

I teach the method of Viniyoga best taught in the personal relationship of student and teacher, with the added dimension of Ayurveda as a means of self-care: Yoga as Therapy, Healing and Prevention. From Yoga Philosophy I apply the Pança Maya model in daily life:

ANNAMAYA

Annamaya is about taking care of the physical body – everything conceivable from exercise, nutrition, massage, how we use our body, and Ritucharya - the seasonal adaptations of āsana practice, nutrition and other appropriate forms of exercise. For instance I am more physically active in the summer through gardening, walking, beachcombing, so my āsana practice changes to accommodate my other physical activities. In the winter I am more sedentary and my joints ache in the cold, so I remedy joint pain with herbs, teas, diet and exercise, a langhana (gentle) yoga practice, and I use a treadmill to simulate my warmer weather walking. I adjust nutritional needs to accommodate the seasons – more protein in winter, more carbohydrates in summer, and a low fat diet (greens) in the spring to burn off any excess fat accumulated in winter. The idea is to nourish our physical bodies to prevent disease and optimize functioning of the neuromuscular/skeletal structure.

PRĀṆĀMAYA

This dimension incorporates Prāṇāyāma (breathing practices) to energize our Prana (vital energy). This encourages the development of the breath to enhance energy, to calm the mind and physiology, and to connect with a deep awareness of our body, mind and emotions. We accomplish this by developing breathing ratios and breath capacity during and after āsana practice in order to further the connection and positively influence the nervous system, respiratory system, circulatory system, and ultimately to manage Prana (vital energy). In the Spring I focus on Kapālabhati (a vigorous Prāṇāyāma to help burn off excess weight or lethargic energy accumulated over the winter months). In Summer I use a cooling Prāṇāyāma technique, Śītalī or Śītkārī, and in Winter, Nāḍī Śodhana. I manage my energy daily and seasonally so that I can function with calmness and equanimity.

MANOMAYA

This dimension is to develop our intellect and directly relates to our capacity to learn and adjust to life circumstances. I continue to develop my mind through education, continuing studies in Ayurveda, Yoga Sutras and Sanskrit, and through developing other interests such as hobbies, travel, and having fun with friends.

VIJÑĀNAMAYA

Our personalities are shaped by many influences, including our past, attitudes, perceptions, values, communication, and our relationships, to name a few. Patañjali's Yoga Sutras are aphorisms that are chanted as tools to refine the mind and personality so we can hone the kernel of who we are (as compared to who we think we are and all the perceptions/misperceptions we encounter in life), and get to the essence of our being and indeed of life itself. I find this dimension to also be the place where I connect to creativity and creative intelligence. This allows me to promote good will, health and harmony for myself, for my familiar relationships, and indeed, for all whom I meet.

ĀNANDAMAYA

Our emotions can rule us and yet they are so fleeting. Sit for a moment when you are angry or sad and simply watch/listen to your thoughts. Then imagine being free of those thoughts so that you respond instead of reacting in a knee-jerk fashion. I access this aspect of my being through meditation, so I can connect to my heart's deepest desires, and live my life through the intention of those desires. My joy of life and living shines through in my actions and words, and helps inspire the lives of others. Prayer connects me to my Divine pure essence.

So what attracts many people to yoga is the physical practice. The physicality certainly attracted me in the beginning. But when those poses were mastered, I was bored. When I was injured, now that is when the journey of discovery and mastery began. I had the "aha" moment of realizing that the āsanas were the beginning of the connection to the innermost places of my mind and heart. Mastery of the mind, liberation from suffering, and connecting with the Divine are the ultimate goals of yoga. And those goals continue to be a life-long endeavor. It matters not where we start or why. Once I began the journey, there was no turning back.

Susan Krantz

www.viniyogajourney.com

Susan Krantz, ERYT (500), RYTT (500) is certified by the American Viniyoga Institute (AVI) as a Yoga Therapist and Yoga teacher/educator.

Susan has been teaching yoga since 1999 offering classes for individuals and groups, and workshops. She has taught in a variety of studio and wellness settings, and has assisted in the training of yoga teachers.

Susan works therapeutically with people with a variety of different conditions: pain management, stress management, post-surgery recovery, shoulder pain, back pain and sciatica, breast cancer, anxiety, arthritis, MS, Fibromyalgia and many other conditions.

Susan also develops and leads workshops such as "Developing a Personal Yoga Practice", "Yoga for Chronic Low Back Pain: Develop a Healthy Back", "Prenatal Yoga", "Osteoporosis and Yoga", and "Restorative Yoga."

Susan is also a certified Ayurvedic Life-Style Counselor through the American Institute of Vedic Studies.

SOMETHING MAGICAL HAPPENS

NATALIE MAISEL

What is yoga? Well, if you think about it, what isn't yoga? It's been my personal quest to prove that yoga is truly for any "body" and everybody, regardless of size, age or physical issues.

I began my yogic adventure when a yoga studio opened up in the heart of Pasadena, TX. And, if any of you are familiar with the rural culture and refineries of Pasadena, TX, you, too, will be amazed that this came to pass in the early 90's.

Being the eternal cheerleader type (petite, flexible and energetic) I started my yoga practice to learn to meditate. Meditation always sounded so mysterious to me. Growing up where I did, you weren't surrounded by those seeming to follow "alternative paths". But, I will say that I've grown to feel differently about that.

I remember tree pose was a huge challenge to me at first. The teacher said that to still the mind is to still the body, and that one can't have a mental circus going on and maintain the pose. Boy, was she right. My young, eager mind jumped from college to work to boyfriends and all around until I finally "got" the pose and found some pathways of cranial clearing. This was my first taste of mental freedom, and I wanted more.

And, so, after staying with the program and graduating into the upper levels of classes, I began my certification process and then started teaching classes on my own, initiating yoga programs in franchise gym locations, as well as opening a yoga studio several years down the road, and still teaching to this day.

I want to debunk the myth that yoga is only serious. Yoga is just like the most complicated human being (which means all of us) -- yoga is soft and fierce, relaxed and energizing, forgiving and demanding, humorous and serene. It's all there. You can run the whole gamut of emotions in just one yoga class, and I believe that's where the transformation lives. And, if we each can just allow the yoga to take its place, filling us up like a sponge, the yoga will go where it needs to go and we will expand and grow with it.

I've always said that one teaches what one needs to learn. I didn't make that up, someone much wiser than I am did, but I do believe it. When I began my practice I hated to sit still. And, at times, it can remain a challenge. But I have to admit that looking forward to a nice, restorative shavasana is truly one of life's simple pleasures. How often do we just "receive"? We are often so busy doing things and going places and making mental agendas, but I've learned that shavasana has healing benefits that no over-the-counter medicine can touch.

In my yogic journey, I've met the die-hards, the purists, the show-offs, the slackers. I've met those who knew Sanskrit from A-Z, and those that didn't know a sutra from a sultan. So, who am I? Well, depending on who you ask, I'm all of those people. But, I will say that the one common thread we all share is that we are each expressing the yogi or yogini within ourselves to our own level of understanding and expression. And THAT, to me, is yoga.

As a teacher something magical happens the moment I sit down to teach. The room becomes quiet, the students begin to settle themselves, the breath begins to resonate audibly, and something bigger and more powerful takes me over and it's as if I've hit some invisible button that re-sets me to the highest place that I can be in. I think this is the greatest benefit that I could possibly receive. Because, when I am in that place in me, it helps others to be in that place in them. And that is the experience of Namaste.

Do I have an extreme and regimented practice? No. But, I do feel that the effects of yoga are cumulative. At least that's what I'd like to believe. At times, I find that I mindlessly, and yes that was not misspoken, I mindlessly find myself in a yoga pose or focusing on my breath without really intending to "do" yoga. I've come to understand that yoga is not always doing. It just happens after it becomes a part of you, almost like putting one foot in front of the other. It's simply there.

Of course I do take time to take classes from others, attend huge yoga conferences, teach at conferences, travel to destination spas to teach, work privately with students, do my own at-home yoga and still bring yoga to the masses at gym locations. I do what I can. I do what works. I try my best not to guilt myself for not doing yoga as much as I sometimes think I should. It's a teacher's excuse, "well, I AM always teaching, you know". The beauty is that it's all there...in every class I teach or participate in, the highest awareness presents itself and I remember that all I ever needed to know or remember is right there in that moment. Omnipresent, omniscient yoga IS there.

Years ago, I moved out of rural USA, and have since moved to southern California where I'm surrounded by all types of people interested in the healing arts, but I recognize that yoga is a lifestyle, not a fad, not a temporary condition, not like last year's spring shoes. I'm thrilled that one can easily find yoga classes even in the most unlikely of places and know that the golden thread of sangha, community, truly does connect us all.

So, after all that, the bottom line is that yoga is truly whatever you think it is and what makes sense to you. May each day, with whatever it brings to your yoga mat, help you connect with the highest place inside, so that you can share that with others.

Natalie Maisel

www.goddessdownload.com

Natalie has been a certified yoga instructor (ERYT) since 1996 and began her teaching in Maui, Hawaii. After moving back to the mainland, she created Sundance Yoga Studio in TX which was named "Best Yoga Studio in Houston 2002".

She has been featured extensively in Gary Kraftsow's book <u>Yoga for Wellness</u>, and has been reviewed and highlighted numerous times in Luxury Spa Finder magazine and other spa publications for her teaching skills, as well as a yoga segment on Gene Simmons Family Jewels. She hopes that was NOT her 15 minutes of fame!

She also keeps it real by teaching to the masses at a local LA Fitness. She teaches all levels from beginner though advanced: hatha, and eclectic improvisational style flow yoga.

When she's not teaching yoga, being fed by her chef husband, or cuddling with her two cool cats, she's performing massage and also facilitating rituals for the lunar phases and seasonal sabbats.

101 BITE-SIZED ANSWERS TO
WHAT IS YOGA IN AMERICA?

DEBORAH S. BERNSTEIN

WHAT IS YOGA?
ANSWERS IN 101 BITE-SIZED PIECES

1. Asking more questions than the number of stories you tell

2. Taking the path of least resistance when it serves you best

3. Noticing what you are thinking about right now

4. Noticing what you are feeling in your body, right now

5. Noticing your intentions; the conscious and unconscious intentions

6. Being aware of the unintended consequences of your actions - and taking them into consideration

7. Choosing silence over disingenuousness

8. Staying in child's pose (balasana) for ten minutes in the middle of a power yoga class

9. Centering yourself in a posture that is comfortable for you at the beginning of a yoga class

10. Noticing when you are stressed; noticing how your body behaves when you are stressed (clenched jaw, hunched shoulders, pursed lips)

11. Not needing to correct other people every time they misspeak

12. Practicing postures that feel good

13. Recognizing that you do not have the answers to everything, but someone does. Seek out people with answers to interesting questions

14. Realizing when you are thinking and behaving in self absorbed way

15. Allowing others to express their own beliefs without needing to interject your own

16. Practicing postures that strengthen your body

17. Practicing postures that improve your balance

18. Becoming aware of what you experience in your body, mind and breath with each yoga posture

19. Being aware of your motivations each time you act and talk

20. Realizing that your world revolves around you and that everyone else's revolves around someone else's....theirs

21. Letting go of the stories about yourself that "define" you

22. Being aware that whatever you are experiencing at this moment is nothing more or less than what you are experiencing at this moment

23. Knowing that this too, shall pass

24. Substituting, "I do yoga" with "I live yoga"

25. Talking 10 deep breaths a day....so deep that they move your belly

26. Asana without using any mats, blocks, blankets or other props -and honoring your body completely by staying in front of your edge (staying only within a safe range of motion for your body)

27. A practice with one asana, savasana

28. Letting what you do on your yoga mat be an extension of your yoga, rather than a start and end point for your practice

29. Asana in bed

30. Adopting a mantra

31. Allowing "dead air time" in your brain

32. Giving away a book that you covet and haven't read in years

33. Practicing asana in a less than ideal setting, and letting go of the annoyances

34. Letting go of attachment to your yoga mat, spot in the yoga studio, favorite yoga teacher, yoga music.....

35. Being truthful and speaking hurtful truth only when necessary

36. Embracing the transition to death

37. Smiling as you are falling asleep, crying as you are falling asleep

38. Taking a long, silent exhale instead of snapping back with sarcasm

39. Showing up on time when someone is waiting for you

40. Listening more than you speak; try it for one day

41. Giving all of your attention to whomever you are speaking with on the phone (no multi tasking with texting/twittering/watching tv, etc)

42. Tools to help you navigate life

43. Touching the earth with both hands as a reminder that you are connected to something greater than yourself and that you are grounded

44. Allowing loved ones to find happiness on their terms, without remarks

45. Allowing loved ones to make mistakes

46. Noticing when you are holding your breath

47. The inner knowledge that you are OK in this moment

48. Understanding that the only thing we ever really "have" is this moment

49. Accepting that there is not a "right" way to be in a posture, only a "safe" way for your body

50. Noticing your ugly thoughts

51. Allowing yourself an unlimited supply of "start-overs"

52. Sun salutations

53. Meditation

54. Exploring sources of nourishment that serve your physical and emotional selves

55. A set of tools to energize you

56. A set of tools to relax you

57. A set of tools to lead an ethical life

58. Accepting uncertainty

59. Framing change as a constant

60. Allowing yourself to contemplate that whatever is on the other side of life might be ok

61. A compliment to religion

62. Seeing the nastiness and the serenity in a raw, rainy November day

63. That inner knowing that somehow you will be ok again

64. Asking for help when you need it

65. Non-judgment of others who eat, pray, process and look differently from you

66. Letting non-essential tasks wait until tomorrow, sometimes

67. Noticing what you are proud of, and why

68. Starting over (again)

69. Letting it be OK to disappoint people when it means doing what is right for you

70. Feeling the full emotions of grief, sorrow, delight, contentment, etc.

71. Knowing that the grief, sorrow, delight, contentment, etc. will pass

72. Leaning into fear, instead of pushing it away

73. Reading the book or magazine you feel like reading instead of the one that you ought to read

74. Eliminating the word "should" from your vocabulary

75. Saying sorry, only when it is sincere

76. Asking the universe (God) for help

77. Knowing when to jump into "solution mode" and when to just listen when someone else is struggling

78. Recognizing the difference between constructive self-exploration and narcissism

79. Noticing and letting go of your entrenched patterns of rumination and behavior

80. Letting go of the wasted energy consumed by regret and guilt

81. Caring about loved ones without feeling responsible for their happiness

82. Knowing the difference between being at your "edge" and behaving recklessly

83. Trying out a new asana because it looks like it might feel great

84. Wobbling in vrikasana (tree pose) without reciting the story of "I'm so off balance today"

85. Giving praise anytime it is appropriate

86. Seeing everyone as human...full of flaws, fears, wisdom, fun, love, wisdom....

87. Trying to forgive

88. Letting peace come to you rather than seeking it out

89. Legs on the wall pose (viparita karani)

90. Cutting emotional "cords", both the pleasant and unpleasant, so that you are not weighed down with other people's energy

91. Giving to others, both when your life is plentiful and depleted

92. Giving from the heart and not the ego

93. Taking a 5 minute timeout....right now

94. Learning something new to nourish your soul rather than your credentials

95. Recognizing that your yoga teacher is human and not to be treated any differently than other person

96. Not needing to perfect any asana....just to experience each asana

97. Starting over, and starting where you are rather than where you think you should be

98. Remembering that you can only resolve your own demons

99. Embracing all of yourself, but letting go of the patterns and the stories that no longer serve you

100. Five minutes a day of stillness, while you are awake

101. Allowing yourself to JUST BE

Deborah Bernstein

http://florianyoga.blogspot.com

Deborah Bernstein is a former management consultant and corporate finance executive turned yoga teacher and entrepreneur. Deborah is the founder and owner of Florian Villa, a yoga retreat center on St. John in the US Virgin Islands and the founder of Roslindale Yoga Studio in Boston, MA.

Deborah and her fiancé and co-owner of Florian Villa, Scott, lead several yoga retreats a year at the villa. The couple also donates the villa and their time to host retreats for families of fallen firefighters and disabled veterans.

Deborah lives in Boston, MA and provides business consulting services and web design to yoga studios and wellness practitioners.